FIFTY KEY SOCIOLOGISTS:
THE FORMATIVE THEORISTS

Fifty Key Sociologists: The Formative Theorists covers the life, work, ideas and impact of some of the most important thinkers within this discipline. This volume concentrates on those historical figures whose main writings were based in the nineteenth and early twentieth century. A–Z entries make this book easy to navigate and figures covered include:

- Jane Addams
- Theodor Adorno
- Gyorgy Lukács
- Pitirim Sorokin
- Max Weber

Interested readers will find the ideas of theorists who were writing predominantly in the second half of the twentieth century discussed in *Fifty Key Sociologists: The Contemporary Theorists*.

John Scott is a Professor of Sociology at the University of Essex. His most recent books include *Sociology: The Key Concepts* (2006), *Power* (Polity Press, 2001), *Social Theory: Central Issues in Sociology* (Sage, 2006) and, with James Fulcher, *Sociology,* (third edition 2007).

Also available from Routledge

FIFTY KEY SOCIOLOGISTS: THE FORMATIVE THEORISTS

Edited by John Scott

Routledge
Taylor & Francis Group

LONDON AND NEW YORK

First published 2007
by Routledge
2 Park Square, Milton Park, Abingdon, Oxon OX14 4RN

Simultaneously published in the USA and Canada
by Routledge
711 Third Avenue, New York, NY 10017

Routledge is an imprint of the Taylor & Francis Group, an informa business

Typeset in Bembo by
Taylor & Francis Books

British Library Cataloguing in Publication Data
A catalogue record for this book is available from the British Library

Library of Congress Cataloging in Publication Data
A catalog record for this book has been requested

ISBN10: 0-415-35257-6 ISBN13: 978-0-415-35257-4 (hbk)
ISBN10: 0-415-35260-6 ISBN13: 978-0-415-35260-4 (pbk)
ISBN10: 0-203-11727-1 ISBN13: 978-0-203-11727-9 (ebk)

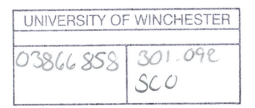

CONTENTS

NOTES ON CONTRIBUTORS

Michael Asch is Professor Emeritus in the Department of Anthropology at the University of Alberta and a Professor in the Department of Anthropology at the University of Victoria. His research on relations between First Nations people and Canada has appeared in *Kinship and the Drum Dance in a Northern Dene Community* (University of Alberta Press, 1988), *Home and Native Land: Aboriginal Rights and the Canadian Constitution* (Methuen, 1984) and *Aboriginal and Treaty Rights in Canada* (editor, University of British Columbia Press, 1998). He is a Fellow of the Royal Society of Canada.

Richard Bellamy is Director, School of Public Policy, University College London, Academic Director, European Consortium of Political Research (ECPR), and co-editor, *Critical Review of International Social and Political Philosophy*. His main books include *Modern Italian Social Theory: Ideology and Politics from Pareto to the Present* (Stanford University Press, 1987), *Liberalism and Modern Society: An Historical Argument* (Pennsylvania State University Press, 1992) and *Liberalism and Pluralism: Towards a Politics of Compromise* (Routledge, 1999). He is the editor of *The Cambridge History of Twentieth Century Political Thought* (with Terence Ball, Cambridge University Press, 2003).

Robin Blackburn is Professor of Sociology at the University of Essex, having studied and taught at the LSE and Oxford in the 1960s. He has been a member of the editorial committee of *New Left Review* since 1962 and was editor from 1981 to 1999. He has been consulting editor of Verso since 1970. Research interests include comparative investigations of slavery and of contemporary financial institutions. His publications include *The Making of New World Slavery: From the Baroque to the Modern* (Verso, 1997), *The Overthrow of Colonial Slavery* (Verso, 1988) and *Banking on Death. Or, Investing in Life: The History and Future of Pensions* (Verso, 2002).

Martin Bulmer is Professor of Sociology at the University of Surrey and Director of the ESRC Social Survey Question Bank. He also edits *Ethnic and Racial Studies*, the international journal published by Routledge. His main research interests are in the methodology of quantitative and qualitative social research, the history of sociology and of social research, and the study of ethnicity and race.

Eamonn Carrabine is Senior Lecturer in the Department of Sociology at the University of Essex. His teaching and research interests lie in the fields of criminology and cultural studies. His books include *Crime in Modern Britain* (with Pamela Cox, Maggy Lee and Nigel South, Oxford University Press, 2002), *Criminology: A Sociological Introduction* (with Paul Iganski, Maggy Lee, Ken Plummer and Nigel South, Routledge, 2004) and *Power, Discourse and Resistance: A Genealogy of the Strangeways Prison Riot* (Ashgate, 2004). He is currently working on a book on *Crime and the Media: Interrogating Representations of Transgression in Popular Culture*.

David Chalcraft is Professor of Classical Sociology, University of Derby, and Visiting Fellow at Lancaster University. He has published widely in the area of Weber studies and is the editor of *The Protestant Ethic Debate: Weber's Replies to His Critics, 1907–1910* (with Austin Harrington, Liverpool University Press, 2001). He is co-founder of the international journal *Max Weber Studies* and editor of the monograph series 'Rethinking Classical Sociology' (Ashgate Press).

James J. Chriss is currently Associate Professor of Sociology at Cleveland State University. His main areas of interest are sociological theory, crime and delinquency, the sociology of police and medical sociology. His forthcoming book *Social Control: History and Current Controversies* will be published by Polity Press.

Mary Jo Deegan is Professor of Sociology and Women's Studies at the University of Nebraska, Lincoln. She is author of *Jane Addams and the Men of the Chicago School, 1892–1918* (Transaction, 1988), *Race, Hull-House, and the University of Chicago: A New Conscience against Ancient Evils* (Praeger, 2002) and *The New Woman of Color: The Collected Writings of Fannie Barrier Williams, 1893–1918* (editor, Northern Illinois University Press, 2002), and she edited the recently discovered edition of George Herbert Mead's *Essays in Sociology* (Transaction, 2001).

Karl Figlio is Director and Professor in the Centre for Psycho-analytic Studies at the University of Essex and a practising psychoanalytic psychotherapist. He is interested in the engagement of clinically based psychoanalytic thinking and methods with sociological thinking and methods. His publications include *Psychoanalysis, Science and Masculinity* (Whurr Publishers, 2000).

Marcel Fournier is Professor of Sociology at Université de Montréal, Canada, and held the Killam Fellowship and Pathy Chair at Princeton University from 2001 to 2003. He is the author of *Cultivating Differences* (with D. White, University of Chicago Press, 1992), *Quebec Society* (Prentice Hall, 1996), *Emile Durkheim, Lettres à Marcel Mauss* (Presses Universitaires de France, 1998) and *Marcel Mauss: A Biography* (Princeton University Press, 2005).

Robert L. A. Hancock is a Doctoral student in the Department of History at the University of Victoria, British Columbia. He specializes in the study of indigenous peoples.

Johs. Hjellbrekke is Associate Professor, Department of Sociology, University of Bergen, Norway. His recent publications include *Innføring i Korrespondanseanalyse* (Fagbokforl, 1999), 'Educational Mobility Trajectories and Mobility Barriers in the Norwegian Social Space' (with Olav Korsnes, *International Journal of Contemporary Sociology*, 2004), 'Social Capital Structures in Norwegian Élites' (with Olav Korsnes, *Tidsskrift for samfunnsforskning*, 2005) and 'The Norwegian Field of Power' (with others, *European Societies*, in press).

Susan Hoecker-Drysdale is Professor Emerita, Sociology, Concordia University, Montréal, and Retired Visiting Professor, Sociology, the University of Iowa. She has been Visiting Fellow, Institute of Historical Research, University of London, and Visiting Fellow, School of Advanced Study, University of London. Her publications include *Harriet Martineau: First Woman Sociologist* (Berg, 1992), *Harriet Martineau: Theoretical and Methodological Perspectives* (co-edited with Michael R. Hill, Routledge, 2001) and *Harriet Martineau: Studies of America 1831–68* (8 vols, Thoemmes, 2004). In 2005 she received the Distinguished Scholarly Achievement Award of the Section on the History of Sociology, the American Sociological Association.

John Hoffman is Emeritus Professor of Political Theory, University of Leicester. He is the author of many works, including *The Gramscian*

Challenge: Coercion and Consent in Marxist Political Theory (Blackwell, 1984), *Beyond The State* (Polity Press, 1995), *Gender and Sovereignty: Feminism, the State and International Relations* (Macmillan, 2001) and *Citizenship Beyond the State* (Sage, 2004).

Alan How is Senior Lecturer in Sociology at the University of Worcester, UK. His previous work includes *The Habermas–Gadamer Debate and the Nature of the Social* (Avebury, 1995) and *Traditions in Social Theory: Critical Theory* (Palgrave, 2003). He is currently working on a book on the role of classic texts in sociology.

David Howarth is Senior Lecturer in Government, University of Essex. He specializes in discourse theory, South African politics and social movements. His publications include *Discourse* (Open University Press, 2000), *South Africa in Transition* (co-edited with Aletta Norval, Macmillan,1998) and *Discourse Theory in European Politics: Identity, Policy and Governance* (co-edited with Jacob Torling, Palgrave, 2005).

Christopher T. Husbands is Reader in Sociology at the London School of Economics. He has published numerous articles on political sociology and biographical studies in lexicography and is the translator and editor of Werner Sombart's *Why Is There No Socialism in the United States?* (Macmillan, 1976).

Wendy James is Professor of Social Anthropology at the University of Oxford and a Fellow of the British Academy. She has carried out research in the Sudan and Ethiopia and her main theoretical interests have concerned the relationship between politics and the enduring aspects of religious, cultural and moral systems. Her recent books include *Marcel Mauss: A Centenary Tribute* (co-edited with Nicholas J. Allen, Berghahn, 1998), *Anthropologists in a Wider World: Essays on Field Research* (co-edited with Paul Dresch and David Parkin, Berghahn, 2000), *The Ceremonial Animal: A New Portrait of Anthropology* (Oxford University Press, 2003) and *The Qualities of Time: Anthropological Approaches* (co-edited with David Mills, Berghahn, 2005).

Barry V. Johnston is Professor of Sociology at Indiana University Northwest. He is the author of *Pitirim A. Sorokin: An Intellectual Biography* (University Press of Kansas, 1995). His works on Pitirim A. Sorokin and the early sociology departments at Harvard University have won a number of awards from international and regional associations. He has begun a new work tentatively titled *One Hundred Years of Sociology at Harvard University.*

Douglas Kellner is Professor in the Graduate School of Education and Information Studies at the University of California, Los Angeles. He is the author of numerous books on culture, media and social theory, including *Jean Baudrillard: From Marxism to Postmodernism and Beyond* (Stanford University Press, 1990), *Postmodern Theory: Critical Interrogations* (with Steven Best, Guilford Press, 1991) and *The Postmodern Turn* (with Steven Best, Guilford Press, 1997), and he has edited *The Collected Works of Herbert Marcuse* (Routledge, 2004 onwards).

David Kettler is Research Professor, Bard College, New York. Author of numerous books on social theory, including *Karl Mannheim* (with Volker Meja and Nico Stehr, Ellis Horwood, 1984) and *Adam Ferguson: Social and Political Thought* (expanded edition, Transaction, 2005). With Volka Meja and Nico Stehr he has edited some of the work of Karl Mannheim, most notably *Structures of Thinking* (Routledge and Kegan Paul, 1982), *Conservatism* (Routledge and Kegan Paul, 1986), and, with Colin Loader, *Sociology as Political Education* (Transaction Publishers, 2001).

Adam Kuper is Professor of Anthropology at Brunel University and a Fellow of the British Academy. His publications include *The Invention of Primitive Society: Transformations of an Illusion* (Routledge, 1988), *The Chosen Primate: Human Nature and Cultural Diversity* (Harvard University Press, 1994), *Anthropology and Anthropologists: The Modern British School* (third edition, Routledge, 1998) and *Culture: The Anthropologists' Account* (Harvard University Press, 1998).

Donald N. Levine is Peter B. Ritzma Professor of Sociology at the University of Chicago. His interests include classical social theory, modernization theory, Ethiopian studies, conflict theory and aikido, and philosophies of liberal education. His many publications include *Greater Ethiopia: The Evolution of a Multiethnic Society* (revised edition, University of Chicago Press, 2000), *Visions of the Sociological Tradition* (University of Chicago Press, 1995), *The Flight from Ambiguity: Essays in Social and Cultural Theory* (University of Chicago Press, 1985) and *Powers of the Mind: The Reinvention of Liberal Learning in America* (University of Chicago Press, 2006). Since 1978 he has served as editor of 'The Heritage of Sociology' series published by the University of

Chicago Press and, in 1971, edited the HOS series volume *Georg Simmel on Individuality and Social Forms*.

Thomas Luckmann is Emeritus Professor of Sociology at the University of Konstanz. He worked closely with Alfred Schutz and he edited and co-authored *Structures of the Lifeworld* for publication. He is the author of *The Invisible Religion* (Macmillan, 1967 [originally 1963]), *The Social Construction of Reality* (with Peter Berger, Anchor Books, 1966), *The Sociology of Language* (Bobbs-Merrill, 1975) and *Life-World and Social Realities* (Heinemann, 1983).

E. Stina Lyon is Professor of Educational Developments in Sociology and Pro Dean in the Faculty of Arts and Human Sciences at London South Bank University. Her research interests include research methodology, the sociology of education, gender, race and ethnicity, and welfare-state ideology. Her present research is focused on the intellectual contributions of Gunnar and Alva Myrdal. She is co-editor of *Methodological Imaginations* (with Joan Busfield, Macmillan, 1996) and *Gender Relations in Public and Private* (with Lydia Morris, Macmillan 1996).

Volker Meja is Professor of Sociology at the Memorial University of Newfoundland. His publications, with David Kettler and Nico Stehr, include *Karl Mannheim* (Ellis Horwood, 1984) and he has edited two collections of the work of Karl Mannheim, *Structures of Thinking* (Routledge and Kegan Paul, 1982) and *Conservatism* (Routledge and Kegan Paul, 1986).

Ann Nilsen is Professor at the Sosiologisk Institutt at the University of Bergen, Norway, where she is also Vice Dean of the Faculty of Social Sciences. She is engaged in comparative research on gender, parenthood and employment. Her publications include *Young Europeans, Work and Family: Futures in Transition* (co-edited with Julia Brannen, Suzan Lewis and Janet Smithson, Routledge, 2001) and 'Individualisation, Choice and Structure: A Discussion of Current Trends in Sociological Analysis' (with Julia Brannen, *Sociological Review* 53(3), 2005).

Mary Pickering received her PhD from Harvard in 1988. She is currently Professor of History at San Jose State University. The second volume of her *Auguste Comte: An Intellectual Biography* will be published shortly.

Lucinda Platt is lecturer in Sociology at the University of Essex. Author of *Parallel Lives? Poverty among Ethnic Minority Groups n Britain* (CPAG, 2002) and *Discovering Child Poverty* (The Policy Press, 2005), her research focuses on ethnic minority disadvantage and on child poverty.

Colin Samson is Senior Lecturer in Sociology at the University of Essex. Having worked in medical sociology and cultural sociology, he is currently working on indigenous peoples in North America and working closely with the Innu people of the Labrador–Quebec peninsula. He has published *Canada's Tibet: The Killing of the Innu* (with James Wilson and Jonathan Mazower, Survival, 1999) and *A Way of Life that Does Not Exist: Canada and the Extinguishment of the Innu* (Verso, 2003).

John Scott is Professor of Sociology at the University of Essex, having previously been Professor at the University of Leicester. Specializing in social stratification, economic sociology and social theory, his most recent books include *Power* (Polity Press, 2001), *Sociology* (with James Fulcher, third edition, Oxford University Press, 2007) and *Social Theory: Central Issues in Sociology* (Sage, 2006).

Susie Scott is Lecturer in Sociology at the University of Sussex, with research interests in interaction, performance and everyday life. Her publications include various articles on shyness and *Shyness and Society* (Palgrave, 2007).

Catherine B. Silver is Professor of Sociology at Brooklyn College and the Graduate Center of the City University of New York. Her book on Frédéric Le Play was followed by research and publications on gender, work and aging from a cross-cultural and socio-psychoanalytic perspective.

Stephen Small is Associate Professor of African American Studies at University of California, Berkeley. He has previously taught at the University of Massachusetts, Amherst, and at the Universities of Warwick and Leicester. His recent publications include *Representations of Slavery. Race and Ideology in Southern Plantation Museums* (with Jennifer Eichstedt, Smithsonian Institution Press, 2002) and *Race and Power. Global Racism in the Twenty-First Century* (with Gargi Bhattacharyya and John Gabriel, Routledge, 2004).

Kenneth Thompson is Emeritus Professor of Sociology at the Open University, Faculty Fellow at Yale University and Visiting Professor at the University of California Los Angeles. His numerous publications on social theory and the sociology of culture include *Moral Panics* (Routledge, 1998), *Emile Durkheim* (Routledge, 2002) and *The Uses of Sociology* (co-edited with Peter Hamilton, Blackwell, 2002).

INTRODUCTION

'Classical' and 'modern' are, perhaps, the most common labels applied to social theorists. Both terms are, however, misleading. Debates over modernity and modernization have made problematic the idea that 'modern' can be used to mean 'contemporary'. Equally problematic is the word 'classical'. In music, art and architecture, classical styles have a particular meaning and can be contrasted with the 'romantic' and other styles. This has never been the case in sociology. Although the term was once used to refer to the status of certain foundational statements as 'classic' works that stand as exemplars, it is now most often used simply with a chronological reference: 'classical' theory is theory that came before contemporary theory.

For all these reasons, this book has been described not as a book of classical social theory but as a book of *formative* social theory. I use the term formative to refer to those theorists who contributed to the formation of a distinctive body of social theory and social research in the period when sociology and the other social sciences were becoming established as distinct disciplines.

This period comprises the bulk of the nineteenth century and the first half of the twentieth century. This is not to say that all social theorists of the period agreed with each other – far from it. What characterizes the period is a common concern for establishing the disciplinary frameworks within which theoretical debate could take place and intellectual disagreements could be thrashed out. The formative writers established a set of common themes towards which they contributed differentially and that formed the basis for all subsequent social theorizing.

Social theory is not the same thing as 'sociology'. The discipline of sociology, as it emerged in the formative period, has, however, been a focus for the development of the most general formulations of social theory. Theoretical ideas have, however, also developed in the more specialized social sciences – in geography, in politics, in social psychology – and a book on key sociologists that seeks to represent the range of social theorizing must include some theorists who stand outside sociology itself. In this book, then, a core of sociologists are joined by a smaller selection of psychoanalysts, political scientists, anthropologists and others who made important contributions to the formative debates around which sociology emerged. The psychoanalyst Sigmund Freud, the linguist Ferdinand de Saussure, the economist Gunnar Myrdal, the anthropologists Lewis Morgan and Bronislaw Malinowski, for example, all demand a place in any definitive list of key sociologists.

Sociology is also more than simply social theory. The formative sociologists were engaged in empirical research and social reform as well as social theorizing. Jane Addams, the founder of the Chicago settlement house movement, Charles Booth and Seebohm Rowntree, the poverty researchers, Helen Bosanquet, the social case worker, and W. E. B. DuBois, the black activist, made important contributions to the establishment of sociology and its key concerns. One particular area of social activism that must be considered within a tradition of sociological thinkers is Marxism: from Marx himself to Gyorgy Lukács and the more academic work of Theodor Adorno and Herbert Marcuse.

Any selection of key sociologists is bound to be contentious. Each person will make their own particular choices and will have their preferred criteria for choice. Ask fifty people to choose fifty key thinkers and you are likely to end up with fifty different lists – well, ·almost. From within the mainstream of sociology certain theorists will find their place in almost any list: Max Weber and Emile Durkheim, for example, are perhaps the strongest contenders for inclusion. Beyond this core of certain inclusions, however, matters become more complex. Many would agree with the inclusion of Georg Simmel and George Herbert Mead, together with earlier theorists such as Auguste Comte and Herbert Spencer – but how far beyond this core would most people be willing to go in counting someone as a 'key' contributor? The further we get from the core, the greater the disagreement that there will be.

My particular selection of key sociologists reflects my own interests and concerns: that is inevitable. I have, however, taken advice in order to ensure that my selection is as representative as possible. My initial selection of writers was referred to a panel of colleagues at Essex University, the leading Department of Sociology in Britain. Colleagues were asked to vote for those they felt should definitely be included and those they felt should be excluded. They were also asked to identify any further writers whom they felt warranted inclusion in the book. A revised list was produced from these suggestions and this was then, in its turn, sent around the panel for further consideration. Finally, the overall list was divided into two lists – of 'formative' and 'contemporary' writers – and each list was trimmed down to the essential fifty thinkers that it seemed reasonable to include in the definitive list.

The entries in this volume have been produced by a variety of international experts. They vary in style and format, but all take a similar approach. Basic biographical details on the life and career of each theorist place them in their historical and intellectual contexts. Contributors also aim to outline the key ideas and studies undertaken by each writer, showing the ways in which their ideas emerged and developed. I have tried to list each theorist simply by their first name and surname, but where they are more conventionally known by an alternative name (e.g. George Herbert Mead and W. E. B. DuBois) they are listed in that way. Each entry concludes with a listing of the major works of each theorist and some suggestions for further reading. Connections with other theorists are indicated by 'See also' cross-references. These cross-references include references to subsequent writers in the companion volume on *Fifty Key Sociologists: The Contemporary Theorists*.

Further reading

Alex Callinicos. 1999. *Social Theory: A Historical Introduction*. Cambridge: Polity Press.

Ian Craib. 1997. *Classical Social Theory*. Oxford: Oxford University Press.

John Scott. 2006. *Social Theory: Central Issues in Sociology*. London: Sage.

Stephen Turner, ed. 1996. *Social Theory and Sociology: The Classics and Beyond*. Oxford: Basil Blackwell.

FIFTY KEY SOCIOLOGISTS: THE FORMATIVE THEORISTS

JANE ADDAMS

Feminist pragmatist, social settlement leader and Nobel Laureate, Jane Addams is a recognized world leader with a sweeping mind, personal charisma and an innovative intellectual legacy. She is one of the most important female sociologists who has ever lived. She was a leader for dozens of women in sociology from 1890 until her death in 1935, although after 1920 most of these women were forced out of sociology and into fields such as social work, home economics, applied psychology, pedagogy and administration in higher education.

Jane Addams was born on 6 September 1860 in the small Midwestern town of Cedarville, Illinois. She was profoundly influenced by her father John Addams, a Hicksite Quaker, state senator and mill owner, but she did not know her mother Sarah Weber, who died when Addams was two years old. In 1877 Addams entered Rockford Female Seminary, one of the pioneering colleges for women. After graduating in 1881, she entered an extended period of unhappiness and depression. In August, her father died and his absence left her confused and despairing. She entered the Women's Medical College in Philadelphia in the autumn, but she soon returned to Illinois. Ill and surrounded by family problems, Addams drifted for a year. Finally taking some action, she travelled to Europe in 1883 but she remained frustrated for the next two years until her return to Europe. Accompanied by her college friend Ellen Gates Starr, Addams found a direction for her life after visiting the social settlement Toynbee Hall in London's East End. This group served the exploited working classes and supported artisans who harmonized their interests in art, labor and the community. Toynbee Hall provided a model for Addams and Starr to co-found their social settlement, Hull-House, in Chicago in 1889. Hull-House became the institutional anchor for women's gender-segregated work in sociology and a link with the most important male sociological centre during this era, the University of Chicago.

The 1890s were lively, controversial years at Hull-House, where anarchists, Marxists, socialists, unionists, and leading social theorists congregated. John Dewey, **George Herbert Mead**, and W. I. Thomas, among others, were frequent visitors, lecturers and close friends of Addams. Chicago pragmatism was born through their collegial contacts and intellectual exchanges. A groundbreaking sociological text, *Hull-House Maps and Papers* was published by Hull-House residents in 1895, predating and establishing the urban interests of the early Chicago male sociologists.

Author of eleven books and hundreds of articles, Addams continued her educational efforts through lectures across the country. She led social reform organizations, campaigned for the Progressive Party, and helped to found numerous government agencies. She practised and advocated 'radical democracy', holding that equality must extend beyond citizenship rights and pervade all aspects of economic and social life. This involved a commitment to African Americans and cultural pluralism. She sought not only answers to problems, but answers in the best interests of all, including the poor and disenfranchised.

Her thought and practice is called 'feminist pragmatism': an American theory uniting liberal values and a belief in a rational public with a cooperative, nurturing, and liberating model of the self, the other and the community. Education and democracy are significant mechanisms for organizing and improving society. Feminist pragmatists study 'social behaviour' and believe each person is born with rudimentary and flexible instincts or 'impulses'. Infants primarily learn by observing, imitating and responding to the 'gestures' of others, particularly their parents. They can abstract the meaning of gestures, particularly vocal gestures, and generalize about 'the other, the group, the community, and institutions'. This 'process' allows the individual to develop a 'mind, intelligence, a self, and the ability to take the role of the other'. The self learns organized 'attitudes' of 'the community' towards 'social situations'. People sharing the same neighbourhood and community develop 'shared experience (which is the greatest of human goods)'. The self emerges from others and is not in conflict with others unless it is taught to be in conflict. 'Education' is a major way to learn about one's community, participate in group decisions and become a 'citizen'.

Women who obey the rules governing the home and family follow the 'family claim'. When they work for others outside the home, they follow the 'social claim'. Conflicts between these claims can result in 'social disorganization', where competing values and attitudes on the same situation are legitimated simultaneously. This creates an instability in society, whereby 'women become a resource for social change'. Women in public life can utilize their cooperative worldview to implement the goals of democracy. The female world is based on the unity of the female self, the home, the family and face-to-face interactions with neighbours in a community. Women can take this pattern and extend it to nurturing others, as 'bread givers engaged in bread labor'. Their model for the home and family when extended to the larger social situation is called 'civic housekeeping'.

Women can be leaders in a new 'social consciousness', indicated in 'newer ideals of peace'. A sign of this awakening consciousness is 'the integration of the objective with the subjective'. This is organized through 'social movements in labor, social science, and women'. The modern city is a new location for these social changes.

Women learn 'folk wisdom' and share a culture based on female myths such as the Corn Mother. This unity crosses racial/ethnic lines while it supports and respects differences including variation by class, age, race, religion, education, sexual preference and disability. Democracy emerges from different groups and represents these distinct perspectives, histories, communities and characteristic structures of the self. Social change must articulate and respond to these various groups' commonalities and differences. 'Old women' also learn and pass on legends, cherish the good in others, develop 'woman's Memory' and engage in 'perfecting the past'. Because women are not full members of the male world, they are in an ideal situation to 'challenge war, disturb conventions, integrate industry, react to life, and transform the past'. 'Women's obligation' is to help create and distribute the world's food supply. The modern woman's family claim is built on a 'consumer role' that should criticize and change industry.

Reuniting the woman and society through economic productivity empowers the woman to make better choices in the home and the marketplace. 'New perspectives on women' can develop through the use of rational facts; alternative attitudes; new social situations; the new social sciences, especially sociology; and changed economics. This can occur through the development of 'working hypotheses' that enter a social situation and change it, thereby generating new working hypotheses. This process is called 'social reconstruction'. Women's clubwork is another source for social change and education.

Areas of concentration within feminist pragmatism form separate literatures, including the study of: (1) the city, (2) crime, (3) the use of qualitative and quantitative methodology, (4) the life cycle, (5) social class and labour relations, (6) the process of making and enjoying art and aesthetics, (7) play, (8) education, (9) social movements, (10) ethics, (11) the development of an international consciousness and political apparatus, (12) immigration, (13) African American life and racial discrimination, and (14) feminine values and the natural environment. Each area often involved dozens of scholars and activists, with Addams as a central figure uniting these disparate interests and activities.

As a pacifist prior to the First World War, Addams was lauded as a 'good woman'. With the building of patriotic feeling from 1914 until

America's entry into the war in 1917, she increasingly became the target of animosity and personal attack. By 1917 she was socially and publicly ostracized, moving from saint to villain. Booed off speaking platforms, abandoned by her friends, colleagues and, most notably here, other sociologists, Addams was a social pariah. This was an agonizing time for Addams. Committed to her values, based on 'female' ideals, she maintained her pacifist position. The culmination of her politically untouchable status occurred in 1919, when she was targeted by the US government as the most dangerous person in America. At this point, her major role as a sociologist diminished and, until recently, she was ostracized by succeeding generations of sociologists.

In 1920, women were granted the franchise, and to Addams this was a major victory. Contrary to her expectation of a powerful women's vote, however, this decade led to an eclipse in the former power of women activists, including Addams. Progressive leadership was squelched and the liberal vision of a changing, optimistic and scientifically rational society was less and less acceptable. Sociologists increasingly applied an androcentric perspective to their definition of the field.

Addams gradually resumed her pubic leadership during the 1920s, but the devastating impact of the Great Depression once again called for radical social analysis and social change. Addams again became a distinguished world leader. Winner of the Nobel Peace Prize in 1931, she spoke for many of the values and policies adopted during the New Deal, especially in social security and other government programmes that altered American capitalism. Dying in 1935, she was mourned worldwide as a great leader and interpreter of American thought.

In addition to her contribution to Chicago pragmatism, Addams engaged with sociological work in Britain, including empiricism, social surveys, social settlements, Fabian socialism and the Arts and Crafts movement. She was interested in the work of Charles Ashbee, **Beatrice Webb**, **Charles Booth**, Patrick Geddes, John Ruskin, and Canon Barnett. Addams was also influenced by Russian sociologists, especially the pacifism and art of Leo Tolstoy and the analysis of human relationships to the land articulated by Piotr Kropotkin. Addams seriously considered the work of Karl Marx and Friedrich Engels, but her dedication to a cooperative rather than a conflict model, based on a triple foundation for human behaviour that included play and art as well as labour, made this approach unworkable for her.

There is a vast literature on Addams, most of it emphasizing her biography, social work and public role in American society. There is a serious lack of study of her intellectual apparatus: her theory of the arts, including the theatre, pageants, drama, literature, sculpture, pottery and the aesthetics of nature; her life-long commitment to political theory; and her vast influence on American race relations, especially those between whites, Mexican Americans and African Americans. This dearth of scholarship in these major areas of her work significantly limits our understanding of her ideas and accomplishments.

A large literature exists in several fields, especially in women's studies, that criticizes white, middle-class women, early social workers, reformers and philanthropists as conservative, exploitative and oppressive. Addams is often the symbolic leader of these various groups and sometimes emerges as a contemporary symbol of the villainy of benevolent ignorance or intentional evil. Thus she is sometimes mentioned superficially in texts where she is stereotyped as a racist, assimilationist, essentialist and atheoretical meddler.

This scholarship contrasts with the early studies of Addams as a sociologist before 1920, when she was highly integrated into the sociological literature, frequently spoke before the American Sociological Society and published in the *American Journal of Sociology*. Addams' stellar leadership in sociology was erased until the publication of my book (Deegan 1988) and a series of related articles on the sociology of Addams and the cohort of women she inspired. Rediscovering her role and influence in sociology has made her increasingly visible and understood within the profession.

Addams' intellectual legacy as a feminist pragmatist has been obscured and sometimes distorted. She articulated radical changes in American life and politics, altering the possibilities for human growth and action for the poor, the working class, immigrants, people of colour, youth, the aged and women. Addams was a central figure in applied sociology between 1892 and 1920 and led a large and powerful cohort of women whom she profoundly influenced. Contemporary scholars often document and either praise or deplore Addams' significant contributions to public life, but her intellectual stature is barely appreciated. Her legacy in sociology is particularly hidden within the mainstream literature in the discipline. Her profound influence on the course and development of sociology is only suggested in most sociological textbooks, books and articles. A growing number of scholars are analysing this great, alternative heritage and tradition in American sociology. They envision a new horizon for a more just and liberated society.

See also: Charles Booth, George Herbert Mead.

Major works

Hull-House Maps and Papers (as 'Residents of Hull-House'). New York: Crowell, 1895.
Democracy and Social Ethics. New York: Macmillan, 1902.
Newer Ideals of Peace. New York: Macmillan, 1907.
The Spirit of Youth and the City Streets. New York: Macmillan, 1909.
Twenty Years at Hull-House. New York: Macmillan, 1910.
A New Conscience and an Ancient Evil. New York: Macmillan, 1912.
The Women at the Hague (with Emily Greene Balch and Alice Hamilton). New York: Macmillan, 1915.
The Long Road of Woman's Memory. New York: Macmillan, 1916.
Peace and Bread in Time of War. New York: Macmillan, 1922.
The Child, the Clinic and the Court, intro. by Jane Addams. New York: New Republic, 1927.
The Second Twenty Years at Hull-House. New York: Macmillan, 1930.

Addams also wrote a large number of articles in many different areas of specialization.

Further reading

Mary Lynn McCree Bryan and Allen F. Davis. 1990. *One Hundred Years at Hull-House*. Bloomington, IN: Indiana University Press.
Allen F. Davis. 1973. *American Heroine*. New York: Oxford University Press.
Mary Jo Deegan. 1988. *Jane Addams and the Men of the Chicago School, 1892–1920*. New Brunswick, NJ: Transaction Books.
John C. Farrell. 1967. *Beloved Lady*. Baltimore, MD: Johns Hopkins Press.
James Weber Linn. 1935. *Jane Addams*. New York: Appleton-Century Crofts.

MARY JO DEEGAN

THEODOR ADORNO

Adorno was an uncompromising thinker and leading representative of the group of critical intellectuals associated with the Institute for Social Research at the University of Frankfurt. A formidable philosopher, versed in the German idealist tradition, as well as a serious musician and composer, he was uniquely placed to develop a complex aesthetic theory and controversial understanding of popular entertainment. As a sociologist, he wrote damning analyses of instrumental reason, modern culture and authoritarian character that drew on **Marx, Weber** and **Freud** in innovative and idiosyncratic fashion. Although Adorno's work addressed a bewildering range of topics and was written in a style that defies easy comprehension, there was a remarkable consistency in his thinking over time. This he came to define as 'negative dialectics', which involves not only revealing how our everyday concepts mask social reality but also demonstrating how the contradiction between truth and illusion says much about how modern life is experienced.

Above all else, Adorno was concerned with human misery. The question of domination animates his entire writings. The unifying theme at the core of his work is that the history of civilization is based on the repression of nature and the consolidation of oppressive social systems that negate human freedom. Adorno's despairing view of modernity and deeply pessimistic understanding of mass culture are offset by the tentative hope of imagining a world free from unnecessary suffering. Even though he refused to describe what this utopian alternative to contemporary society might look like, he remained convinced of the value of utopian beliefs, whether these were realistic or not.

Adorno was born in 1903 and grew up in Frankfurt as the only child of a Jewish wine merchant and his Catholic wife, a professional opera singer. The relative affluence and liberal cosmopolitanism of his background enabled him to pursue his prodigious musical and intellectual talents. He began reading German classical philosophy at fifteen with Sigmund Kracauer, a family friend and who would become one of the Weimar Republic's most celebrated cultural critics. In the early 1920s he met Max Horkheimer, a young philosopher who shared many of his aesthetic interests, and Walter Benjamin, a radical thinker who sought to combine Marxist philosophy with Judaic mysticism. Both would become life-long friends and shape his intellectual development immeasurably. By the mid-1920s, Adorno had moved to Vienna to study music composition and train as a concert pianist.

For a time it seemed as if Adorno was able to combine two careers at once: as musician and philosopher. However, both suffered setbacks. His musical critiques were not well received by his Viennese circle and, while he continued to compose music for the rest of his life, he concentrated his energies on an academic career. His initial attempt to gain qualifications as a university lecturer was thwarted when, following his return to Frankfurt, his dissertation supervisor raised concerns over his thesis in 1927, forcing him to take up another topic (a critique of Søren Kierkegaard's existential philosophy). During this time his ties with Horkheimer brought him into loose contact with the recently founded Institute of Social Research at the University of Frankfurt.

The Institute, or Frankfurt school as it was later to become known, was established in 1923 as a centre for socialist scholarship and initially pursued research of a broadly orthodox Marxist kind. From the outset the Institute reflected the need felt by the Left intelligentsia to reappraise Marxist theory in the light of the unexpected Bolshevik victory in Russia in 1917 and the subsequent defeat of Central European revolutions. Over the years that followed, the Institute produced largely empirical work with little theoretical imagination. However, the Institute radically changed direction when Horkheimer became director in 1930. The differences in approach soon became apparent when philosophy, rather than economics or history, came to prominence. Cultural questions began to assume significance, with various attempts at integrating dialectical Marxism with Freud's psychoanalysis appearing. More generally, Horkheimer sought to distance the Institute from the workers' movement, in a further effort to break with orthodox Marxism, and to give it an essentially academic identity. He coined the term 'critical theory' to define the new approach emanating from the Institute. This new direction included such luminaries as the philosopher **Herbert Marcuse**, psychoanalyst Erich Fromm and sociologist Leo Löwenthal, amongst others.

Adorno's inaugural lecture, 'The Actuality of Philosophy', was presented in 1931 at the University of Frankfurt and introduced the key elements of his thinking that would inform his subsequent work. He outlined his own distinctive combination of 'dialectical' and 'materialist' thinking as a means of demystifying social practices. However, as Susan Buck-Morss put it, 'although it was indebted to Marx and might even be termed "Marxism", it was not Marxism . . . throughout his life he differed fundamentally from Marx in that his philosophy never included a theory of political action'.

A crucial influence on Adorno's understanding of Marx was the work of the Hungarian **Gyorgy Lukács** in *History and Class Consciousness*. Lukács's theory of 'reification', which refers to the ways in which commodity fetishism saturates all social relations in capitalist societies, produced a searing moral condemnation of capitalism. Adorno shared this understanding of the destructive consequences of commodity fetishism, but was never swayed by Lukács's optimism that the revolutionary working-class consciousness would overcome reification.

With the Nazi seizure of power in 1933, Adorno's future as a German academic was bleak. Horkheimer's Institute, as a Marxist think tank staffed almost exclusively by Jewish men, was one of the first intellectual groups forced into exile. Its members fled via Geneva to arrive in New York and set up loose connections with Columbia University. Adorno left for England and was reduced to the status of an 'advanced student' at Merton College, Oxford, where he would spend most of the next four years. His projects here included a study of the philosopher Husserl, and various articles on music. The scathing 'On Jazz' (written under the apt pseudonym Hektor Rottweiler) was published in 1936, while the second, 'On the Fetish Character of Music and the Regression of Hearing', appeared two years later. These pieces establish how structural changes in late capitalism have altered the character of art. Rather than promising freedom and having a genuine use value that people can enjoy, all significance becomes invested in art as an object of exchange and a standardized commodity – themes that he would develop in his future work.

Adorno arrived in New York in 1938 to direct a research programme into radio listeners with the sociologist Paul Lazarsfeld. The differences between Lazarsfeld's empiricism and Adorno's philosophizing soon became irreconcilable, and his role on the project terminated in 1940. However, the move to America enabled Adorno to develop his intellectual ties with Horkheimer and he soon joined the latter in southern California. The pair worked closely together and produced a landmark document of their now joint position: *The Dialectic of Enlightenment*, first published in 1947, combined Marx with Weber and Nietzsche's understandings of reason and domination. The book came to prominence in the 1960s and is the defining statement of the Frankfurt school. It explores the self-destructive tendencies of modern societies and its central argument is that instrumental rationality – the form of reasoning that separates facts from value by being solely concerned with practical purposes – has undermined the emancipatory potential of enlightenment. Fascism, for instance, used many of the tools of instrumental reason and modern science in its barbaric destruction and brutal repression.

However, democratic states as much as authoritarian ones possess dehumanizing tendencies. These are more subtle but no less damaging, a claim examined in Horkheimer and Adorno's analysis of what they call the 'culture industry', which obliterates individuality and silences critical thinking through 'mass deception'. As they put it, in 'the culture industry the individual is an illusion not merely because of the standardization of the means of production ... Pseudo individuality is rife: from the standardized jazz improvisation to the exceptional film star whose hair curls over her eye to demonstrate her originality'. As might be expected, these arguments have proved to be highly controversial. This characterization of a monolithic culture industry and an elitist denial of the aesthetics of popular entertainment have all been roundly and routinely criticized. Most obviously disputed is the extent to which the 'mass' is deceived by the products of the culture industry. However, Horkheimer and Adorno were keenly aware that the 'triumph of advertising in the culture industry is that consumers feel compelled to buy and use its products even though they see through them'.

Adorno develops this possibility of seeing through yet obeying in a subsequent study of the astrology column of the *Los Angeles Times*, written in the 1950s but published only in 1994 as 'The Stars Down to Earth'. The overall aim is to analyse and understand 'the motivations of some large-scale phenomena involving irrational elements in a peculiar way'. Rather than dismissing astrology as simply irrational, he argued that the instrumental rationality of capitalist societies gives astrology a degree of coherence with which to provide for the readers of columns the means of living with conditions beyond their apparent control. Yet for Adorno, astrology avoids fatalism. The reader of horoscope columns is continually exhorted to make choices, though in the end this is an empty autonomy that produces social conformity. The column's implicit rule is that the reader must adjust to the command of the stars, while appealing to the narcissism of the individual and portraying the reader as someone able to change their circumstances through their personal 'assets' (such as deploying 'charm', 'magnetism' or 'intuition' in particular situations). The result is that individuality 'itself is submerged in the process of transformation of ends into means'.

Adorno extended this concern with social conformity and mass irrationality in his collaborative work on *The Authoritarian Personality*, a large-scale empirical study carried out in the USA at the end of the Second World War. The central claim is that there is a correlation between personality structure and the support likely to be given to mass irrational movements like fascism. Using psychoanalytic categories, he argued that late capitalism produces submissive 'narcissistic' personalities that seek strong models to identify with (such as charismatic film stars or authoritarian political leaders). The study quickly became controversial for overstating the psychological causes of fascism, and it is highly ironic that, in the words of Jay, it had 'the effect of identifying Adorno in the minds of most Americans with the type of social scientific research that was peripheral at best to his main interests'.

Much more representative of his overall approach, and arguably his greatest achievement, is the collection of aphorisms in *Minima Moralia: Reflections from Damaged Life*, written during his American exile. Adorno described this collection as a work of 'melancholy science'. Written under the shadows of fascism, Stalinism and Hollywood, it offers the stark warning that '[w]rong life cannot be lived rightly'. Adorno returned to Frankfurt in 1949 and quickly established himself as a leading German intellectual. As well as helping to rebuild the Institute of Social Research, he eventually became its director in 1958. Adorno continued to write prolifically. In 1952 he brought out *In Search of Wagner*, a critique of the composer. *Prisms* – a collection of essays on cultural criticism – appeared three years later, and *Dissonances: Music in the Administered World* appeared three years after that. Up until his sudden death in 1969 he published at an incredible rate on a diverse range of musical and literary themes – his collected works comprise some twenty-three volumes.

The fortunes of Adorno's thought have fluctuated since his death. A familiar complaint is that he was a dour elitist whose thinking offers little to our very different times. Certainly, Adorno's star has been eclipsed by Walter Benjamin's more optimistic understanding of popular culture, while his work has been dismissed as abstract speculation by mainstream social scientists and Marxists alike. Karl Popper, for instance, accused him of 'simply talking trivialities in high-sounding language'. There is no doubt that Adorno can be incredibly difficult to read, but this is quite deliberate. He viewed language itself as distorting and refused to simplify his complicated ideas. It is as if he demanded of the reader an almost fierce concentration of effort to live up to his dictum that 'the splinter in your eye is the best magnifying glass'.

One of the most searching criticisms of Adorno's project is contained in Jürgen Habermas's assessment of the *Dialectic of Enlightenment*. Habermas – one of Adorno's former students – argues that instrumental reason is nowhere near as pervasive or all encompassing as Adorno maintained. If Adorno is to be believed, there is no escape. Politically, this precludes the possibility of realizing the aims of critical theory, and philosophically it excludes the possibility of Adorno's rational analysis of these conditions. Habermas accuses Adorno of lapsing into a 'performative contradiction', but one that acutely anticipates the main dilemmas of social theory in the second half of the twentieth century. Habermas's critique helped pave the way for poststructuralist readings of Adorno, while postcolonial theorists have located in *Minima Moralia* lucid accounts of exile and feminists have used his 'negative dialectics' to unravel subjectivity. To be sure, Adorno's work is easily caricatured, yet it is the subtlety and depth of his thinking that ensure it remains at the forefront of contemporary social theory.

See also: Sigmund Freud, Georg Lukács, Herbert Marcuse, Karl Marx, Max Weber.

See also in *Fifty Key Sociologists: The Contemporary Theorists*: Jean Baudrillard, Jürgen Habermas.

Major works

Dialectic of Enlightenment (with Max Horkheimer). 1947. London: Penguin, 1973.
The Authoritarian Personality (with Else Frenkel-Brunswick, Daniel J. Levinson and R. N. Sanford). 1950. New York: Norton, 1969.
Minima Moralia: Reflections from Damaged Life. 1951. London: New Left Books, 1974.
The Stars Down to Earth and other Essays on the Irrational in Culture. 1952–3. London: Routledge, 1994.
Prisms: Cultural Criticism and Society. 1955. London: Neville Spearman, 1967.
Negative Dialectics. 1966. London: Routledge, 1973.
The Culture Industry: Selected Essays on Mass Culture. Various dates. London: Routledge, 1991.

Further reading

Susan Buck-Morss. 1977. *The Origin of Negative Dialectics: Theodor W. Adorno, Walter Benjamin, and the Frankfurt Institute*. New York: Free Press.
Nigel Gibson and Andrew Rubin, eds. 2002. *Adorno: A Critical Reader*. Oxford: Blackwell.
Simon Jarvis. 1998. *Adorno: A Critical Introduction*. Cambridge: Polity Press.
Martin Jay. 1984. *Adorno*. Cambridge, MA: Harvard University Press.

EAMONN CARRABINE

CHARLES BOOTH

Born in 1840 into a commercial family in Liverpool, Charles Booth was apprenticed to a shipping firm at the age of sixteen. He joined his brother, Alfred, in the leather trade in 1862 and they subsequently established a successful shipping firm together, and Charles remained actively involved with it until his retirement in 1912. Booth became alienated from the dominant, nonconformist business class of Liverpool into which he had been born, and, following his marriage in 1871 to Mary Macaulay, the couple settled in London. Influenced earlier by positivism, he embarked in 1886 on the major survey of London 'life and labour' for which he became famous and which is commonly regarded as initiating the systematic study of poverty in Britain. The scale of the survey meant that, while results were published serially, it took over fifteen years before the full seventeen-volume edition was published. His work on the study and his concern with the problems of poverty led to an involvement in campaigning for old-age pensions and promoting the decasualization of labour. He died from a stroke in 1916.

The survey of life and labour began with a pilot study in Tower Hamlets. Booth then recruited numerous researchers to assist with the full study of the whole of London, which investigated the three main topics of poverty, occupations and religion. Among his researchers were many, such as **Beatrice Webb**, who went on to make names for themselves in social investigation. Hubert Llewellyn Smith, another of these original researchers, became a noted social researcher and, in 1928, undertook a 'repeat' of Booth's survey called the *New Survey of London Life and Labour.*

Booth's survey aimed not only to identify the poor and those engaged in different occupations, but also to classify them. This stress on classification and subdivision into types can also be seen in the work of the Charity Organisation Society (*see* **Helen Bosanquet**) and in the much earlier detailed journalism of Henry Mayhew. For the purposes of poverty measurement, Booth divided the working population into eight classes, from the poorest to the most well off and he labelled these A–H. These categories summarized economic circumstances but also had a moral dimension, with 'A' representing the 'feckless, deviant or criminal' groups.

Using this classification, Booth determined that about 30 per cent of the population were living in poverty. Some of this poverty he attributed to a lack of thrift or management or to 'idleness'; but his survey also revealed the low wages associated with unskilled labouring jobs and, more importantly, the problem of interrupted or unreliable work – the class of 'casual workers' who were deemed to be 'very poor'. His work revealed some sympathy with the situation of the poor and the insecurity of their situation in the face of circumstances such as age or trade cycles that were beyond their control. On the other hand, and in line with the attitudes of the time, he was often inclined to locate the causes of poverty in failings of character. The difficulty in identifying causes for poverty was one he struggled with, not being able to attribute responsibility between 'irregularity of earning and irregularity of conduct', and recognizing that 'a man is apt to drink when he is idle, as well as to lose his work because of intemperate habits'.

Having divided the population into different classes, Booth could map the distribution of these classes. One of the most striking aspects of the study was the poverty maps, which classified streets by colour according to their class. In this he revealed a conviction that there is a spatial component to poverty – that who your neighbours are matters for your own circumstances. The maps also evidence a concern with the environmental context of poverty. Edwin Chadwick had, in 1842, made the connection between differential mortality rates and differences in living conditions across areas. But before Booth's maps, environmental explanations tended to remain of interest primarily to local medical officers of health. Booth thus brought environmental issues into empirical sociological investigation.

The survey has been much criticized for its methodology. Booth used school board visitors – those who undertook to ensure the attendance of children at school – to collect information on the circumstances of families. However, his extrapolation from these findings to families without school-age children was speculative. Moreover, his 'definitions' of the poverty levels of household 'classes' were general descriptive categories that did not equate to specific criteria. Indeed, the whole seventeen volumes, while dense with often fascinating detail, remain primarily descriptive rather than analytical.

Nevertheless, the study made a big impact on Victorian society and on social investigation. The maps, the systematic accounts of occupations, the warnings about the problems of irregular work, the inference about the role of spatial or environmental factors in contributing to poverty, and the extensive amount of poverty that Booth identified all ensured wide-ranging interest. As well as Llewellyn Smith's repeat London survey, Booth's work was the impetus behind **Seebohm Rowntree**'s influential survey of York, which attempted to analyse York according to Booth's classes while also developing a far more systematic measure of poverty. Moreover, for Booth himself, his research stimulated a particular concern with the plight of the impoverished elderly and the impact of casual employment on the workforce as a whole. He campaigned strenuously for old-age pensions up until the introduction of a state pension scheme in 1908.

For contemporary readers, interest in *Life and Labour* is more as a historical document than for the appropriateness of its methodology or the accuracy of its poverty analysis. In scope and scale it remains unmatched and it is of interest for its combination of a range of different materials – such as analysis of the census alongside the survey data itself – as well as for its range of approaches: observation, inquiry, numerical calculations and geographical description. The study also offers a unique resource in that the original field notebooks and other support material have been preserved, generating another layer of detail to the published results and providing direct insight into the methods of survey research employed. Access to the notebooks, lodged at the London School of Economics, and also to online versions of the maps has been made possible by an extensive online resource (http://booth.lse.ac.uk/), providing a fascinating insight into patterns of life in London at the end of the ninenteenth century.

See also: Helen Bosanquet, Seebohm Rowntree, Beatrice Webb.

Major works

The Life and Labour of the People in London. 17 vols. 1902–3. London: Macmillan.

Further reading

Mary Booth. 1918. *Charles Booth: A Memoir*. London: Macmillan.
Josie Harris. 2004. 'Booth, Charles (1840–1916)', in H. C. G. Matthew and B. Harrison, eds. Oxford Dictionary of National Biography: in association with the British Academy: from the earliest times to the year 2000, Oxford: Oxford University Press.
Ernest P. Hennock. 'Concepts of Poverty in the British Social Surveys from Charles Booth to Arthur Bowley', in M. Bulmer, K. Bales and K. Kish Sklar, eds. 1991. *The Social Survey in Historical Perspective*. Cambridge: Cambridge University Press.
Rosemary O'Day and David Englander. 1993. *Mr Charles Booth's Inquiry: Life and Labour of the People in London Reconsidered*. London: Hambledon Press.

LUCINDA PLATT

HELEN BOSANQUET

Helen Bosanquet (née Dendy) was a social theorist concerned with poverty and a pioneer of modern social work practice. She was born in Manchester in 1860 and completed her education in 1889 at Newnham College, Cambridge, where she studied moral sciences. On graduating, she moved to London and took up employment as District Secretary to the Shoreditch Committee of the Charity Organisation Society (COS). She continued to be closely involved with the COS throughout the rest of her active life. Her interest in moral philosophy led her to the London Ethical Society, where she met the philosopher Bernard Bosanquet, whom she married in 1895. She gave up paid employment on her marriage and spent more time putting her ideas and prescriptions into writing; between 1909 and 1921 she edited the *Charity Organisation Review*, the organ of the COS. Bernard died in 1923 and she wrote a memoir of his life; she herself died in 1925.

The 'problem of poverty', that is, the visible existence of deprivation and squalor in the midst of affluence, was a prominent issue for late Victorian society, and social theorists and activists sought explanations for this phenomenon. The COS viewed it as a problem of 'the poor' themselves and looked for solutions in a professional and efficient approach to charitable giving. While its original emphasis was on the effective co-ordination of philanthropic effort at local level, the COS shifted its focus to a concern with working effectively with applicants for charity to enhance their long-term self-sufficiency. Helen and Bernard Bosanquet provided a theoretical underpinning for this work and clearly defined the role and skills of case work.

It has been argued that the spirit and philosophy of the COS can be dismissed as reactionary and without further interest, given its strenuous opposition to unplanned charity and its stress on thrift and family responsibility. Nevertheless, its development of case work and the establishment of professional social work training with both generic and specialist components was both innovative and central to the development of the British welfare state. This duality of conservative theory underpinned by progressive practice does not, however, fully reflect the complexity of the COS's approach to poverty. There were clearly *laissez-faire* elements within the COS that were rigidly unsympathetic to 'the poor', regarding them as a class apart, and viewing all doles as undermining incentives to work and all applications for support as morally reprehensible. But the principles and practice of the COS, as articulated by Helen Bosanquet, were more complex (see, for example, *Social Work in London*).

Bosanquet stressed the potential for development and the active citizenship of the destitute. Optimistic about the potential of working-class families, and particularly working-class women, she argued that individuals and families should be assisted to tackle and rise above their misfortune. It was important to understand the cause of poverty in terms of the individual's capacity to deal with it – their character – and the COS volunteer (or case worker) should then work with the individual and their family to focus on increasing their understanding of their predicament and its long-term solution, assisting them to take appropriate action. This might include encouraging emigration where unemployment had resulted from industrial change or providing education in child welfare.

For Bosanquet it was essential that the different classes should become familiar with each other (see *Rich and Poor*). Rather than simply 'leading by example', Bosanquet argued that case workers should understand the perspective of the recipients of their help. However, she also expected the case worker to come to a 'true' understanding of their client's predicament and its causes through detailed investigation, including making enquiries of family and neighbours.

The dignity of the individual was important to Bosanquet, and the case-work approach was contrasted with what were regarded as degrading and often insufficient doles. However, little acknowledgement was made of the intrusive nature of the detailed investigations and how much such intrusion might be resented. The family unit was seen as the basis of individual development, and the source of interdependence and responsibility (see *The Family*). Any state usurpation of family roles was regarded as dangerous and counterproductive. Thus, free school meals were strongly resisted on the grounds that they would undermine parental responsibility. However, case workers themselves would attempt to support 'proper' family relationships and, by making judgements on appropriate roles, had the potential to disrupt family life.

The emphasis on highly competent case workers to diagnose, at family level, the causes of poverty and then to support family members in bettering themselves required trained professionals. In 1903 the COS's School of Sociology was founded to initiate professional social work training in the UK. Bosanquet was influential in determining what was taught and that the training should cover both practical skills and more general education. The School was incorporated into the London School of Economics in 1912, and many aspects of its curriculum and approach were carried through in social work training into the post-Second World War welfare state.

From her early work with the COS, Bosanquet had direct experience of living among 'the poor'. She brought this experience into her analysis of working-class families, and it provided her with apposite examples for her writings. For her, it was not inappropriate to make general statements on the basis of anecdotes, since it was her philosophy rather than her investigation that drove her accounts. Indeed, she was critical of attempts to draw causal accounts from a demonstration of 'the facts' and was largely suspicious of statistics. Thus she prioritized her 'knowledge' over the evidence presented by **Rowntree**'s 1901 findings on the extent of poverty in York. Resisting the idea that those in regular employment could have insufficient incomes adequately to support a family, which would undermine much of the basis of what the COS was trying to do, she vehemently contested both his methods and his results.

Bosanquet was appointed to the Royal Commission on the Poor Laws in 1905, to review the workings of a system of state relief that was considered to be under substantial pressure. Alongside Bosanquet on the Commission was **Beatrice Webb**. While Bosanquet was the driving force behind the majority report, Webb wrote her own minority report and disparaged Bosanquet in her autobiographical writings. The majority report was concerned to ensure that the Poor Law continued to operate as a system of last resort, even if not necessarily in an excessively punitive way (except in relation to those deemed to be able bodied and 'work shy'). It stressed that the Poor Law should not provide for non-paupers; and that every effort should be made to encourage the development of character – and thus the avoidance of pauperism – by an extension of the case-work approach.

However, the appeal for an extension of case work came at a time when voluntary activity was declining rather than increasing and key developments in state welfare – strongly at odds with the COS view of the good society – were imminent. By the time the Commission reported in 1909, state pensions and school meals had been introduced. Professional social work was to continue but increasingly as part of, rather than as an alternative to, the development of state welfare.

See also: Charles Booth, Seebohm Rowntree, Beatrice Webb.

Major works

Rich and Poor (as Mrs Bernard Bosanquet).1896. London: Macmillan.
Social Work in London, 1869–1912.1914. Brighton: The Harvester Press, 1973.
The Family. 1915. London: Macmillan.

Further reading

Jane Lewis. 1991. *Women and Social Action in Victorian and Edwardian England*. Cheltenham: Edward Elgar.

Royal Commission on the Poor Laws. *The Poor Law report of 1909: a summary explaining the defects of the present system and the principal recommendations of the Commission, so far as relates to England and Wales* (The Majority Report). London: HMSO.

LUCINDA PLATT

AUGUSTE COMTE

Auguste Comte is generally hailed as the founder of sociology, a term he coined in 1839 to refer to the nascent science of society. He also established a new philosophy, positivism, which stressed the importance of limiting knowledge to what could be observed. This philosophy led him to create a new secular religion: the Religion of Humanity. In addition, he pioneered a new academic field – the history of science – which put scientific developments into their historical context. Comte was born in Montpellier, France, in 1798 at the end of the French Revolution, which had overturned traditional institutions and beliefs. A consensus no longer existed as to what constituted a legitimate government or how society should be organized. Comte shared the longing of his contemporaries for new certitudes and a new cohesive community. As a teenager, he rejected his parents' loyalty to the monarchy and the Catholic Church. A brilliant student in mathematics, he was accepted at an early age at the Ecole Polytechnique, a prestigious engineering school in Paris. Expelled in 1816 for his rebellious attitudes, he worked from 1817 to 1824 as a writer for the social reformer Henri de Saint-Simon. Thanks to him, Comte learned to think in terms of rebuilding a society on the basis of industry and a 'positive philosophy' that was to be grounded in the sciences, especially the study of society. Always seeking the middle way, Comte was also influenced by thinkers on both the left and right, such as Mary Wollstonecraft, David Hume, Montesquieu, Condorcet, Johann Herder, Immanuel Kant and Joseph de Maistre. In 1826, Comte made his first effort to synthesize knowledge in a public lecture course but, suffering from manic depression and paranoia, he was hospitalized. He worked as a journalist for the Saint-Simonians on his release from an asylum a few months later, though he distanced himself from this sect. He eventually secured a job as a teaching assistant in mathematics and admissions officer at the Ecole Polytechnique, where he worked from 1832 to 1851. After his dismissal from this post, his disciples supported him until his death in 1857.

Comte's greatest work, the *Cours de philosophie positive*, was published in six volumes between 1830 and 1842. It introduced positivism, which represented a synthesis of all knowledge based on the scientific – that is, positive – method. Comte argued that scientific knowledge had to derive from the observation of concrete phenomena. Yet empiricism had its limits, for the mere accumulation of facts could not lead to a full grasp of reality, which was in any case impossible to attain. Moreover, facts could not even be perceived without the guidance of provisional *a priori* theories. These theories had to be verified by induction and deduction, both of which were crucial to scientific investigation. Likewise, rationalism had to complement empiricism, for sciences could not be reduced to the purely experiential. Abstraction and the use of the imagination were essential to constructing scientific laws from observations. The essence of these scientific laws consisted of the ability to make predictions. According to Comte's classification of the sciences, there were six fields that had reached or were attaining scientific status. Positivism embraced these six core sciences, which developed in the following order: mathematics, astronomy, physics, chemistry, biology and sociology. Comte treated the history of each science, showing its relationship to the development of other sciences and society at large. Although he never succeeded in attaining a chair in the history of science, a professorship in this field was created at the Collège de France in 1892.

Comte argued that sociology, the last science, was just entering the positive stage and represented the keystone of the positivist system. Once the study of society, which included politics, became a positive science, social theory would have the authority of theories in the natural sciences and its rational principles could be used to reconstruct the post-revolutionary world. Sociology was divided into two parts: social statics and social dynamics, which cultivated, respectively, feelings of solidarity with other members of society and a sense of connection with past and future generations. Focused on the organization of society, social statics studied the basis of social order and investigated the family and moral values. Treating the development or progress of society, social dynamics was the scientific study of history.

The main law of sociology, or, more exactly, social dynamics, was Comte's famous law of three stages. This law stated that every branch of knowledge and every social and political structure went through a theological, metaphysical and positive stage of history. In the theological stage, people attempt to understand the world around them by tracing occurrences to the action of one or more gods. (There were three substages: fetishism, polytheism and monotheism.) Supernatural ideas were used to link observations. In the transitional metaphysical stage, abstract entities like Nature or Reason replaced God. The positive stage of history was about to begin. In this stage, people would eschew the issue of origins or first causes and focus on explaining how, not why, phenomena worked. Replacing gods and metaphysical abstractions, scientific laws would be descriptive.

Each of the six sciences went through these three stages according to their distance from man and the simplicity of the phenomena that they studied. Dealing with the most complex phenomena, those closest to man, sociology developed last. Because all aspects of knowledge were interrelated and the mind was driven to make all ideas homogeneous, the scientific or positive method would inevitably be applied to social phenomena. Once all ideas became scientific, the positive philosophy, comprising all six sciences, would be completed and unified. Knowledge would be brought together not on the basis of a Newtonian-like law, which had been Saint-Simon's and other thinkers' hope, but on the grounds of having a common method, the scientific method, and a common object of study, that is, society. (Every scientific theory had to relate to social needs.) All knowledge would be 'positive', which meant, to Comte, certain, precise, real, constructive, useful and relative. Convinced that theory preceded practice and that ideas ran the universe, he argued that the intellectual harmony coming from positivism would usher in a stable industrial society.

Yet, living during the romantic period, Comte believed that reason could not satisfy all our needs and that emotions shaped our ideas and actions and determined our happiness. Humans were characterized not only by their intellect but also by their innate sociability: phrenology, he held, proved that people were naturally 'good' and loving beings. The consensus underlying society had to be subjective as well as intellectual. But a consensus did not exist in Comte's own home. After fighting with his wife, Caroline Massin, Comte agreed to her demands for a separation. In 1842, their seventeen-year-old marriage terminated. Three years later, Comte fell madly in love with Clotilde de Vaux, a young aspiring novelist, who died in 1846. Their friendship reinforced his interest in sentiment. He presented her as the muse who inspired his second major work, the *Système de philosophie positive*, published in four volumes between 1851 and 1854. It transformed his philosophy into a religion designed to bring people together in order to effect the improvement of society, that is, Humanity. A non-metaphysical entity, Humanity had to be placed at the centre not only of people's intellectual world, but of their emotional and practical lives. One of his primary purposes was to encourage the development of 'altruism', a word he coined. He made morality the seventh science to highlight the role of individuals in society.

In constructing his Religion of Humanity, Comte drew on disparate traditions to rejuvenate people's emotional life, which he believed was endangered by the growing 'positivity' or scientism of modern existence. Influenced by the revolutionaries, Comte set up festivals and a new calendar to commemorate the great figures of the past, such as Aristotle, Caesar and Dante. The cult of the dead was seen as important in reinforcing the sense of human continuity. His Catholic background was evident in his insistence that new sacraments be created to remind people of their connections to the community. Imitating Napoleon, he also stressed the importance of establishing positivist schools to inculcate intellectual and moral principles. The arts would be revived to offset the 'dryness' of the sciences, whose research would be restricted to matters relevant to human needs. In addition, Comte wanted positivism to embrace fetishism, which he made into a construct epitomizing benevolent feeling, spontaneity, humility and concreteness. Positivists would not worship gods in concrete objects as primitive fetishists did. Instead, they would venerate abstract, collective beings: the 'Great Being' (Humanity), the 'Great Fetish' (Earth) and the 'Great Milieu' (Space). Comte highlighted the fetishist aspects of positivism to demonstrate that his religion, unlike Catholicism or Protestantism, would be welcomed by Africans, Oceanians and American Indians. It could 'civilize' these primitive peoples without destroying their uniqueness. By becoming universal, the Religion of Humanity would unify the entire world.

Comte's politics defy easy explanation. Having lived through monarchies, republics and empires, he attacked his contemporaries for focusing too much on political experimentations. To him, an intellectual revolution had to come first. It would lead to a moral revolution and then a social and political overhaul of society. Every society reflected the prevailing synthesis of knowledge. To characterize social development, Comte blended his law of three stages with his principle of the 'separation of powers', whereby the temporal power supervised human actions while the spiritual power oversaw opinions and ideas. In the theological period, society was governed by priests and military men and monarchs tended to rule. In the metaphysical period, metaphysician and lawyers were in charge and parliaments proliferated. In the positivist era, republics would be the norm. Society would be dominated by scientists and industrialists, who would apply scientific knowledge. Comte did not advocate a totalitarian government of scientists. Indeed, he thought that the scientists of his day were narrow-minded, selfish specialists. The scientists who represented the spiritual power would be positive philosophers or sociologists with a wide knowledge of all the sciences, which Comte assumed would make them generous. Preaching in temples of Humanity, they would advise industrialists and check their tendency to abuse their power. Likewise, the industrialists would make sure that the positive philosophers limited themselves to education and counselling; they could not exercise political or practical power. In charge of encouraging sociability and a spirit of cooperation, the spiritual power would be helped by women and workers, who were more emotional than the other members of society.

Comte advocated the Cult of Woman, which reflected the nineteenth century's gender biases. He claimed to be eager to emancipate women, whom he regarded as experts in the emotions. They would have a major role to play in countering the shallowness of men and creating a compassionate society. Comte revived the salons to give them their own space in which to mingle with men and shape public opinion. Yet his patriarchal tendencies were evident in his insistence that women not exercise economic or political power. Comte idealized workers and sympathized with their marginal status in bourgeois society. They should be able to form associations (unions), own their own abodes for the sake of stability, and meet in cafés. Temples of Humanity, salons and cafés were important public spaces for making social connections. Supportive of the workers during the revolution of 1848, Comte condemned their employers for their materialism and egoism. Indeed, until the industrialists were regenerated, he recommended that positivist republics be ruled by a dictatorship of three workers concerned for the interests of the entire society. An opponent of nationalism and imperialism, he wanted the future global society to be broken up into small city-states, which could better connect families to Humanity. If the world was made up of small, approximately equal republics and people received a similar secular, scientific education, there would be less chance of war.

Comte's impact was widespread in politics and academia. On the one hand, his anti-clerical, scientific, republican philosophy, with its stress on progress, was used by opponents of the status quo in France's

Third Republic and Latin America, especially Brazil. Positivism also attracted American leftists, such as Edward Bellamy and Herbert Croly, and prominent English reformers and writers, including John Stuart Mill, **Harriet Martineau** and George Eliot. On the other hand, Comte's authoritarianism and stress on duties, hierarchy and order were much appreciated by right-wing movements, such as the Action Française. In addition, Comte's scientific approach to society and history influenced philosophy, literature, historiography and sociology (especially that of **Emile Durkheim**). Comte's fears of social atomization, musings about the effects of scepticism, attacks on scientific specialization, denunciation of egoism and selfishness in a capitalist society, criticism of one-dimensional humans, longing for a religion in a secular age, and stress on socialization through education and public rituals are still relevant today.

See also: Emile Durkheim, Harriet Martineau.

Major works

Cours de philosophie positive. 1830–42. Condensed and translated as *Positive Philosophy of Auguste Comte*. 2 vols. New York: D. Appleton, 1853.
A Discourse on the Positive Spirit. 1844. London: William Reeves, 1903.
System of Positive Polity. 6 vols. 1851–4. London: Longman Green, 1875–7.
Catechism of Positive Philosophy. 1852. London: John Chapman, 1858.
Appeal to Conservatives. 1855. London: Trübner and Co, 1889.
Subjective Synthesis. 1856. London: Kegan Paul, Trench, Trübner, 1891.

Further reading

Pickering, Mary. 1993. *Auguste Comte: An Intellectual Biography*, vol. 1. Cambridge: Cambridge University Press.
Scharff, Robert C. 1995. *Comte after Positivism*. Cambridge: Cambridge University Press.
Wernick, Andrew. 2001. *Auguste Comte and the Religion of Humanity: The Post-Theistic Program of French Social Theory*. Cambridge: Cambridge University Press.

MARY PICKERING

CHARLES COOLEY

Cooley's position within the sociological hall of fame is well deserved but quite surprising, given his personal history. A shy, reclusive character who found social situations both exhausting and confusing, he began his career as a mechanical engineer and drifted into sociology almost accidentally. Cooley was an introspective, self-reflective man who was somewhat prone to daydreaming. He read selectively and wrote sporadically, as and when his artistic temperament allowed. Nevertheless, he had an extraordinary ability to sit back and reflect upon the nature of human beings and of society. Cooley is now most famous for his theoretical insights into the self and for his influence upon the symbolic interactionist tradition, although he also wrote extensively on many other aspects of social and political theory.

Charles Horton Cooley was born in Ann Arbor, Michigan, on 17 August 1864, the fourth child of Thomas Cooley and Mary Elizabeth Horton. His father had a successful career in law and was eventually made a Justice of the State Supreme Court of Michigan. He was a gentle, modest man whom Charles resembled in both character and constitution. The boy was small, slight and physically weak, and so would spend a lot of his time resting at home, where he found solace through his escape into books. Shy, self-conscious and somewhat unused to social contact, Charles found himself teased for his effeminate voice and passive manner. Throughout his life he remained extremely concerned about what others thought of him and was eager for approval. In his journals he recalled how he would fantasize about situations in which he performed heroic deeds and imagined how other people might then change their opinions of him. As Edward Jandy remarked, it is likely that this tendency to retreat into a rich inner world was what shaped Cooley's interest in perceptions of self and others.

Despite frequent interruptions to his education because of poor health, Cooley graduated from the University of Michigan in 1887 with a bachelor's degree in mechanical engineering. He had intended to pursue graduate studies in this subject, but instead found himself more interested in social theory and political economy. He was influenced by the dominant idealist philosophy, and particularly by the work of Ralph Emerson, Johann Wolfgang von Goethe and Henry Thoreau. He also read **Herbert Spencer**'s sociology, the idea that societies were like biological organisms appealing to his interest in the 'mechanics' of evolution. However, Cooley was very critical of the way in which such models neglected the more personal and experiential side of social life and lacked a 'human' element. His 1894 PhD thesis on 'The Theory of Transportation' explored the idea of transport systems as holistic, organic entities based on efficient lines of communication, and this foreshadowed the ecological approach that he would later take to the study of society.

Cooley was appointed to an academic job at the University of Michigan, where he remained throughout his career. Rising through the ranks from assistant professor to full professor of sociology, he remained modest about his achievements and was shy in the company of his colleagues. He saw himself as an outsider to mainstream sociology, which was dominated by statistical analyses of 'social problems'. Cooley's own work focused on more fundamental lines of enquiry about the nature of society and of the social self. He was a charismatic lecturer and very popular with his students, in particular those who attended his graduate seminars. Research, for Cooley, entailed reading and reflecting on social theory, and he used his journals to record his developing ideas. Cooley saw himself not as a social scientist but as an artist-philosopher, who depicted his vision of society through carefully constructed prose. He wanted his writing to be accessible to the educated lay reader as well as to academics, and so avoided the conventions of traditional, 'scientific' writing in favour of a more creative and imaginative style.

His first book, *Human Nature and the Social Order*, was published in 1902. Cooley was concerned that it was somewhat autobiographical and might reveal too much about his private thoughts and feelings, but in fact it reads as an impressive theoretical text. The main argument of the book is that the mental processes that we experience as individuals are nevertheless tied to social processes and the structure of the social world. In emphasizing the interconnectedness of mind, self and society, Cooley echoes the ideas of **George Herbert Mead**, another key influence upon the symbolic interactionist tradition. In Cooley's view, the mind is a product of its social environment and we develop our personalities through internalizing social processes such as interaction and communication. This posed a challenge to psychoanalytic and sociobiological theories, which treated human nature as existing innately and independently of the social world. By contrast, Cooley's theory suggests that the mind is socially shaped and emerges as a product of the social process. Indeed, his approach is sometimes described as 'mentalistic', in that it focuses on the way in which we create mental representations of other people and objects, including 'society'. In this respect, Cooley's theory is compatible with **Durkheim**'s notion of the collective representations that shape the way individuals think and feel.

Drawing on the ideas of William James, Cooley distinguished between the empirical self, which can be observed by others, and the social self, as a collection of feelings about who 'I' am and what is 'mine'. Whereas Mead identified the 'I' and the 'me' as two phases of an internal conversation, Cooley focused on the former, suggesting that it was the 'phases of I' that form the nucleus of the social self. For example, he pointed to the various ways in which people use the word 'I' in conversation to express different 'self-feelings', such as desires, declarations and ambitions. This reminds us that language often has a performative element, as we can use statements about how we think, feel or perceive things as a way of displaying identity to others. Indeed, Cooley argued that it is impossible to think of oneself without also thinking of other people or objects in the world and differentiating ourselves from them; we define ourselves relationally. As he put it, '[t]here is no sense of "I" ... without its correlative sense of you, or he, or they'. The social self therefore represents a collection of thoughts and feelings about oneself – 'self-sentiments' – that emerge from the communicative life of society.

Central to this argument is Cooley's notion of the looking-glass self, an image of oneself from the perspective of other people. This is rather like Mead's idea of the 'me' in that it involves taking the view of the other towards oneself as a social object. Cooley, however, focused on the attitudes we attribute to these audiences and their effects on the self. He suggested that the looking-glass self has three elements: the imagination of our appearance to another person, the imagination of his or her judgement of that appearance, and the resultant self-feelings, such as pride, shame or mortification. Thus the way in which we think about ourselves is based not on an objective, mechanical image of 'me', but on these imputed sentiments which *others* seem to have of us. This also means that we can have many different social selves, as the looking glasses that different audiences in different situations hold up to us will reveal a wide range of images. This idea of the self as fluid, dynamic and socially negotiated reminds us again of the influence that Cooley had upon symbolic interactionism.

Cooley's second book, *Social Organization*, was published in 1909; it drew upon more classic sociological theory and so was more readily accepted by his contemporaries. In it he addressed the question of what 'society' is and how it is ordered, considering in particular the relationship between larger, formal organizations and the smaller groups of which they are composed. For example, the social class system is an example of the way in which certain values, such as meritocracy and individualism, can help to keep order and prevent conflict between groups which have conflicting interests. Cooley argued that it is the task of these larger, more complex forms of social organization to co-ordinate the actions of individuals and interest groups. In this respect, he was recognizing the structural forces at play in society, and showing his allegiance to the organicist theories of Spencer and Durkheim. However, other ideas discussed in *Social Organization* reveal Cooley's continuing interest in social processes of interaction and their role in personality development. His notion of the 'primary group', for example, refers to those groups of people who provide the individual with his or her first experience of social unity, and who remain a source of 'intimate face-to-face association and cooperation'. For example, the family, the peer group and the neighbourhood community can all help to shape the ideas and beliefs of the developing child, and thus act as agents of socialization. Cooley believed that our feelings of sympathy and identification with primary groups help to connect the self to the social world and create a sense of common purpose. Although he maintained that these groups could be characterized by conflict as well as love and harmony, they were 'not independent of the larger society, but to some extent reflect its spirit'. In this respect, Cooley reminds us of his argument that human nature is shaped by social processes: rather than existing inherently in the individual, it is a 'group-nature' or condition of the social mind. Echoing Durkheim, he argued that 'society and individuals are inseparable phases of a common whole, so that wherever we find an individual fact we may look for a social fact to go with it'.

Cooley's third book, *Social Process*, was published in 1918 and reflected his increasing interest in social conflict and political competition. Here, Cooley considered what would happen when there was a clash of interests between the values of primary groups and institutional values, such as religious beliefs and ideologies. He wrote this book during the First World War, as he became progressively disquieted by the actions of the American government. Cooley was a firm believer in democracy, which he thought could be achieved through more humanistic, peaceful means. He also warned against the dangers of wealth and power being concentrated in the hands of a few, and argued for a more egalitarian distribution of economic and political power. The task of reconciling conflicting interests was a central problem for all types of social organization, Cooley thought, but one that could nevertheless be achieved.

In the last decade of his life, Cooley became more settled and contented. He was now recognized by his colleagues as an eminent scholar, and had been president of the American Sociological Society. Although he continued to feel nervous about giving papers and speeches, he began to enjoy the social side of academic life much more. In 1927, he published his final book, a collection of articles, quotations and musings from his journals, which was intended to inspire those pursuing academic careers. He called this collection *Life and the Student*. It was as personal and self-revelatory as his first book, but less ashamedly so. He was beginning to research a new interest in the question of sociological method when he became ill with cancer. Cooley died on 8 May 1929, at the age of sixty-four.

See also: George Herbert Mead.

See also in *Fifty Key Sociologists: The Contemporary Theorists*: Howard Becker, Erving Goffman.

Major works

Human Nature and the Social Order. 1902. Glencoe, IL: The Free Press.
Social Organization. 1909. Glencoe, IL: The Free Press.
Social Process. 1918. New York: Charles Scribner's Sons.
Life and the Student. 1927. New York: Knopf.

Further reading

Edward C. Jandy. 1942. *Charles Horton Cooley: His Life and His Social Theory*. New York: The Dryden Press.

SUSIE SCOTT

OLIVER COX

Oliver Cromwell Cox is a significant but widely neglected analyst of capitalism, race relations and fascism, publishing five books and more than thirty articles during his lifetime. Political factors were important in the neglect of Cox while he was alive. He was neglected in the United States because of racism against black scholars, because of his leftist thinking and because of the significant influence of Marxist analysis in his work. Much of his work appeared at a time when politicians and the public in the United States feared Marxism and communism more than they feared disease. Cox was also ignored because of his criticisms of the dominant sociological model of race relations in the mid-twentieth century, the caste school of race relations largely shaped by Chicago University's Department of Sociology. In consequence he was confined to teaching in small and little-known colleges.

Despite the hardships that he faced, and the racial discrimination and the hostility addressed to his work, Cox continued relentlessly pursuing his analysis, publishing and occasionally lecturing. The foremost writers of his day, nevertheless, did not frequently cite his work, and he was little known outside the United States before the 1970s. He received no formal acclaim from the sociology establishment until he was awarded in 1971, as the first ever recipient, the DuBois–Johnson–Frazier award by the American Sociological Association. As a result, Cox's work has been more widely read in the USA since the 1970s, and there is now a greater appreciation of his analysis and concepts. His life is a testimony to hard work and persistence.

Cox was born in 1901 in Trinidad, where he received his schooling before migrating to the United Sates in 1927 to study Law at Northwestern University, Chicago. While in the United States, he succumbed to poliomyelitis, which left him permanently crippled in both legs, and he spent the rest of his life walking with crutches. His initial intention had been to return to Trinidad to practise law, but he felt that a future in law was now unlikely and turned to the study of economics. He earned a Master's Degree in 1932, and then a PhD in sociology in 1938, both from the University of Chicago. Though he found economics inadequate for explaining social phenomena, the influence of his economics training was consistently evidenced in his future work. He carried out these studies at a time when the Great Depression highlighted social inequities across the nation, particularly for blacks.

Racial discrimination and Jim Crow segregation in the United States meant that there were no opportunities for Cox to teach at the more prestigious and resource-rich universities and his first teaching position was at Wiley College, a small Baptist school in Marshall, Texas. He moved to Tuskegee Institute in 1944 and that school hoped that Cox's presence would bring them prestige. They were not wrong and his publication record was impressive. While there, however, he was not supportive of the Booker T. Washington approach, either in his personal relations or in his analysis. He moved to Lincoln University in 1949 and to Wayne State University in 1970. He died in 1974.

He published 'Social Focus – The Modern Caste School of Race Relations' in 1942 and *Caste, Class and Race*, his best known work, was published in 1948. The consistent theme in these works is the failure of the caste school to clearly distinguish between caste, class and race as analytical concepts. Cox also rejected the dominant school's focus on individual prejudice and attitudes, and he argued that **Gunnar Myrdal**'s famous study *An American Dilemma*, published in 1944, was but one example, albeit the epitome, of all 'classical scholarship on the subject of race relations' in the United States. Cox questioned the imprecise definition of 'caste' provided by this school, and he challenged their claims to originality in the face of many clear precedents. Above all, he articulated the limited applicability of the concept of caste to blacks and whites in the American South, given its conceptualization in another time and place, that is India, since ancient times. Instead of seeking the cause of racial inequality, as the dominant schools did, in the 'hearts of the American people' and thus seeking the solution with the 'guardians of morals', Cox turned his attention to the ways in which capitalist society benefited from the presence of a distinctive and exploitable class of workers. *Caste, Class and Race* is an analysis of the broad principles of inequality and social stratification across all human societies. He argued that 'Our hypothesis is that racial exploitation and race prejudice developed among Europeans with the rise of capitalism and nationalism'. Because 'racial antagonism is part and parcel of this class struggle', '[t]he interest behind racial antagonism is an exploitative interest'. For Cox, racism emerged with the rise of modern European capitalism and racial antagonism was a central component of class struggle.

Cox saw fascism as an extreme type of racism and he compared oppression of black Americans with the rise of fascism in Europe and Asia. Both had to be understood, he argued, in terms of what they contributed to class domination. He rejected the dominant explanations of the day – in which fascism was somehow caused by working-class authoritarianism or an authoritarian personality. An understanding of fascism is important, he argued, because it is fascism that promotes nationalism and racism. Fascism is one politically organized aspect of capitalist class consciousness and '[i]n any fascist movement emphasis upon race superiority and racial antagonism or intolerance helps to confuse the masses and to develop a degree of racial egocentrism'.

Since the time that Cox wrote, a massive volume of writings on Marxism, class and race has appeared, and so Cox's work seems somewhat antiquated. Several of his key arguments are now regarded as too simple. However, his work introduced and crafted key concepts, and he elaborated the relationships between them in ways that have been incorporated into this literature, and we ought not forget our debt to him. Cox wrote three works on the nature and dynamics of world capitalism. Immanuel Wallerstein, the foremost analyst of world systems theory, has praised Cox for establishing the foundations and all the key principles of that approach to the analysis of capitalism. For students new to the analysis of class and race, it would be wise to consult Cox. While more recent writing reveals attention to complexities that Cox was not able to anticipate, Cox remains rewarding because of his directness, the clarity of concepts and arguments, and because his work, without showiness, is impressive and elegant in its formulations.

See also: Karl Marx, Lloyd Warner.

See also in *Fifty Key Sociologists: The Contemporary Theorists*: Immanuel Wallerstein.

Major works

Caste, Class and Race. 1948. New York: Monthly Review Press. Republished as *Race: A Study in Social Dynamics*. New York: Monthly Review Press, 2000.
The Foundations of Capitalism. 1959. London: Peter Owen.
Capitalism and American Leadership. 1962. New York: Philosophical Library.
Capitalism as a System. 1964. New York: Monthly Review Press.

Further reading

Herbert M. Hunter. 2001. *The Sociology of Oliver C. Cox: New Perspectives* (Special Issue of *Research in Race and Ethnic Relations*, vol. 11).
Adolph Reed. 'Race and Class in the Work of Oliver Cromwell Cox', *Monthly Review*, February, 2001.
Christopher McAuley. 2004. *The Mind of Oliver C. Cox*. Notre Dame, IN: University of Notre Dame Press.

STEPHEN SMALL

W. E. B. DUBOIS

The problem of the twentieth century is the problem of the color line – the relation of the darker to the lighter races of men in Asia and Africa, in America and in the islands of the sea.

DuBois is still widely considered the pre-eminent African American intellectual of the twentieth century. Scholars from sociology, history, politics, literature, philosophy and the recently established interdisciplinary fields of African–American studies and cultural studies continue to pay homage to the many enduring concepts, methodologies and theories that he contributed. DuBois' early contributions were in the field of sociology – though intellectually he became far more than a sociologist. He published history, novels, essays and poetry, and he edited journals. He was quintessentially a late-nineteenth century intellectual – broad in scope across many disciplines and penetrating in depth. His legacy still endures, and today it is well nigh impossible to consult the most popular African American or African diaspora magazines, newspapers or journals without finding references to him.

DuBois' work was a response to the dramatically changing circumstances of the United States, and the world, from the 1870s to the 1960s. It is difficult to judge his contribution independent of the fact that, as an African American, he lived in a period of legal racial segregation in the USA, and of widespread violence and discrimination against black people there and in the colonies of the British, French and Portuguese Empires. His work demanding equality was carried out at a time when, with the full knowledge of state officials, African Americans were being castrated and lynched. These social facts affected him directly and his life's work was largely a response to his analysis of them. Like most of the renowned black thinkers of the past 100 years, DuBois travelled across continents and countries as if distance was of no consequence. Travel across the African diaspora (that is, the regions and countries outside Africa with populations of African descent) was deemed indispensable to his mission.

Born in 1868 in the small town of Great Barrington, Massachusetts, in the USA, and raised by his mother alone, William Edward Burghardt DuBois received a BA in 1888 from Fisk University (a segregated university for African Americans only). He got a second BA, as well as his MA and PhD, at Harvard University, his graduate work being mainly in history and sociology. He also spent two years at the University of Berlin – at that time the most respected centre in the world for the study of history. Despite having a PhD from Harvard, no white university would recruit him as a professor, and his first job was at a small black college – Wilberforce – where he taught Latin and Greek. He taught the same topics at the University of Pennsylvania before moving to Atlanta University to teach sociology and conduct sociological research. He spent several decades teaching there – between 1897 and 1910, then again from 1934 to 1944.

A different writing career began in 1910 when he became editor of the news journal of the newly established multi-racial organization the National Association for the Advancement of Colored People (NAACP). In this journal he challenged the injustice of the Jim Crow system of segregation, implored middle-class blacks to act on behalf of all blacks, and provided a forum for a diverse range of black writings on history, politics, culture and art. He played a role in the Harlem Renaissance of the 1920s, a period of unprecedented creativity and publication by African Americans in the fields of art, literature, biography and music. In his journal he published a number of the prominent authors, such as Langston Hughes and Countee Cullen. He founded an academic journal, *Phylon*, in 1940 and was editor of that journal from 1940 to 1944.

In sociology, DuBois has been called the first black sociologist, and the first American sociologist of any colour, to carry out a large-scale research survey. This research was published in *The Philadelphia Negro*, a survey of the conditions of blacks in Philadelphia conducted in the 1890s, with much of the actual research carried out by DuBois himself. Sociology as a discipline was in its infancy and DuBois was greatly inspired by the promise of the application of scientific knowledge to profound and enduring issues of social organization, stability and conflict. He saw the study of blacks across the world as one way to articulate and apply the principles of the discipline of sociology, as well as to contribute knowledge to the resolution of the social problems of race relations.

DuBois contributed several key concepts that were innovative at the time and which are still central to sociological analyses today. The most important concept, that of the colour line, remains a compelling idea for interpreting racial inequality. While **Durkheim**, **Weber** and **Marx** all, for different reasons, predicted the decline of race or ethnic consciousness in the social organization of western society, DuBois saw just the opposite. Race would remain a tenacious and reprehensible social division. At the start of the twenty-first century, when blacks in the USA and Britain, despite some significant gains, are still far more likely than whites to be found in poverty, unemployment and prisons, and where race remains a fundamental aspect of social organization, it is clear that a colour line still shapes people's lives.

Most of what DuBois contributed to sociology was ignored in his day. He was not welcomed at sociology conferences organized by whites, and his work was hardly ever published in the major sociology journals. This has now changed and DuBois is currently recognized as one of the most important contributors to American sociology. The American Sociological Association's annual meeting in 2005 included several sessions on DuBois and organized a tour of the neighbourhoods where he carried out his research for *The Philadelphia Negro*.

DuBois' most famous book is *The Souls of Black Folks*, a collection of essays published in 1903. This was part autobiography, part history, cultural and philosophical inquiry, and part sociology. In it he expanded upon two concepts that were already evident in his work – 'double consciousness' and 'the talented tenth'. Challenging the hypocrisy of US segregation and violence against blacks, combined with the promise of equality and humanity and freedom for all people, he saw the consequences for African Americans:

> One ever feels his two-ness – an American, a Negro; two souls, two thoughts, two unreconciled strivings; two warring ideals in one dark body, whose dogged strength alone keeps it from being torn asunder.

This concept of double consciousness remains one of the most enduring and insightful concepts in an evaluation of black life in the United States today. With the concept of the 'talented tenth', DuBois argued that the most highly educated and talented African Americans should take responsibility for leading other less fortunate blacks in the quest for racial uplift. DuBois' own life was lived out exemplifying such an effort. Others, like sociologist E. Franklin Frazier, challenged the idea that the rich would help the poor – he saw wealthy blacks of the first half of the twentieth century as forming a 'black bourgeoisie', living in pathetic imitation of rich whites and with complete disdain for poor blacks. The concept continues to be significant and the most prominent debate in the sociology of African Americans today has to do with the role of class divisions.

DuBois wrote several books on Africa and on Africans throughout the world, building on work by Alexander Crummell and Edward Wilmot Blyden, America's first prominent black writers on these topics. He published a short book called *The Negro* and another, *The World and Africa*, that documented the role of Africans in the unfolding of civilizations. He wrote and published numerous articles on African history, culture and art in the NAACP journal. These contributions underpin much of the work done in African-American studies departments today.

Concurrently with his academic activities, DuBois was involved in political and social campaigns for racial equality. In the United States, where blacks faced racial discrimination and violence, DuBois felt an urgent need for hands-on political activity. He wrote: 'One could not be a calm, cool, and detached scientist while Negroes were lynched, murdered, and starved'. DuBois challenged colonialism and imperialism in the European empires that dominated most of Africa. He helped establish Pan-Africanism as an international political and cultural movement. Pan-Africanism promoted the international collective organization of blacks to achieve economic, political and social autonomy from Europeans. A primary goal was the end of colonialism in Africa. He played a central part in the organization of the first Pan-African Congress in Paris, in 1919, and he contributed to several subsequent conferences, being honoured at the 1945 Pan-African Congress. During this work he became colleague, friend or advisor to some of the most prominent black leaders of the century – including Kwame Nkrumah, the first president of Ghana, and Jomo Kenyatta, the first president of Tanzania.

But he also came into conflict with many black leaders. He challenged the political philosophy of Booker T. Washington, the most powerful and influential African American at the end of the nineteenth century. Washington encouraged blacks to forgo political rights and focus on economic progress in agricultural work. DuBois felt acceptance for a temporary period would become permanent and the two clashed frequently. DuBois was central to the establishment of the Niagara Movement that began in 1905. This movement involved a group of prominent black thinkers and educationalists and activities that offered a counter movement to Washington. They favoured agitation and confrontation of racism as principles for racial uplift. DuBois was also in conflict with Marcus Garvey, the leader of the largest movement of blacks in the history of the twentieth century – the Universal Negro Improvement Association – which had its heyday in the 1920s. While both favoured Pan-Africanism, they brought different priorities and approaches. DuBois was highly educated, aloof and often haughty. Garvey was working class, with a trade union background and limited formal education. It did not help that DuBois was light skinned and Garvey dark skinned – Garvey accused light-skinned blacks of advancing themselves at the expense of dark-skinned blacks. Political differences were aggravated by personal attacks and the two were life-long enemies. DuBois also clashed with Walter White, head of the NAACP.

DuBois' frustration with the inefficacy of neutral academic research in achieving social change was matched by his frustration with appeals to the dominant groups in the capitalist and racially segregated United States. His interest in Marx began while a student in Berlin and over time his work revealed the growing influence of

Marxism. One of his most important books, *Black Reconstruction in America*, is strongly influenced by such ideas. DuBois was closely associated with Paul Robeson, who also shared many socialist ideas and Pan-African ideals. He visited the Soviet Union in 1926, when the USSR was just nine years old.

DuBois' sympathy for the Soviet Union and his identification with leftist thinkers and ideals – especially international concerns like the peace moment and nuclear weapons – meant his work became less influential by the 1950s. Most blacks at this time were more directly focused on civil rights and the dismantling of Jim Crow segregation. Some saw inconsistencies in his work: for example, his continued appeal to racial solidarity, and especially to rich blacks to help poor blacks. Those quick to criticize what look like inconsistencies in his work forget that his analysis spanned nine decades, including two world wars, the independence of India and most African and Caribbean nations, and the invention of the car and aeroplane. Lest we forget that few concepts or analyses can transcend socio-historic specificity, we might remember the words of John Maynard Keynes: 'When the facts change, I change my opinion sir, what do you do?'

DuBois' work is powerful today, not only for its enduring contribution, but also as a reminder of the relationship between social thought and social practice. DuBois risked much in his work and writing. He was accused, variously, of being elitist, a separatist, a communist; he was denied access to immense research and education funds because of his radical stance and the opposition to him of Washington, and later on because of his socialist principles. He was forced into retirement by Atlanta University in 1944; he was fired from his NAACP job in 1948; he was indicted, briefly imprisoned and denied a passport by the US government for most of the 1950s. His life was directly threatened by racist whites on numerous occasions, particularly before the Second World War, and he fled from his office on a number of occasions to avoid being lynched. He got his passport back in 1958 and toured the Soviet Union and communist China. He visited Ghana in 1960 for the inauguration of Kwame Nkrumah as its first president. He joined the Communist Party in 1961 and left the United States permanently for Ghana, to begin work on *The Encyclopaedia Africana*. He renounced his US citizenship in 1963, becoming a citizen of Ghana, where he died six months later, on 27 August 1963, at the age of ninety-five. If he suffered much, he was also greatly revered. His work, his writings, his ability to combine sophisticated analysis with political action and insight, and his wide range of skills in different disciplines continue to inspire students, scholars and activists.

Major works

The Philadelphia Negro. 1899. Philadelphia: University of Pennsylvania Press, 1996.
The Souls of Black Folk. 1903. New York: Library of America, 1986.
The Negro. 1915. Philadelphia: University of Pennsylvania Press, 2001.
Black Reconstruction in America. 1935. New York: Free Press, 1998.
The World and Africa. 1947. New York: International Publishers, 1979.

Further reading

David Levering Lewis. 1993. *W. E. B. Du Bois: Biography of a Race, 1868–1919*. New York: Henry Holt.
David Levering Lewis. 2000. *W. E. B. Du Bois: The Fight for Equality and the American Century 1919–1963*. New York: Henry Holt.
Michael B. Katz and Thomas J. Sugrue, eds. 1998. *W. E. B. DuBois, Race, and the City: The Philadelphia Negro and Its Legacy*. Philadelphia: University of Pennsylvania Press.

STEPHEN SMALL

EMILE DURKHEIM

Durkheim is often ranked alongside **Karl Marx** and **Max Weber** to form a triumvirate of key figures whose influence on the development of sociology is unparalleled. To many sociologists he epitomizes the founding figure in academic sociology. Unlike Marx or Weber, he actually defined his vocation in terms of a mission to develop sociology as an accepted and esteemed discipline within the university world, and he identified closely with that professional role.

He was born on 15 April 1858, at Epinal, capital city of the department of Vosges in the Lorraine region of France. His father was chief rabbi of the Vosges and Haute-Marne, and it seemed that Emile was destined for the rabbinate, following in the footsteps of his father, grandfather and greatgrandfather. However, apart from a brief mystical experience under the influence of a Catholic schoolmistress, he seems to have abandoned all religious belief by the time he finished his schooling. Although his subsequent position was that of a rationalist-humanist, he was to give religion a prominent place in his sociology and even came to regard it as the key to understanding social life. It may be that he never forgot the bonds of community that bound together the Jews of Alsace-Lorraine, which had been strengthened further by the experience of anti-Semitism following the occupation by Prussian troops in 1870.

Although Durkheim was an outstanding student at the school in Epinal, he seems to have gone through a more difficult period in securing entry to the elite Ecole Normale Supérieur in Paris. Once there, however, he benefited from exceptional teachers, such as the philosophers Charles Renouvier and Emile Boutroux, and the historian Fustel de Coulanges. He was also a participant in the philosophical and political debates among the students, including such future luminaries as the socialist Jean Jaures (who became a life-long friend), the philosophers Henri Bergson and Maurice Blondel, the historians Henri Berr and Camille Julian, and the psychologist Pierre Janet. After completing his studies, he had a brief spell teaching philosophy in secondary schools. In 1887 he was appointed to teach social sciences and education at the University of Bordeaux, where he introduced the first course of sociology in France. At the age of thirty-five he secured his doctoral degree at the University of Paris, with a dissertation on the division of labour in society, which was in addition to a shorter dissertation in Latin dealing with the thought of Montesquieu. His first published articles were on German philosophy and social science. It was these writings that caught the attention of Louis Laird, the director of higher education in France, who resented German pre-eminence in social science and wished to develop education in the Third Republic on the basis of the kind of secular scientific morality that Durkheim seemed to be advocating. This was the beginning of Durkheim's influential role in spreading his version of sociology through the training of teachers in France. The scope of his influence widened when he was appointed to a chair in education at the University of Paris (Sorbonne) in 1902. It was not until 1913 that his chair was made one in 'Education and Sociology', but the advantage was that his teaching on the history and theory of education in France had become a compulsory part of teacher training. Some critics spoke of it as 'state Durkheimianism'.

Durkheim's position at the Sorbonne had been earned by the strength of his achievements during the fifteen years at Bordeaux, which were perhaps the most productive period of his life as far as variety of subjects taught and books written were concerned. In addition to the education courses he also lectured on the family, suicide, legal and political sociology, social solidarity, psychology, criminology, religion, the history of socialism and the history of sociological theories. His publications included *The Division of Labour in Society* and a study of Montesquieu, *The Rules of Sociological Method*, and *Suicide*; and articles on such topics as incest, the individual and collective representations, the definition of religious phenomena, the 'Two Laws of Penal Evolution' and totemism. He had also founded one of the first international journals of sociology, *L'Année sociologique*, in 1898.

His contributions to sociology mirror the problems, issues and disputes of his time, but they also have had a lasting significance. He dealt with questions concerning the course of social development, the scientific status of sociology, methods of social research, the need for precise research rather than sweeping generalizations, the place of values in sociology, social aspects of economic life and of law, social control and solidarity, 'primitive' and 'civilized' mentalities, social characteristics of knowledge and cognition, group psychology, professional ethics, democracy and the state, and the forms and problems of education.

The most famous works are: *The Division of Labour in Society, The Rules of Sociological Method, Suicide: A Study in Sociology* and *The Elementary Forms of the Religious Life*. In *The Division of Labour in Society*, he argued that societies have evolved from a simple form, in which there was mechanical solidarity based on a low specialization of roles and functions, to complex societies with an organic solidarity deriving from the interdependence of specialized roles. According to his rules of sociological method, sociology studies 'social facts' that are distinguished by their generality and by the fact that they are external to the individual and exercise constraint over individual behaviour. His study of suicide explained differences in rates of suicide for different countries, regions and groups in terms of the degree of social and moral integration they possessed. Too low a degree of integration might be due to a lack of shared norms ('anomie'), or too much individualism and a lack of integration into social relationships ('egoism'). In *The Elementary Forms of the Religious Life*, he used examples from totemic religions among Australian and American Aborigines to show how the most fundamental 'collective representations' (concepts, symbols and beliefs) reflect past and present social organization. Certain 'sacred' collective representations, such as the totem, serve the function of giving members of society a common identity and excite allegiance.

The definition of sociology as the study of social facts, as mapped out in the methodological discussion contained in *The Rules of Sociological Method*, may seem self-evident today, but that is because of the success of Durkheim's argument insisting that there are constraining and determining factors of a social nature that must be taken into account in explaining human behaviour. Durkheim was arguing against the prevailing tendency to reduce such explanations to the level of individual psychology or biology. The other three substantive works published in his lifetime – *The Division of Labour in Society, Suicide* and *The Elementary Forms of Religion* – all have a similar structure of argument, despite the differences in topic and data. In each work the argument is arranged in three parts. First, he gives a definition of the subject matter. Second, he presents various suggested explanations of the phenomenon, usually of a psychologistic or individualistic explanatory nature. He then uses a combination of argument and data to show the inadequacy of such 'reductionist' explanations and the need for a sociological explanation that focuses on the social causes of social phenomena. For example, he rejects the arguments claiming that the division of labour results from individuals' pursuit of increased happiness, that suicide rates are explicable in terms of insanity, and that religion can be explained as the outgrowth of cosmic or natural forces. Finally, in each case, he puts forward his own sociological explanation in which the social fact in question – the growth of the specialized division of labour, the different rates of suicide, totemic beliefs and practices – is explained in terms of other social facts. In *The Division of Labour*, the growth in population volume, population density and then in 'moral density' produced a growth in social differentiation, specialization of functions and the emergence of organic solidarity based on complementarity of the parts. This was in contrast to the mechanical solidarity of more simple societies that was based on resemblance of the parts and the dominance of the collective consciousness over individuals. This also explains the evolutionary change in the character of law and punishment, from the repressive type under mechanical solidarity to the restitutive type characteristic of societies with organic solidarity. In *Suicide* the comparative rates of suicide, as between such groups as Catholics and Protestants, married and unmarried people, rich and poor, and as between periods of national crisis or relative quiet, are determined by different suicidogenic currents related to four types of imbalance in the relation of the individual to society: one pair relates to the degree of integration or interaction in a group (egoism – too little; and altruism – too much), the other pair refers to the degree of moral regulation (anomie – too little; and fatalism – too much). In *The Elementary Forms* he argues that religion serves certain functional needs that bind people together, and that what people worship is really society itself.

Apart from their effective demonstration of the Durkheimian sociological method, these studies are full of thought-provoking and counter-intuitive findings. In *The Division of Labour* it is suggested that punishment of crime is designed to act more on the law-abiding citizen than on the criminal. Among the findings in *Suicide* is one which suggests that marriage is harmful to women (without children) judging by the suicide rate; and another which suggests that economic booms increase suicides, whereas revolutions and wars do not. *The Elementary Forms of the Religious Life* uses evidence on totemism among Australian and American aborigines to explore the social functions of religion, but also produces a sociology of knowledge which suggests that not only our ideas of God are collective representations of the social order itself, but also our ideas of time, space and causation.

The proof of the lasting significance of Durkheim's sociological ideas lies in the extent to which they have continued to attract interest today, as witnessed by the references to him in many topical debates and new theoretical developments. One direction in which a re-reading of his works can be seen to have had an impact is that of the so-called 'cultural turn' taken by sociology in the latter part of the twentieth century. More than any other of the early sociologists, Durkheim has provided useful conceptual tools for investigating symbolic structures and processes – those concerned with meaning-making and its patterned reproduction. An example is his insight into the significance in all societies of binary categories, such as the sacred versus the profane, the pure and the polluted, the 'we' and the 'other', as discussed in *The Elementary Forms of the Religious Life* and with his nephew Marcel Mauss in *Primitive Classification*. This was to form the basis of the structuralist analysis developed by Claude Lévi-Strauss and others, which swept through the humanities and social sciences. It provided a new appreciation of the relative autonomy and causal significance of cultural logics once they have become established.

Durkheim died in 1917. Among the posthumously published works that have attracted renewed attention are *Professional Ethics and Civic Morals* and *The Evolution of Educational Thought*. The former has proved particularly relevant to recent debates about civil society, while the latter is now found to be relevant to the study of educational ideologies and their institutionalization. Durkheim's political sociology, which was once regarded as almost non-existent or of little contemporary relevance, is now appreciated as offering a communication theory of politics that seems quite contemporary. He distinguishes between the administrative, coercive and intelligence functions of political and state institutions. The discussion of the state's intelligence functions in *Professional Ethics and Civic Morals* –

which is concerned with the formulation of collective representations distinguished by their higher degree of consciousness and reflection, and so distilling and elevating the ideals and beliefs of the pre-reflective masses – is particularly relevant for analyses of ideology, public opinion and the public sphere of civil society. It is in relation to analyses of the narratives and discourses that appear in the public sphere of civil society that Durkheim's ideas about binary codes have also been found useful. An example of a recent American political episode that can be subjected to such a Durkheimian analysis is that of the Watergate crisis, which has been viewed as a public drama of ritual cleansing involving narratives composed of binary sets of good and evil characters. Another fruitful Durkheimian concept is that of moments or episodes of 'collective effervescence'. Durkheim used examples ranging from primitive religion to the French Revolution to illustrate these potentially creative and dynamic moments. They served not just to reproduce society through the experience of a heightened sense of collective identity, but also to transform social relations and to rework social solidarities in certain situations. This type of Durkheimian analysis calls into question earlier criticisms of Durkheim for allegedly focusing solely on social reproduction and for failing to offer a theory of social change other than the social evolutionary. The Durkheimian theme of the revival of the sacred and collective effervescence has reappeared in studies of new social movements. It is suggested that the contemporary trend towards excessive individualism is intolerable to many people, who react by seeking a sacred bonding through commitment to movements or groups which offer means of 'keeping warm together' against the cold winds of modernity and the alienating experience of the economic-political order. Durkheim's writings on moral education and moral values have also been found to have relevance for debates between the rival political philosophies of communitarianism and individualism, especially in the face of pressures from a revived neo-liberalism. Similarly, some contemporary economists have begun to react against the ascendancy of neo-liberalism in economics and are inclined to follow his lead in considering the normative side of economic behaviour as set out in *Professional Ethics and Civic Morals* and in his discussion of 'abnormal' forms of the division of labour, in *The Division of Labour in Society*. Finally, certain ideas in moral education have been found relevant to recent debates around Michel Foucault's theory of 'governmentality' and forms of self-governance in liberal-democratic society. While Durkheim and Foucault would probably not have agreed about what should be the balance in the relations between individual and community, it is intriguing that they both focused on the significance of the development of forms of moral regulation based on self-governance as characteristic of modern liberal-democratic society.

See also: Maurice Halbwachs, Marcel Mauss, Alfred Radcliffe-Brown.

See also in *Fifty Key Sociologists: The Contemporary Theorists*: Basil Bernstein, Mary Douglas, Talcott Parsons, Georges Gurvitch, Claude Lévi-Strauss.

Major works

The Division of Labour in Society. 1893. Trans. G. Simpson, New York, Macmillan, 1933. New translation by W. D. Hall. London: Macmillan, 1984.

The Rules of Sociological Method. 1895. Trans. Sarah A. Soloway and John H. Mueller. Chicago: University of Chicago, 1938. New translation by W. D. Halls. London: Macmillan, 1982.

Socialism and Saint-Simon. 1895–6. Trans. Charlotte Sattler. Yellow Springs, OH: Antioch Press, 1958. First published in French, 1928.

Suicide: A Study in Sociology. 1897. Trans. John A. Spaulding and George Simpson. Glencoe, IL: Free Press, 1952.

Primitive Classification (with M. Mauss). 1903. Trans. Rodney Needham. London: Cohen & West, 1963.

Sociology and Philosophy. 1898–1911. Trans. D. F. Pocock. London: Cohen & West, 1956. Published in book form in French, 1924.

Education and Sociology. 1903–11. Trans. Sherwood D. Fox. Glencoe, IL: Free Press, 1956. Published in book form in French, 1922.

The Elementary Forms of the Religious Life. 1912. Trans. J. W. Swain. London: Allen & Unwin; New York: Macmillan, 1915.

Moral Education. 1912. Trans. Everett K. Wilson. Glencoe, IL: Free Press, 1961. Published in book form in French, 1925.

The Evolution of Educational Thought. 1913. Trans. Peter Collins. London: Routledge & Kegan Paul, 1977. Published in book form in French, 1938.

Professional Ethics and Civic Morals. c.1917. Trans. Cornelia Brookfield. London: Routledge & Kegan Paul, 1957. Published in book form in French as *Leçons de sociologie*, 1950.

Further reading

Steven Lukes. 1973. *Emile Durkheim: His Life and Work.* London: Allen Lane.

William S. F. Pickering, ed. *Emile Durkheim: Critical Assessments of Leading Sociologists*, third series, London and New York: Routledge, Taylor and Francis, 2001.

Ken Thompson. 2002. *Emile Durkheim*, revised edn. London: Routledge.

KENNETH THOMPSON

EDWARD EVANS-PRITCHARD

Evans-Pritchard, born in 1902, was the son of an Anglican clergyman and was educated at Winchester College before going on to Oxford, where he studied history. However, his background and career were less conventional than this might suggest. His father was from Caernarvon and spoke Welsh, while his mother's family came from Liverpool. It was his dissatisfaction with the 'kings and battles' approach to history that made fieldworking anthropology, with its promise of exploration and adventure, seem more attractive. This led him to join the courses being taught at the London School of Economics by the senior anthropologist Charles Seligman and **Bronislaw Malinowski** in the mid-1920s. Following in Seligman's footsteps, he then immersed himself in periods of fieldwork in the Sudan between 1926 and 1940, and in Cyrenaica (Libya) during the wartime British military administration of that country. He succeeded **Alfred Radcliffe-Brown** in the chair of social anthropology at Oxford (1945–70) and fostered a productive postgraduate and research institute which achieved worldwide fame and trained many professional teachers of the discipline. He was able to secure a new respect for social anthropology not only in the social sciences, but also among scholars in humanities such as theology, philosophy, linguistics and comparative literature. He died in 1973.

Evans-Pritchard's importance for social anthropology rests mainly on the originality and high quality of his fieldwork and his theoretical reflections on the life of peoples in areas of the world little known, at that time, to scholarship. He produced, especially in later life, a range of theoretical essays and assessments, in the main extremely critical of naïve stereotypes of 'primitive' humanity and modes of thought. However, the classic works on which his reputation rests are the analytical monographs derived from his ethnographic research. On the basis of these, even before his death, Evans-Pritchard had become something of a 'household name' in anthropology. His main quest was for a comparative understanding of the distinctively social, shared nature of the forms of human life and experience (see, for example, his *Social Anthropology* of 1951).

His analysis of Azande ideas about the human sources of evil and misfortune and the practices needed to control them became widely influential in the debate opening up within philosophy over the social foundations of knowledge. The Azande and their doggedly 'rational' and clever way of justifying the identification of witches through oracles (still quite surprising to many readers) have helped to define what modern anthropology is about. Ironically, the appeal of the Azande has more recently converged with new and easy forms of cultural relativism which lead students to ask, 'Why *shouldn't* the Azande believe in witchcraft, if it suits their way of life, and who am I to criticize them?' This is not Evans-Pritchard's line. On the contrary, he shows how most ordinary Azande themselves are not at all comfortable with the presence of witchcraft. It is those in privileged positions who are able to turn their accusations on the relatively helpless. The oracles are ultimately controlled by (sometimes cruel) kings and princes. Even at the household level it is only senior men who have access to them, while women constitute a large proportion of the accused. Evans-Pritchard's analysis is set explicitly in a political and historical context which offers a more nuanced reading than that of simple relativism, and ultimately it can be argued that this extra depth is what gives the text its lasting qualities.

The Nuer, as a people, and *The Nuer*, as Evans-Pritchard's first book on them, entered the life and language of academic anthropology in 1940. This was the first time that 'œcology' had explicitly been selected for analysis in a field monograph. It was also the first demonstration of rational principles behind the apparent anarchy of factional hostilities and expedient regroupings among herders moving over hundreds of miles of territory: principles cast by them in the strong rhetoric of paternal descent. Structured conceptions of space and of time were shown to shape genealogies and to constitute a framework of shared understandings within which political action could be analysed outside the framework of any state.

The final volume in Evans-Pritchard's trilogy devoted to the Nuer also established a new baseline for conversations with a neighbouring discipline. *Nuer Religion* was written quite provocatively as a challenge to academic theology, requiring its specialists to take tribal systems of belief and practice seriously. Evans-Pritchard's presentation of Nuer trust in *kwoth*, the 'spirit of the above', has the schematic character of a creed, but at the same time a lived and shared reality. He portrays for us in almost biblical tone an elemental confrontation between God and Man, demanding recognition across the gulf between the historical religions and their sacred texts on the one hand and the worlds they often denigrate on the other as erring paganism or blind custom. The work is presented as social analysis, emphasizing how diversity of perception and representation reflects the relativity of points of view within Nuer society established in his first book.

Evans-Pritchard drew much inspiration from the French sociological school of **Durkheim**, and especially perhaps from the work of

Durkheim's nephew and collaborator **Marcel Mauss**. He sponsored a series of translations of classic essays from the *Année sociologique*, starting with Mauss's essay on *The Gift*, which remains a foundation text in the teaching of anthropology. A project he undertook in the 1960s was the launching of the Oxford Library of African Literature, a series which flourished over the following two decades and had considerable influence in developing anthropology's openness to art, performance, narrative and the uses of indigenous textual material generally.

From the mid-1960s on, in common with others whose lives had become involved in the Sudan in one way or another, Evans-Pritchard was shocked and angry about the deepening civil war in the country and its effect on people he remembered, and who remembered him, and partly because of this he had no taste for responding to critics of his earlier writings. But his work remains fresh to many. He put very vividly those paradoxes of multiple belonging or 'positionality' which the modern student ponders, focusing in a still helpful way on the relativities of 'self and other' in the making of personal and group identities, as we might rephrase the relevance of segmentary theory today. He placed 'dialogue' both between the Azande themselves and between himself and his informants firmly at the heart of the analysis of knowledge and belief which he carried out among them. He respected, explicitly, the privacy and inner religious consciousness of the Nuer, whose world became in so many other ways public property through his work. It is clearly true that in many respects Evans-Pritchard failed to take 'colonialism' into account in his analyses, or to allow for historical change; but then again, looking back, he is foremost among those who worked to reorient anthropology towards history. His treatment of field research was never as an end in itself; field research was only one of many methods, though an essential one, for anthropological analysis.

See also: Emile Durkheim, Marcel Mauss, Bronislaw Malinowski, Alfred Radcliffe-Brown.

See also in *Fifty Key Sociologists: The Contemporary Theorists*: Mary Douglas.

Major works

Witchcraft, Oracles, and Magic among the Azande. 1937. Oxford: Clarendon Press. Abridged edn issued in 1976.

The Nuer: A Description of the Modes of Livelihood and Political Institutions of a Nilotic People. 1940. Oxford: Clarendon Press.
The Sanusi of Cyrenaica. 1949. Oxford: Clarendon Press.
Kinship and Marriage among the Nuer. 1951. Oxford: Clarendon Press.
Social Anthropology. 1951. London: Cohen and West.
Nuer Religion. 1956. Oxford: Clarendon Press.
Essays in Social Anthropology. Various dates. London: Faber and Faber, 1962.
The Position of Women in Primitive Societies, and Other Essays. Various dates. London: Faber and Faber, 1965.
The Zande Trickster, ed. 1967. Oxford: Clarendon Press.
The Azande: History and Political Institutions. 1971. Oxford: Clarendon Press.

Further reading

Talal Asad, ed. 1973. *Anthropology and the Colonial Encounter.* London: Ithaca.
Wendy James. 2003. *The Ceremonial Animal: A New Portrait of Anthropology.* Oxford: Oxford University Press.
Peter Winch. 1958. *The Idea of a Social Science, and its Relation to Philosophy.* London: Routledge & Kegan Paul.

WENDY JAMES

SIGMUND FREUD

Sigmund Freud was born in 1856 in the Moravian town of Freiberg, now Příbor in the Czech Republic. When he was three, his family moved to Vienna, a city of intense intellectual and cultural activity, and he remained there until friends brought him to London in 1938, to escape Nazi persecution. Originally a neurologist, Freud created psychoanalysis and has become one of the major intellectual figures of modern times. The twenty-four volumes of the *Standard Edition* of his psychological oeuvre follow a substantial body of non-psychoanalytic work, both from a research career in neuroanatomy, including the embryology and histology of the nervous system, and from a clinical career as an expert in children's neurological diseases, on which he published major works on infantile paralysis and aphasias.

Freud's psychoanalytic work falls into three categories: clinical, theoretical and methodological. His clinical writings include his *Studies on Hysteria* (with Josef Breuer) (1893–5), *The Interpretation of Dreams* (1900) and several extensive case studies, on which he based his concepts and models of the psyche. Many of his concepts have become commonplace, such as the unconscious, repression, projection, slips of the tongue, ego, id, super-ego. He codified these ideas in theoretical writings in 1915 that comprise his 'metapsychology', most particularly 'The Unconscious', 'Repression', and 'Instincts and Their Vicissitudes'.

His methodological thinking was based on the concept of transference as a means of studying the unconscious. Transference refers to a primal tendency to replace one object of loving and hating by another – perhaps replacing mother or father with a wife or husband or psychoanalyst – making the 'transference' figure into one's (fantasy laden) version of mother or father. The unconscious was a reservoir of these past relationships, and the experience of these transferences gave the psychoanalyst an insight into them.

The unconscious, which Freud made the object of systematic inquiry, was not the 'descriptive unconscious' (what is out of awareness), but the 'dynamic unconscious' (what is held unconscious by the force of repression). Different principles obtain here: no time, no contradictions, and ideas merge (condensation) or shift with respect to each other (displacement). Freud distinguished this 'primary process' of the unconscious from the 'secondary process' of conscious thinking, and sought the meaning of dreams and of psychoneurotic symptoms in the analysis of these bizarre, unconsciously driven, mental productions.

As Freud's understanding of transference evolved, he mapped the psyche and described its functioning. The transference relationship, in which the analyst could stand for many different figures, or even aspects of them, such as criticizing, teaching, supporting, revealed the psyche to be a society of internal figures in relationships quite different from – often more extreme than – the external figures, say parents, on which they seemed to be based, and in conflict with each other. He divided the psyche into three agencies, producing his famous structural model of the id (drives), ego (centre of perception and will) and super-ego (parent-like ideals and authority).

Freud was a social thinker – something that is easily hidden beneath his vast scientific and clinical achievement. These internal agencies are 'projected' into external relationships, so that they, too, have an 'internal' structure. Although the richest accounts of 'internal' processes are in his case studies, the most direct connections between his clinical discoveries, his model of the psyche and his theory of social organization occur in *Group Psychology and the Analysis of the Ego* and in *Civilisation and Its Discontents*. In the former, social groups are seen as formed from love and deference to a leader; in the latter, society more broadly is seen as formed from the conflict between love and hate.

The authority of a leader, as of parents, derives partly from the actual experience of children with their parents, and therefore from an extension of infantile life into adult life. But it also derives from the internal roots of the super-ego (sometimes distinguished from an ego-ideal). The super-ego is a precipitate in the psyche of the Oedipus complex; that is, the conflict between its love, usually of the parent of the opposite sex, and its prohibition, usually by the parent of the same sex. The ego-ideal is the residue of the persistent yearning for the infant's early bliss. The merging of Oedipal subjugation, maintained internally by the super-ego, and yearning for the ego-ideal as lost bliss results in an agency of extraordinary power.

Although the relationship between super-ego and ego is utterly authoritative, eliciting the total deference of the ego, it is also loving ('libidinal'). The ego loves the super-ego as a child loves its parents, craving love in return and its early bliss. Social groups are formed from the same passionate bond. Each individual invests the leader with his/her super-ego, forming a collective super-ego. Simultaneously, with their super-ego held in common, the members identify with each other in their egos, forming the glue of the social group.

Society is built from the diversions of sexual aims from their direct expression (sublimations), enforced by the super-ego, into all the arrangements and endeavours that we call civilization. But there is a contradiction at the heart of society, because inhibition and sublimation of sexual aims both create society and undermine its sexual roots. Social bonds are also undermined by aggression. Aggression is aroused partly by the frustration of the inhibition and sublimation of libidinal drives, but also by a primary anti-libidinal aggressiveness arising from the death drive (*Beyond the Pleasure Principle*).

The super-ego captures this aggression, deflecting it from external objects, and sends it back to the ego as the instrument of conscience. But here, as in the case of libido and its inhibition, there is a contradiction inherent in society. The inhibition of aggression by the super-ego only leads to more aggression from the ego, as it renounces the pleasure of the expression of its aggressive drive. The intrinsic conflict of forces, in the individual and in society, is central to Freud's thinking. In society, he referred to an unhappy state of unease, malaise or psychological poverty or misery (*Unbehagen; psychologische Elend*, translated as 'discontent').

These unconscious processes persist as an internal world that infuses external reality, as in transference. They generate social life and simultaneously undermine it. Freud might seem pessimistic about the chances of social improvement, but he might better be seen as realistic and relentlessly opposed to illusion. For example, he was not persuaded by communist ideology that character could be modified by abolishing the external reality of private property. The internal reality of the aggressive drive to dominate others would simply move from property to the sexual domination of women.

Freud's intellectual and cultural context, like his own thinking, might be typified as a 'subjective turn', in that experience is the basis of all knowledge. Leading intellectual figures of his time, such as Wilhelm Dilthey, Edmund Husserl, Ernst Mach and Arthur Schnitzler, argued in a similar way for a new grounding of knowledge, in physics, philosophy, the human sciences and literature. Subjectivity did not mean an idiosyncratic or distorted observation of the world by a separate, individual 'I', but an integral process of passionate involvement. Transference was such an experience of a relationship. Freud reflected this subjective turn, but added so much to it that the poet W. H. Auden said he had become 'a whole climate of opinion'.

See also: Theodor Adorno, Herbert Marcuse.

See also in *Fifty Key Sociologists, The Contemporary Theorists*: Gilles Deleuze, Melanie Klein.

Major works

Studies on Hysteria. 1895. With Josef Breuer. In *The Standard Edition of the Complete Psychological Works of Sigmund Freud*, vol. 2. London: The Hogarth Press.

The Interpretation of Dreams. 1900. In *The Standard Edition of the Complete Psychological Works of Sigmund Freud*, vol. 4–5. London: The Hogarth Press.

The Psychopathology of Everyday Life. 1901. In *The Standard Edition of the Complete Psychological Works of Sigmund Freud*, vol. 6. London: The Hogarth Press.

Jokes and Their Relation to the Unconscious. 1905. In *The Standard Edition of the Complete Psychological Works of Sigmund Freud*, vol. 8. London: The Hogarth Press.

Totem and Taboo. 1912–13. In *The Standard Edition of the Complete Psychological Works of Sigmund Freud*, vol. 13. London: The Hogarth Press.

Introductory Lectures on Psycho-Analysis. 1916–17. In *The Standard Edition of the Complete Psychological Works of Sigmund Freud*, vol. 15–16. London: The Hogarth Press.

Beyond the Pleasure Principle. 1920. In *The Standard Edition of the Complete Psychological Works of Sigmund Freud*, vol. 18. London: The Hogarth Press.

Group Psychology and the Analysis of the Ego. 1921. In *The Standard Edition of the Complete Psychological Works of Sigmund Freud*, vol. 18. London: The Hogarth Press.

The Ego and the Id. 1923. In *The Standard Edition of the Complete Psychological Works of Sigmund Freud*, vol. 19. London: The Hogarth Press.

The Future of an Illusion. 1927. In *The Standard Edition of the Complete Psychological Works of Sigmund Freud*, vol. 21. London: The Hogarth Press.

Civilization and Its Discontents. 1930. In *The Standard Edition of the Complete Psychological Works of Sigmund Freud*, vol. 21. London: The Hogarth Press.

Many of Freud's writings have been gathered, edited and introduced in a reader by Peter Gay: *The Freud Reader*. New York: Norton; London: Vintage.

Further reading

Ian Craib. 1989. *Psychoanalysis and Social Theory.* Hemel Hempstead: Harvester Wheatsheaf.

Hannah S. Decker. 1991. *Freud, Dora and Vienna*. New York, Free Press.

Anthony Elliott. 2004. *Social Theory Since Freud: Traversing Social Imaginaries,* London: Routledge.

Karl Figlio. 2000. *Psychoanalysis, Science and Masculinity* London: Whurr.

Peter Gay. 1988. *Freud: A Life Time.* London: Dent.

Ernest Jones. 1953–7. *The Life and Work of Sigmund Freud*. 3 vols.. New York: Basic Books.

Howard Kaye. 2003. 'Was Freud a Medical Scientist or a Social Theorist? The Mysterious "Development of the Hero"', *Sociological Theory* 21.

Paul Roazen. 1968–70. *Freud: Political and Social Thought*. New York: Alfred A. Knopf.

Carl Schorske. 1980. *Fin-de-Siècle Vienna: Politics and Culture.* New York: Knopf.

KARL FIGLIO

ANTONIO GRAMSCI

Born in Ales, Sardinia, in 1891, Gramsci was the son of a clerk in a registrar's office at Ghilarza. He was brought up in poverty, particularly during the years his father was in prison for alleged embezzlement. As a child, Gramsci was constantly ill and withdrawn, and his anguish was compounded by physical deformity. He was compelled to leave school at the age of twelve, but following his father's release from prison he was able to resume his education at Santa Lussurgia and Cagliari. On winning a scholarship to the University of Turin in 1911 he came into contact with the future communist leader and fellow Sardinian Palmiro Togliatti. During the elections of 1913 – the first to be held in Sardinia with universal male suffrage – he became convinced that Sardinia's acute problems of under-development could be solved only in the context of socialist policies for Italy as a whole. He retained a lively interest in his native Sardinia throughout his life and wrote a major essay on 'The Southern Question' in 1926.

Like many of his generation at the university in Turin, Gramsci was deeply influenced by the liberal idealism of Benedetto Croce, often regarded as Italy's Hegel. Gramsci's hostility to positivism made him a fierce critic of all fatalistic versions of Marxism. By 1915 he was writing regularly on cultural questions for the socialist journals *Il Grido del populo* (the cry of the people) and *Avanti* (forward), stressing the importance of educating the workers for revolution.

During a four-day insurrection in Turin in August 1917, Gramsci became a leading figure in the workers' movement. He welcomed the Russian Revolution, describing it, in Crocean style, as a 'Revolution against *Das Kapital*', and in May 1917 he collaborated with Angelo Tasca, Umberto Terracini and Togliatti to found *L'Ordine nuovo* (the new order) as an 'organ of proletarian culture'. As the paper saw it, the factory committees in Turin were Soviets in embryo – the nuclei of a future socialist state. Thousands responded to the call to establish workers' councils in the Turin area, and during the 'red years' of 1919 and 1920 there was a general strike and factories were occupied. *L'Ordine*'s critique of the passivity and reformism of the Socialist Party won the approval of the Soviet leader Lenin, and although Gramsci would have preferred to continue working in the Socialist Party at a time of rising fascist reaction, a separate Communist Party was formed at Livorno in 1921.

Gramsci became a member of its central committee, but the party was dominated by Amadeo Bordiga, a powerful figure whose dogmatic elitism brought him into increasing conflict with the Third Communist International (the Comintern). Gramsci became his party's representative on the Comintern, and it was while he was recovering from acute depression in a Moscow clinic in 1922 that he met his future wife, Julia, with whom he had two children.

In October 1922 Mussolini seized power. The head of the Communist Party was arrested and Gramsci found himself party leader. He was elected parliamentary deputy in 1924, and by 1926, at the party's third congress in Lyons, he won wide membership support for his Leninist strategy of an alliance with the peasants under proletarian hegemony. In his one and only speech to the Chamber of Deputies,

Gramsci brilliantly analysed the distinctive and lethal character of fascism, with Mussolini describing him as a 'Sardinian hunch-back' with a 'brain of undeniable power'. In 1926 he was arrested and two years later brought to trial. 'We must prevent this brain from functioning for twenty years,' declared the prosecutor, and Gramsci spent the first five years of his imprisonment in the harsh prison in Turin. He was able to start work on his famous *Prison Notebooks* in 1929, but by the middle of 1932 his health was beginning to deteriorate rapidly. Gramsci was suffering from (among other ailments) Potts disease and arteriosclerosis, and pressure from an international campaign for his release led to his transfer to a prison hospital in Formia. By August 1935, however, he was too ill to work. Transferred to a clinic in Rome, he died in April 1937 after a cerebral haemorrhage.

Despite some happy moments before his imprisonment, his relationship with Julia had been fraught. She was in poor mental health, and Gramsci's imprisonment meant that communication between them more or less ceased. Julia's sister, Tatiana, however, was devoted to Gramsci's well-being during the torturing years of incarceration, providing him with some companionship. On his death, Tatiana had his thirty-three notebooks smuggled out of Italy and taken to Moscow in a diplomatic bag.

These notebooks, despite the rudimentary state of their drafts, are undoubtedly Gramsci's masterpiece. They contain sharply perceptive pieces of Italian history, Marxist philosophy, political strategy, literature and linguistics, and the theatre. At their core stands Gramsci's overriding preoccupation with the need to develop critical ideas rooted in the everyday life of the people, so that the communist cause acquires irresistible momentum. Opposed to Bordiga's elitism and to the sectarian policies of the Comintern between 1929 and 1934, Gramsci emphasized the importance of intellectual and moral factors in the political process. Hic concept of 'hegemony' foregrounded the need to create a new and radical 'common sense' so that people would see socialist ideas as relevant to their daily needs and organically linked to folklore and traditional wisdom. Gramsci argued that every person was a theorist and that it was important to bring out the political relevance of everyday ideas.

In the late 1960s student radicals turned to the Gramsci of the Turin Council movement for inspiration. In the 1970s, some communists in the West began to distance themselves, for electoral reasons, from the classical Marxist theses on the state and the 'dictatorship of the proletariat' and they came to see Gramsci's concept of hegemony as a counterweight to a Leninist emphasis on political coercion. Gramsci was acclaimed the 'Father of Eurocommunism' – the Marxist who had forged a happy compromise between reform and revolution.

Yet Gramsci's emphasis upon *class* leadership became increasingly contentious as commentators argued that other identities – linked to gender, nationality, religion and so on – needed to be taken into account, and Gramsci's argument for a strategy based upon winning consent was detached from its roots in class and war. Yet the notion of hegemony has remained influential, as has Gramsci's dislike of a mechanistic determinism that undermines the centrality of will and agency. The idea that political rule has an important cultural dimension is seen as insightful and valid.

Gramsci's interest in his great Renaissance ancestor Machiavelli has continued to fascinate commentators. Machiavelli argued that there were 'two ways of fighting' – by law and by force – and Gramsci's emphasis upon the two aspects of the political process has continued to seem relevant, as has Gramsci's broad view of the state that sees the political character of social relations.

See also: Karl Marx, Gyorgy Lukács.

See also in *Fifty Key Sociologists: The Contemporary Theorists*: Louis Althusser, Paul Gilroy, Stuart Hall.

Major works

Selections from Political Writings 1910–1920. London: Lawrence and Wishart, 1977.
Selections from Political Writings 1921–1926. London: Lawrence and Wishart, 1978.
Selections from Prison Notebooks. 1929–35. London: Lawrence and Wishart, 1971.
Selections from Cultural Writings. Various dates. London: Lawrence and Wishart, 1985.

Further reading

Perry Anderson. 'The Antinomies of Antonio Gramsci'. *New Left Review* November–January, 1976–7.
Giuseppe Fiori. 1970. *Antonio Gramsci: Life of a Revolutionary*. London: New Left Books.
James Martin. 1998. *Gramsci's Political Analysis: A Critical Introduction*. Basingstoke: Macmillan,

Paolo Spriano. 1979. *Antonio Gramsci and the Party: The Prison Years*. London: Lawrence and Wishart.

JOHN HOFFMAN

LUDWIG GUMPLOWICZ

Ludwig Gumplowicz was born into a Jewish family in Poland in 1838. His native country was annexed by Austria-Hungary, and Gumplowicz spent much of his life working in Austria. Trained in law at the University of Kraków, he worked initially as a lawyer but took a teaching post in 1875 in political science and administration at the University of Graz, where he was to spend the rest of his career. His experience of living within a multi-national and multi-ethnic state led him to a sharp awareness of ethnic division and conflict as a major factor in social development. He made this the cornerstone of his general social theory, set out in his *Outlines of Sociology*, and he used the basic framework to produce a theory of state formation (*Geschichte der Staatstheorien*) and militarism (*Der Rassenkampf*). By the time that he had completed his final book, Gumplowicz had been diagnosed with cancer and he and his wife committed suicide in 1909, the same year that the book was published.

His conception of sociology was broadly Comtean, seeing a progressive growth of complexity through inorganic, organic, psychic and social phenomena, each of which can be studied through the formulation of its distinctive laws. Psychic laws have their basis in the individual mind and express the activities of the 'soul' or psyche. Social laws, on the other hand, arise through the aggregation of individuals, and Gumplowicz began his first book with an account of the various social aggregates that are the basis of all social phenomena and form the elements of social life. The simplest and most fundamental social element, he argued, is the primitive horde, once the basis of all human life. The horde comprises a small group based around a hunting and gathering lifestyle. Following Johann Bachofen's arguments on the 'mother right', Gumplowicz – like Engels – saw the horde as sexually promiscuous and having no stable 'family' relations or any conception of 'kinship' other than that between mother and child.

Hordes were gradually aggregated – 'compounded' in Spencer's terminology – into larger forms of association such as tribes, communities, states and nations. The driving force in this process of aggregation is contact between social groups and the consequent reciprocal influences between them. For Gumplowicz, however, contact and influence are rarely harmonious and peaceful. Contact invariably involves the attempt by one group to secure advantages relative to another, and their association leads to conflict, conquest, exploitation and the stratification of more complex societies. Contact and conflict among hordes were motivated by the taking of women and it was this that Gumplowicz saw as leading from the early matriarchy to more complex patterns of patriarchal domination. The patriarchal family became the fundamental unit of wealth-holding, and power was the basis on which property relations in land and moveable goods were firmly established. The emerging forms of stratification were the basis on which states were formed.

This led Gumplowicz to his conflict model of social change. States are organized around the control of a minority over a majority. Initially involving the conquest of a large population by a smaller and better organized population, complex state forms must always be controlled by those small minorities that **Gaetano Mosca** and **Vilfredo Pareto** were to analyse as 'elites'. The motivation behind state formation is economic, as those who form the dominating elites of complex societies seek to establish and enlarge the systems of 'industrial' organization that can generate higher levels of material wealth. Hunting and gathering gave way to farming, which became increasingly complex thanks to the technical development of the forces of production. It was on this basis that Gumplowicz saw the strengthening of stratification as relations among social classes and the development of state societies into complex structures with a variety of intermediate classes between the upper-class 'masters' and the lower-class 'subjects'.

The early human populations were, Gumplowicz argued, racially diverse, as they had originated from various migrant stocks with distinct biological characteristics. Subsequent contact and conflict had produced more racially mixed populations and had established forms of racial conquest and racial stratification. Racial theorizing was common in European thought in the late nineteenth century and was often linked with Darwinian views of evolution through variation and natural selection. Gumplowicz's arguments echoed and contributed to this theorizing. Although his principal concern was with the *ethnic* distinctiveness and diversity of populations, he saw these as having a basis in the now largely abandoned categories of biological race. He used the term 'race' where most would now use 'ethnicity'. Contemporary 'races', he argued, are the product of an interplay between biological characteristics and social conditions. Contact and social mixing produced the ethnically diverse populations of his day. The multi-ethnic Habsburg empire of Austria-Hungary provided the model for such complex and diverse societies, with its populations of Germans, Poles, Czechs, Jews, Hungarians, Slavs and others organized into a political formation in which one ethnic group – the Austrian Germans – was the dominant power. Ethnic differentiation, social stratification and political rule ensured that social conflicts persisted and became ever more organized and militaristic. His final book on racial conflict predicted the outbreak of a world war among the leading European nation-states.

Although the name of Gumplowicz is rarely heard today, his ideas have had a major influence in social theory, especially among those working in political and historical sociology. His compatriot and contemporary Gustav Ratzenhofer took up many of his ideas on racial conflict and sought to ground these in an individualistic theory of action. It was largely through the influence of Ratzenhofer on **Albion Small** that these ideas were taken up in the work of the Chicago sociologists as a way of understanding ethnic competition and cultural diversity. These ideas formed the core of the influential pluralist approach to politics. Gumplowicz's ideas on ruling minorities and states were central to the subsequent work of Mosca and the elite theorists and shaped the development of theories of state formation set out by writers such as Franz Oppenheimer and elaborated more recently in the 'conflict theory' of Ralf Dahrendorf and the comparative investigations of power carried out by Michael Mann.

See also: Gaetano Mosca, Albion Small.

Major works

Outlines of Sociology. 1885. Philadelphia: American Academy of Political and Social Science, 1899. 2nd edn of 1905 published New Brunswick, NJ: Transaction, 1980.
Geschichte der Staatstheorien.1905. Innsbruck: Wagner.
Der Rassenkampf.1909. Innsbruck: Wagner.

Further reading

James A. Aho. 1975. *German Realpolitik and American Sociology*. Cranbury, NJ: Associated University Presses.

JOHN SCOTT

MAURICE HALBWACHS

A French sociologist, strongly influenced by **Emile Durkheim**, Halbwachs was a pupil of Henri Bergson at Lycée Henri IV, Paris. He first studied philosophy at the Ecole Normale Superieure, before, influenced by his close friend François Simiand, he joined Durkheim's school of sociology in 1905. In the years that followed, Halbwachs became one of the central contributors to *L'Année socio-logique*, and was the first to introduce the works of Keynes, **Pareto**, **Veblen** and **Weber** in France. As professor of sociology and pedagogy at the University of Strasbourg from 1919 to 1935, he also exerted influence on what was to become the Annales school in history. After being called to the chair in sociology at the Sorbonne in 1935, he was later elected to the chair in collective psychology at Collège de France in 1944, a position he never came to occupy. Halbwachs was arrested by the Gestapo in July 1944, deported to Germany and died in Buchenwald in March 1945.

Halbwachs' work can be grouped into four main categories: the economic sociology of social classes and consumption, social morphology and methodology in general, the sociology of suicide and the sociology of collective memory.

His sociology of social classes combines Durkheimian, Marxist and Weberian elements. In his doctoral thesis of 1913, *La Classe ouvrière et les niveaux de vie*, Halbwachs separated social and non-social arenas, and sought to analyse the influence of the one on the other as this manifests itself in the consumption patterns of the various social classes, with the working class as the primary case. The factory is seen as a non-social arena where the worker may experience alienation from fellow workers because he or she, unlike members of other classes, must concentrate on the machinery instead of taking part in social life. Following the Durkheimian analytical injunction that social representations can be caused only by other social facts, Halbwachs argued that the division of labour cannot *per se* be the cause of class-consciousness. Instead, class-consciousness arises from the hierarchical comparisons that workers make with other social classes outside the factory gates when they enter the social sphere of consumption, that is, through a comparison of social distinctions as these arise from hierarchical structures in the market. Alienation and exploitation are therefore not analysed as a product of the labour process and the opposition between labour and capital, but instead as the product of a lack of integration and participation in social life where it is lived at its most intense: the family. If a person is socially alienated, the disposition to give priority to the family in his or her consumption behaviour will also be weaker than the dispositions of the socially integrated. Halbwachs' analysis of class-specific psychological dispositions was later further developed in the posthumously published *The Psychology of Social Class*.

In both his work on suicide and his work on social morphology, Halbwachs is considered to be more aware of group-specific fluctuations than was the case with his mentor, Emile Durkheim. Where Durkheim sought to uncover almost time-invariant trends of stability, Halbwachs, armed with a more sophisticated arsenal of statistical tools, also put emphasis on variation and social transformation. He was also more aware of possible interaction effects between several variables. For instance, religion was not analysed as a cause or an institution that could, in itself, protect or expose an individual to suicide, but rather was seen as an element embedded in a broader life-style – a *genre de vie* – that could do so. For example, whereas Catholicism was primarily a rural way of life, Protestantism was part of an urban life-style.

Since the late 1970s, Halbwachs' work on collective memory has been given the greatest attention and is generally also considered to be the most innovative part of his work, by historians, anthropologists and sociologists. True to his Durkheimian legacy, in *Les Cadres sociaux de la mémoire* Halbwachs presents a structural theory of memory, clearly oriented away from all forms of individual and psychological explanations. However, collective memory was not understood as something given. Nor did he claim that the group itself has a mind and a capability of its own to remember. Remembering is always done by individuals, but they do it by mentally 're-entering' or reconstructing social groups. In short, Halbwachs' argument is that memory is a social fact, structured and sustained by the social groups an individual has encountered and been a member of during his or her lifetime. In order to remember, each individual reconstructs the social frameworks in which a specific event or process happened or evolved. This reconstruction takes place in the present, and is therefore also strongly affected by current social structures. For Halbwachs, memory is thus a product of a social practice that is heavily structured by and is functional for our present group memberships.

In his later work on collective memory, the key category is *lieux de mémoire*: a material object or physical location that is perceived as important, is assigned a symbolic meaning by a given group and is functional to the group's collective memory. In a detailed analysis based on various religious texts and historical accounts, he showed that the localization of the holy places in the Gospels has varied throughout history and that the reconstruction of sites is the result of an active commemorative effort on behalf of Christian groups, especially the crusaders. In this way, collective memory can be inscribed and achieve support from objects in material space. Once established, a *lieu de mémoire* also gains a stability of its own, in part because of its function for the group's collective memory, but also because of group resistance to dramatic changes in the physical environment. The perception and representation of these sites and of space in general will also vary from group to group: 'there are as many ways of representing space as there are groups'.

Even so, for all its merits and innovation, Halbwachs' theory becomes rather ahistoric, static and more oriented towards the reproduction of existing structures than towards social transformation. Once a *lieu de mémoire* is established, the actors seem to be locked into two sets of structures, one social and one socio-material, and easily end up more like passive receivers of a materialized past than agents that are also capable of reacting against such symbols. This said, in studies of social or collective memory, Halbwachs' work has been and remains a major source of inspiration.

See also: Emile Durkheim, Marcel Mauss, Thorstein Veblen, Max Weber.

See also in *Fifty Key Sociologists: The Contemporary Theorists*: Georges Gurvitch.

Major works

La Classe ouvrière et les niveaux de vie. 1912. Paris: Alcan.
The Social Framework of Memory. 1925. Partial translation in *On Collective Memory*, Chicago: University of Chicago Press, 1992.
The Causes of Suicide. 1930. London: Routledge & Kegan Paul, 1978.
L'Evolution des besoins dans les classes ouvrières. 1933. Paris: Alcan.
Population and Society: An Introduction to Social Morphology. 1938. Glencoe, IL: Free Press, 1960.
The Psychology of Social Class. 1938. London: William Heinemann, 1958.
La Topographie légendaire des Evangiles en Terre Saint. 1941. Partial translation in *On Collective Memory*, Chicago: University of Chicago Press, 1992.
The Collective Memory. 1950. New York: Harper-Colophon, 1980.

Further reading

Annette Becker. 2003. *Maurice Halbwachs, un intellectuel en guerres mondiales 1914–1945*. Paris: Agnes Viénot Editions.

Lewis Coser. 1992. 'Introduction: Maurice Halbwachs 1877–1945'. In Maurice Halbwachs. *On Collective Memory*. Chicago: Chicago University Press, 1992.

Christian Montlibert, ed. 1997. *Maurice Halbwachs 1877–1945*. Strasbourg: Presses Universitaires de Strasbourg.

JOHS. HJELLBREKKE

LEONARD HOBHOUSE

It is often said that British sociology produced no theorists of note between **Herbert Spencer** and Anthony Giddens. In fact, there were many British contributions to social theory. Among these theorists, Leonard Hobhouse was the most systematic, producing a sociology that was comparable in scope to that of the nineteenth-century French and German founders of sociology. Hobhouse set out a view of sociology that focuses on the structures of whole societies and the ways in which they change over time. At the same time, however, he saw social life as grounded in the interaction of individual actors. He also set out a substantive theory of the development of citizenship in modern societies, though recent discussions of this have largely ignored the contribution of Hobhouse.

Leonard Trelawny Hobhouse was born into the prosperous middle classes in 1864. He was educated at Oxford, where he studied philosophy and psychology and became a fellow of Corpus Christi College. It was at Oxford that he became involved in labour and cooperative politics, and he was closely involved with the work of the Fabian Society. Through these connections he took an interest in social work and was for a time active in the Toynbee Hall settlement in London. In 1897 he resigned his fellowship to pursue journalism and political work, becoming a leader writer for the *Manchester Guardian*, and he began to work through a number of issues in the new liberalism. He was by temperament an academic intellectual. While at Oxford he had published a study in the philosophy of knowledge and he followed this up with an investigation into the psychology of knowledge that drew on experimental studies in which he had been involved. His psychology was evolutionary, based on a Darwinian approach, and he began to work on the wider issue of the evolution of moral ideas. Invited through his Fabian connections to lecture on politics at the newly established London School of Economics, he began to take a closer interest in sociology and in Victor Branford's Sociological Society. A chair in sociology had been endowed by Martin White, a wealthy Scottish merchant who had intended that the chair should go to Patrick Geddes. The School, however, preferred Hobhouse, and in 1907 he became the first full-time professor of sociology to be appointed in Britain. In the same year he became the editor of the new *Sociological Review.*

Hobhouse had produced a comparative sociology of morals shortly before his appointment, and he continued to develop these ideas and to relate them to his political concerns. He made little or no reference to the work of Spencer, yet the sociology that he began to construct was firmly in the Spencerian mould. His major works had already taken an evolutionary standpoint and he pulled these together into a synthetic statement of the evolutionary idea, published in 1913, that summarized the key ideas that he had worked on since his time at Oxford. He went on to apply this orienting idea to a series of programmatic statements of sociological ideas published between 1918 and 1924, and described these as his 'Principles of Sociology'. This work, and particularly the central and definitive book on *Social Development*, extended and enlarged his evolutionary theory of mind and culture. He remained at the London School of Economics throughout his career, recruiting Morris Ginsberg, who became his faithful disciple and the publicist for his ideas. Hobhouse died in 1929.

Hobhouse saw the social world as a network or tissue of social relations within which relatively fixed and enduring social structures could be formed. These structures include families, churches, voluntary associations and nations. Social structures are organized through a 'social mentality' that is maintained from generation to generation through processes of communication and by socialization into a culture or tradition. Although Hobhouse described this network as a 'social mind' or 'social mentality', he did not follow the particularly strong statements of the Oxford idealists about the autonomy and reality of this mentality. The social mentality is not an actual mind that exists over and above individual minds. It is, for Hobhouse, simply a network of minds in communication and the means through which habits, dispositions and commitments to social institutions are built and sustained. Rather like **Durkheim**, Hobhouse was emphasizing that people *share* ideas and that they are social in origin. To stress the distinctiveness of his ideas, Ginsberg and Robert MacIver contrasted it with the 'group mind' thesis that they claimed to find in the Oxford idealists and in Durkheim. Although this interpretation cannot be sustained, it is certainly the case that Hobhouse was at one with the symbolic interactionists in recognizing that social life consists only of individual minds in communication.

Hobhouse grounded this in his social psychology. He saw the physical basis of mind as the product of biological evolution and as common to all human beings. It is this common inheritance that gives the capacity for intelligent and purposive thought and allows the production of a culture that can be passed on from one generation to the next. Cultural learning, then, is the key to social advance. Human biology, however, is not completely determining: there may be fixed impulses to do things, but the particular ways in which these can be done are not generally fixed. A variety of cultural solutions are available to shape the expression of instincts and impulses, and all actions combine instinct with intelligence. Language is the key mechanism through which intelligence can reflect upon and judge impulses and the available means to their satisfaction. Thus human actions range from the completely instinctive to the completely purposive. It is through engaging in purposive action that people are able to produce a sense of self and to establish a basis for mutual understanding with those with whom they interact.

The collective mental process of communication that lies at the heart of society involves, in its most fundamental respects, the shared rules that provide people with an understanding of acceptable and unacceptable forms of behaviour. A population that shares a specific set of rules is a community, and such rules are sustained by sentiments shared within the population. When rules are accepted unreflectively they are 'customs' and are the basis of habitual conformity; when they are consciously declared and enforced by a state or administrative body they are 'laws'. Rules cluster together as 'institutions' concerned with specific types of activity. Property institutions, for example, regulate scontrol over the use and transfer of material objects, while the institution of marriage regulates reproduction and kinship. Social structures, then, comprise 'institutionalized' social relations.

Any society that persists over a long period of time can be characterized as an 'organic' whole. It has a unity and a life of its own, and its various parts work together and reinforce each other. This integration, Hobhouse argued, is a result of evolution, of natural selection. Sentiments and ideas that help the adaptation and survival of society will tend to persist, and societies that fail to nurture these sentiments will decline. It is through such processes of selection that long-term processes of change occur, and Hobhouse saw evolution as having traced a branching pattern of change that led, at the level of humanity as a whole, from simpler to more complex forms of social structure. Hobhouse looked at evolution through a sequence from kinship-based societies, organized around 'primitive' thought and religious ideas, through 'civilized' societies with authoritarian states and complex religious systems, to modern societies based around scientific ideas and with 'civic' states. Thanks to natural selection, any society develops through increases in its scale and the efficiency with which it handles its resources and organizes its activities. This is a condition for enhancing individuality, freedom and mutual co-operation. In Hobhouse's model, advances in human thought and knowledge make possible forms of adaptation that enhance human productive powers and control over nature, and these, in turn, enhance the abilities of people to pursue their goals in rational and more effective ways. For Hobhouse, social development was directional and virtually inevitable and could be characterized in moral terms as 'progress'.

This account of social development was the basis for one of Hobhouse's most important and influential ideas. Modern societies, he argued, are not simply rational, industrial societies; they are societies in which political power has become less authoritarian than in traditional societies. Nation-states are organized around the extension of democratic control over political activity. The freedom and mutuality of modern societies lie behind the 'civic' character of their states. Modern states treat their members as 'citizens' rather than merely as 'subjects'. They have established rights of legal and personal liberty, rights to a minimum standard of living and rights to education and welfare. These rights ensure 'full membership' in a society, with all members having an equal claim to participate in the 'common good'. The fuller development of citizenship was, then, the long-term result of social development. In setting out this theory of citizenship, Hobhouse laid the basis for the further work carried out by his colleague **T. H. Marshall**.

See also: T. H. Marshall, Herbert Spencer, Edward Tylor.

Major works

The Labour Movement. 1893. London: T. Fisher Unwin.
The Theory of Knowledge. 1896. London: Methuen.
Mind in Evolution. 1901. London: Macmillan.
Democracy and Reaction. 1904. Brighton: Harvester, 1972.
Morals in Evolution. 1906. London: Macmillan.
Liberalism. 1911. In James Meadowcroft, ed. *Hobhouse: Liberalism and Other Writings*. Cambridge: Cambridge University Press, 1994.
Social Evolution and Political Theory. 1911. WI: Port Washington: Kennikat Press, 1968.

Development and Purpose. 1913. London: Macmillan.
The Material Culture and Social Institutions of the Simpler Peoples. 1914. With G. C. Wheeler and Morris Ginsberg. London: Routledge and Kegan Paul, 1965.
The Metaphysical Theory of the State. 1918. Vol. 1 of *Principles of Sociology*. London: George Allen and Unwin.
The Rational Good. 1921. Vol. 2 of *Principles of Sociology*. London: George Allen and Unwin.
The Elements of Social Justice. 1922. Vol. 3 of *Principles of Sociology*. London: George Allen and Unwin.
Social Development: Its Nature and Conditions. 1924. Vol. 4 of *Principles of Sociology*. London: George Allen and Unwin, 1966.
Various essays from 1907 to 1930 were posthumously published in his *Sociology and Philosophy*. London: G. Bell and Sons, 1966.

Further reading

Hugh S. Carter. *The Social Theories of L. T. Hobhouse*. Port Washington: Kennikat Press, 1968 (originally 1927).
Stefan Collini. *Liberalism and Sociology: L. T. Hobhouse and Political Argument in England, 1880–1914*. Cambridge: Cambridge University Press, 1979.
John A. Hobson and Morris Ginsberg, eds. 1931. *L. T. Hobhouse: His Life and Work*, London: George Allen and Unwin.

JOHN SCOTT

FRÉDÉRIC LE PLAY

A French industrial and mining engineer and a major figure in the development of elite technical education in France, Pierre-Guillaume-Frédéric Le Play was centrally involved, as practitioner, teacher and consultant, in the industrialization of Russia and other European countries. Born in a small village in Normandy in 1806 into a conservative Catholic family, Le Play graduated from the Ecole Polytechnique and the Ecole des Mines. He took a professorship in metallurgy but resigned his position after the revolution of 1848 and devoted his time to creating a 'science of society' modelled upon metallurgy, chemistry and statistics. He rejected both the rational individualism of capitalism and the newly self-conscious traditionalism of conservative political thinkers. He thought that the Enlightenment's exaltation of pure reason was a way to avoid the difficult task of acquiring scientific knowledge through empirical investigation.

Le Play argued that the science of government could be improved by using a view of statistics as a mixture of geography, history, law, political science and public administration (*General Considerations on Statistics*). But he became convinced that social research should focus on the study of the private lives of citizens, rather than on population characteristics or national resources, and that it should rely on the systematic use of direct observation. Le Play's major empirical work, *The European Workers*, published in 1855, represents the first instance of large-scale empirical research based on a standardized method that combined both qualitative field observation and quantification. Family monographs were living portraits of families capturing all the nuances of 'social happiness' in different types of societies. Le Play conceived of the family as the basic unit of society and believed that 'social happiness' depended on 'familial happiness'. He proposed to demonstrate that happy families, like happy societies, were the ones that satisfied two basic needs: 'daily bread' – that is, regular employment and economic means – and the 'moral law' of responsibility towards family members, respect for authority and frugality. *European Workers* contains thirty-six monographs (the second edition has fifty-seven) on individual families scattered throughout Europe in the first half of the nineteenth century, families whose members included British factory workers and artisans; Russian, Spanish and French peasants; German miners of the upper Hartz mountains; a Swiss clock-maker; and a Parisian rag-picker.

Le Play's monographic method used observation and interviewing. He spent time with families, selected with the help of local 'social authorities', interviewed the head of the household and the oldest child, and elicited information from local informants. He also used this approach to study institutional arrangements that might account for a family's success or failure to satisfy the two basic needs. In this he focused especially on work relations, land tenure, ecology, professional organizations and voluntary associations. Le Play conceived of a two-dimensional property-space where the horizontal axis presents four different types of system of social organization (nomadic, non-voluntary work agreement, patronage, industrial employment) and the vertical axis presents seven types of workers (domestic worker, day worker, piece-worker, worker-tenant, master artisan, worker-owner and proprietor). Each monograph was located at an intersection of the two dimensions, providing a distribution of family monographs with at least one in each cell.

Le Play did not believe in the search for general causal laws. He sought generalizations of a different type by studying the way families functioned, to determine which institutional and work arrangements were most likely to lead to social happiness (*The Organization of*

Work). It is worth noting that Le Play used complex classificatory devices to collect information for family budgets as a central part of family monographs. Le Play thought that by matching the totals of a family budget of receipts with the totals of its expenditures he would verify that he had accounted for every aspect of family life. The budget of receipts was designed to show the variety of ways in which workers' families made a living. It included all sources of revenue – cash revenue, revenue in kind and the value of all property owned. Regarding expenditures, all details of family life regarding food, dwelling, clothing, moral needs and financial expenses (taxes, interest, debts, insurance and mutual aid societies) were recorded in minute detail and patterns of production and consumption analysed in ways that anticipated current analyses of standards of living.

Of all of Le Play's contributions, the elaboration of family types (in *The Organization of the Family*) has received the most attention from followers and commentators. Le Play compared the 'patriarchal' family, the 'stem' family and the 'unstable' family on the basis of the nature of property ownership, family composition and relationships, and inheritance laws. The patriarchal family was based on collective property, with authoritarian family relations and inheritance to the oldest male (primogeniture); the stem family was based on a system of private ownership, the selection of one child to inherit family property, and the heir taking responsibility for aging parents and siblings who did not migrate; finally, the unstable family was based on private property, with an erosion of parental authority, the equal division of inheritance between all the children and no responsibility towards isolated elderly parents. The stem family represented the ideal balance between tradition and change found in small towns and villages in Anglo-Saxon countries, while the unstable family was primarily found in large urban centres in countries like France where inheritance laws favoured equal division of property.

Le Play's monographic method has been criticized for being too descriptive, for making inferences from individual families to whole societies (*The English Constitution*) and as biased by its focus on social harmony and cooperation and failing to report conflicts and antagonism in the family and community. Despite these criticisms, it is no exaggeration to claim that this is the first time that the largely silent and illiterate masses of peasants and workers of Europe were studied in a scientifically intelligible way, with methods that essentially resemble modern-day sociological and anthropological procedures. Concerned with the problems of social mobility and change in a time of rapid economic and political development, Le Play made the decisive leap into what later became known as empirical sociology.

Le Play's works are full of scientific concerns and ideological statements which may be difficult to reconcile. But the apparent contradictions may simply reflect a different idea of social science, conceived during the first half of the nineteenth century when the discipline was just emerging. He never hid the connection between his scientific research and the moral beliefs he wanted his research to serve. His interpretation of society combined conservative and liberal ideas about social order and social change that he pushed as a nominated member of the French Senate within a problem-solving perspective (*The Essential Constitution of Humanity*).

As a social reformer, convinced that he had scientifically discovered social truths, he translated his findings into ideological statements denouncing the false dogma of the French Revolution (equal inheritance laws) and preaching a return to religion, local sovereignty, traditions and parental authority. After his death in 1882, students and followers continued over several decades to publish family monographs in *The Workers of Two Worlds*. Le Play's ideas had an enduring effect, through the creation of two competing journals, in both France and, especially, England. However, the repeated failure of his followers to keep reformist and ideological preoccupations in check led to their marginalization in academic circles and the limited diffusion of the monographic method.

Le Play's approach and ideas are important because they show that, even in its incipient stages, sociology offered a genuine alternative to Comtean positivism. Perhaps no internally consistent scheme of analysis, either reactionary or liberal, could have produced the kinds of concerns and tensions to which Le Play's groundbreaking empirical and comparative sociology was a response, underscoring his continuing relevance in a period concerned with policy analysis.

See also: Charles Booth, Seebohm Rowntree.

Major works

Vues générales sur la statistique. 1840. Paris: La Nouvelle Encyclopédie.
Les Ouvriers européens. 1855. 6 vols. Tours: Mame. 2nd edn 1877–9. Partial translation of vol. 1 in C. Zimmerman. *Family and Society*. London, 1936.
L'Organisation de la travail. 1870. Tours: Mame.
L'Organisation de la famille. 1871. Tours: Mame.

La *Méthode de la science sociale.* 1879 Tours: Mame. Re-edited 1989: Paris, Meridiens-Klincksieck.
La *Constitution essentielle de l'humanité.* 1881. Tours: Mame.
Les *Ouvriers des deux mondes.* 1857–1912. Monograph Series, Paris: International Society of Practical Studies of Political Economy.
Extracts can be found in Catherine Bodard-Silver, ed. 1982. *Frederic Le Play: On Family, Work and Social Change.* Chicago: University of Chicago Press.

Further reading

Catherine Bodard-Silver. 1982. 'Introduction'. In Catherine Bodard-Silver, ed. *Frederic Le Play: On Family, Work and Social Change.* Chicago: University of Chicago Press.
Michael Z. Brooke. 1970. *Le Play, Engineer, and Social Scientist: The Life and Work of Frederic Le Play.* Harlow: Longman.
B. Lecuyer. 1992. 'Frederic Le Play fondateur de la "science sociale"'. *Extraits de communications du groupe d'études des methodes de l'analyse sociologique,* vol. 54. Paris: CNRS/Paris IV.

CATHERINE B. SILVER

GYORGY LUKÁCS

As both political philosopher and literary theorist, Lukács has been among the most influential of twentieth-century thinkers. The book that belatedly attracted most attention in the social sciences was *History and Class Consciousness*, a work that has influenced left-wing thought from **Adorno** and **Marcuse** to Merleau-Ponty and Raymond Williams; from Lucien Goldmann to Walter Benjamin. Moreover, his circle of friends included some of the century's most famous names, including **Max Weber**, **Georg Simmel**, Ernst Bloch, **Ferdinand Tönnies**, **Karl Mannheim**, Karl Korsch, novelist Thomas Mann and composer Bela Bartok.

Lukács was Hungarian by birth and grew up in Budapest. German was the language in which he wrote, as, for him, it offered the richest source of philosophical expression. His mother grew up in Vienna and naturally acquired German; his father, on the way to becoming the managing director of the Hungarian General Credit Bank, learned several foreign languages in his spare time, including German. Lukács' own university education took place in Budapest, but also in Berlin and Heidelberg, where he studied under Simmel and Weber and published as Georg Lukàcs. Though not overtly rebellious in his youth, he remained a controversial figure throughout his life. In building his work around Hegelian Marxism as a philosophy of practice, he twice took up the unenviable task of rendering theory into practice as a government minister: first in 1919 as deputy commissar for education in the Hungarian Soviet Republic and second in 1956 as minister of culture in Hungary. While these were brief episodes, we can understand his work in part as an attempt to resolve a tension between his inherently romantic, utopian spirit and his wish to support the rational-bureaucratic demands of the Soviet regime. In effect, his work was a life-long effort to resolve the difference between 'spirit' and 'reality'.

Lukács' early, pre-Marxist work in *Soul and Form* captures this dilemma. It consists of ten essays written between 1907 and 1910, in which he wrestled with the dismaying fact that the rich, chaotic nature of life (soul) always falters as it comes to fruition (form). Indeed, for soul to come into form means its inevitable defeat. When the endless rush of life halts for the sake of some fixed ideal, be it artistic or personal, it loses its essential vitality in the name of a spurious closure. Themes appeared here that resurfaced differently later. He challenged Hegel's claim that there was a hidden rationality behind life's incoherence, and he rejected the possibility of a unified 'totality' that resolves the opposition between soul and form. Similarly discarded was the literary Romanticism of Georg Novalis, which sought unity solely through a poetic inwardness that bypassed reality. Such rejection of individual experience extended to the use of a psychology that would reduce the meaning of events to the motives people had in realizing them.

The significance of 'totality' reappeared only slightly more positively in the later *Theory of the Novel*, where there is a shift away from the impossibility of overcoming the opposition between (Kantian) categories towards a more Hegelian search for a unified 'totality': something Lukács pursued *via* literary art. In the modern world hopes for this are slender, but in the grandeur of Homer's *Odyssey* and *Illiad* he found the unities for which he longed. In these epics of ancient Greece there is no gap between desire and duty, no split between the individual and the world, no separation between subject and object. This unified worldview knows nothing of history and change; the character of the individuals in the *Odyssey* remains the same throughout, even though the events happen over ten years. Only subsequently, with changing art forms, does a sense of temporality emerge involving a descent from the unities of the epic.

By contrast, the modern novel – with a few exceptions – is able only to express nostalgia for this lost totality. The fragmentation and

arbitrariness of modern life, with its attendant loss of meaning, produces only novels of disillusionment that reflect what Lukács called
our 'transcendent homelessness'. Modern individuals are no longer
truly at home in the world; they may manipulate it for their own
ends but search in vain for any inherent meaning. Whether under the
influence of Weber or not, this idea is close to the latter's belief that
the modern western process of 'rationalization' entails the 'disenchantment' of the world. Certainly, Weber (and Thomas Mann) read
and approved of Lukács' book. As with Weber, however, one should
beware of seeing his contribution as merely romantic pessimism.

There are continuities between this and subsequent work, but in
History and Class Consciousness, published in 1923, both tone and
content change. Whatever final judgement is made of this work, it
represented then the most sophisticated affirmation of Marxism to
date. After *History and Class Consciousness*, dismissing Marxism for its
economic determinism or accusing it of having a naïve, 'positivist'
view of history was no longer tenable. Moreover, its effects are still
with us. Concepts such as 'reification' and 'commodity fetishism',
first aired centrally there, are now part of the embedded vocabulary
of any critical sociology. Where Marx identified these as economic
phenomena, Lukács placed them at the heart of things, arguing they
had overflowed the economy and permeated all aspects of society.
The overweening power of the commodity even reached inside the
individual, stamping 'its imprint on the whole consciousness of man'.
Qualities and abilities that were once an organic part of the personality became things that 'he can own or dispose of like the various
objects of the external world'. Whether one looks at the work of the
Frankfurt school, Giddens' account of the 'pure relationship' or
Baudrillard's of the subject lost in hyper-reality, the concept we now
call the commodification of identity is Lukács' legacy. In effect,
Marxism as a critical academic discourse began here.

Lukács identified Marxism as superior to other approaches because
'totality' was central to its method. Where his pre-Marxist work saw
'totality' as a brief moment of unity and subsequent history a pale
imitation, in this it takes on a dynamic, progressive hue. It refers to
'everything' that has emerged in the self-formation of humanity
through history to culminate in communism. 'Totality', though, is
not an object that can be analysed from the outside. It is an encompassing historical process that embraces subject and object. Indeed,
Marxism, no less than the proletariat, exists within and as an outcome
of this process. Marxism is both the product of the process and the
one theory that can grasp the totality. Tacking back and forth

between subject and object, Marxism's dialectical method is able to get behind empirical appearances and see how 'facts' emerge. Rejecting positivism's fixation with empirical facts is a commonplace today, but Lukács was amongst the first who obliged us to see that facts are only meaningful when placed within the context that produced them.

Tightening the knot even further in emphasizing its praxis, he identified the proletariat as the 'identical subject–object of history'. The 'subject of history' meant that the proletariat was the main mover in bringing history to fruition; it was the universal class which could install a unified totality. It was also the object of history in being the end-state or purpose of it. In claiming this, he melded Marxian and Hegelian ideas together. Capitalism rested on the exploitation and alienation of the proletariat, and because of its structural position the proletariat's struggle for existence represented the most complete possibility of transcending capitalism (**Marx**). The epistemological problems of the subject gaining proper knowledge of the world of objects would also be overcome. For the first time, unclouded by distortion, our understanding of the world would correspond to the way it was, and the world would correspond to our understanding of it (Hegel).

Of course, the flaws in conceiving a social class in almost metaphysical terms were bound to emerge when faced with the political turmoil of Europe between 1917 and 1924. Lukács fused the destiny of the proletariat with the Marxist knowledge held by the Communist Party. The Party was to mediate between the proletariat and history, the proletariat between the Party and history. It was to be a reciprocal relation. However, if the actual consciousness of the proletariat lagged behind what it ideally should be, the Party must 'impute' to it a correct version. The chequered history of Lukács' book has hinged on this dilemma. For Lenin, the Party had to be pre-eminent if socialism in one country was to work: giving the proletariat equal status to the Party only hobbled the revolution. Lukács was subsequently obliged to recant his own position in favour of Lenin's.

These issues have recently resurfaced in unexpected places. When contemporary feminists such as Sandra Harding advocate 'standpoint' theory in opposition to feminist empiricism, they tacitly echo Lukács' claim that empirical facts only make sense when understood within the context that generated them. Similarly, just as Lukács claimed that the proletariat's structural position enabled its standpoint to reveal the truth of capitalism, so Harding claims that only women's standpoint reveals the truth of patriarchy. The problems that follow are similar. If women's actual, empirical consciousness fails to live up to what it 'should' be, feminist theory must intervene and revise it. Indeed, there has been a shift in terminology from 'women's standpoint' to 'feminist standpoint' theory. Contemporary feminists such as Stanley and Wise, though, are aware that the manipulative implications of this view are antipathetic to feminism, and make efforts to refute them. Certainly, with the emergence of black, lesbian and post-modernist feminisms, the idea of women as a seamless, universal group is no more defensible than Lukács' idea of the universal 'proletariat'.

Although *History and Class Consciousness* has attracted most attention, Lukács' interests moved away from the overtly political during the 1930s. His engagement with literary modernism in general and (German) Expressionism in particular involved vehement debates with Ernst Bloch and Bertolt Brecht. Bloch had applauded Expressionism as an apposite response to the increasingly inchoate nature of life in the early decades of the twentieth century. For Lukács, though, the emphasis on feeling and affect at the expense of reference meant that Expressionism failed to uncover the repressive nature of the wider totality. Expressionists shared in the ideological obfuscation of the times by playing on a merely subjective, 'expressive' response to harsh realities. In response Brecht and Bloch pointed out how far removed Lukács' ideas were from the realities of artistic production. Brecht, as a (Marxist) playwright, provided a marvellously caustic riposte, arguing that in advocating the supposedly objective prose norms of great nineteenth-century writers such as Balzac, Dickens and Tolstoy, Lukács ignored the fact that the historical totality had changed and, with it, artistic norms.

There is certainly a tendency in Lukács to gloss ideas and measure them in terms of his presumed superior knowledge of the totality. This reductionism is most apparent in *The Destruction of Reason*, where he criticized a whole range of thinkers – Schelling, Dilthey, Kierkegaard, Mannheim, **Scheler** – bluntly judging them irrationalist because not Marxist. He went on to write further on aesthetics and produced a study of social ontology, left incomplete at his death in 1971. While the failings in his work are obvious, few authors have created a systematic theory with such range and normative ambition. If provoking thought is a measure of a theory's success, he succeeded.

See also: Theodor Adorno, Karl Mannheim, Max Scheler.

See also in *Fifty Key Sociologists: The Contemporary Theorists*: Zygmunt Bauman, Jürgen Habermas.

Major works

Soul and Form. 1910. London: Merlin Press, 1974.
Theory of the Novel. 1914–15. London: Merlin Press, 1974.
History and Class Consciousness. 1923. London: Merlin Press, 1971.
Lenin. 1924. London: New Left Books, 1970.
A Defence of History and Class Consciousness: Tailism and the Dialectic. 1925, unpublished. London: Verso, 2000.
The Historical Novel. 1937. Harmondsworth: Penguin, 1976.
Studies in European Realism. 1946. London: Merlin Press, 1972.
The Destruction of Reason. 1952. London: Merlin Press, 1980.
The Meaning of Contemporary Realism. 1958. London: Merlin Press, 1963.
The Ontology of Social Being. 1971. Vol. 1: *Hegel* and vol. 2: *Marx*. London: Merlin Press, 1978.

Further reading

Frederic Jameson, ed. 1977. *Aesthetics and Politics*. London: NLB.
Martin Jay. 1984. *Marxism and Totality*. Berkeley, CA: University of California Press.
Istvan Meszaros. 1972. *Lukács' Concept of Dialectic*. London: Merlin Press.
Liz Stanley and Sue Wise. 1993. *Breaking Out Again*. London: Routledge.

ALAN HOW

BRONISLAW MALINOWSKI

Bronislaw Kasper Malinowski once wrote that his family belonged 'to the dispossessed, impoverished small Polish nobility, shading into the *intelgiencja*'. He was born in 1884 in Cracow, the capital of a cosmopolitan province of the Austro-Hungarian Empire, and he studied at the Jagiellonian University in the city, where his father was professor of philology. He won the Imperial Prize for his doctoral thesis, and like his father he undertook postgraduate work at the University of Leipzig, moving on, in 1910, to specialize in ethnology under Edvard Westermarck at the London School of Economics. He remained loyal to the multi-ethnic Austro-Hungarian Empire, and during the Second World War he became something of a Polish nationalist, but Malinowski made his professional career in the Anglo-Saxon world, doing fieldwork in New Guinea while based in Australia and later turning down the chance of an appointment to a chair at the Jagiel-lonian University in order to take up a permanent position at the London School of Economics in 1923 – he confessed to 'a mystic cult of British culture'. In 1939 he moved to Yale University, where he died of a massive heart attack in 1942.

Malinowski went out to Australia in 1914 to attend a grand imperial meeting of the British Association for the Advancement of Science. Trapped by the outbreak of war, he found himself an enemy alien. The Australian authorities allowed him to carry out his planned research in their colonial territory of Papua, and even helped to finance his work, and after a preliminary study on mainland New Guinea he undertook ethnographic research on the Trobriand Islands (1915–18), in the course of which he revolutionized field methods in social anthropology. Breaking with the established ethnographic tra-dition, he insisted that the investigator 'must relinquish his comfor-table position on the verandah, where he has been accustomed to collect statements from informants'. Instead he should pitch his tent in the village, cultivate a garden, exchange gifts, listen in to con-versations, flirt, argue and generally hang about. Intimate personal histories, neighbourhood feuds, the tug of a man's emotional loyalties against his legal obligations, all this was accessible only to an observer who immersed himself in everyday life in the village. Getting the rules down from some expert did not tell you how the game was played. Witchdoctors disagreed among themselves, just like medical doctors. And people tend to say one thing but do another, for 'whenever the native can evade his obligations without the loss of prestige, or without the prospective loss of gain, he does so, exactly as a civilised business man would do.'

Malinowski pioneered methods for recording and ordering field data, and he also believed that the ethnographer should interrogate himself as carefully as he studied his subjects. He had kept a diary intermittently for years, since first reading Nietzsche as a teenager. Now it became an instrument of research, as he monitored his physical and spiritual condition and whipped himself on to work harder. 'Main thing to do,' one note reads, 'is to reflect on the two branches: my eth-nological work and my diary. They are well-nigh as complementary as complementary can be.' Malinowski's field notes are largely in Eng-lish, although he jotted down increasingly long passages in Kiriwinian as his command of the language improved; but the private diary was written in Polish. It served among other things as a safety valve through which he could let his emotions boil over, and its pages were punc-tuated with outbursts of irritation, even rage, against the Trobrianders.

Malinowski once wrote of 'the ethnographer's magic, by which he is able to evoke the real spirit of the natives, the true picture of tribal life'. If not magic, it was certainly an art, but one that had to be grounded in empirical research. As an undergraduate studying physics and chemistry, he had specialized in the philosophy of science. He wrote a thesis on Mach's positivism, though he ended up with a more permissive empiricist doctrine, 'nothing without experience'. 'The main principle of my work in the field: avoid artificial simplifications. To this end, collect as concrete materials as possible: note every informant; work with children, *outsiders, and specialists. Take side lights and opinions.*' However, working in the Trobriands he sometimes felt himself 'almost swamped by detail'. Experience had to be shaped. Theory must come before description. 'Every precise description of facts requires precise concepts', he had written in a theoretical essay in 1911, 'and these can be provided only by theory'. The goal was to tease out the various strands – magic, economics, kinship, politics – that were woven together in even the most essential work, like house building, sailing or gardening. The atmosphere, what Malinowski called the *Stimmung*, had to be rendered as well, in the artistic pursuit of realism.

Malinowski was the first ethnographer to represent 'savages' as rational actors. His Trobrianders used myths to make property claims, rituals to extend their power, marriages to gain influence. Yet his descriptions lacked a vital dimension, for his ethnographies very largely ignored the colonial context. The government officer, the missionary and the trader appear as shadowy stereotypes in his published books and papers. In a confessional appendix to his final Trobriand monograph, published in 1935, Malinowski himself wrote: 'The empirical facts which the ethnographer has before him in the Trobriands nowadays are not natives unaffected by European influences but natives to a considerable extent transformed by these influences.' His neglect of the colonial reality was, he admitted, 'perhaps the most serious shortcoming of my whole anthropological research in Melanesia'. At the London School of Economics in the 1930s, he was to promote a new brand of anthropology, which he called 'the anthropology of the changing native'. Yet the ethnographies retain their power because the cosmopolitan Malinowski regarded the Trobriander as being essentially rather like himself.

Between 1923 and 1939 he built up the leading school of social anthropology in Europe at the London School of Economics and trained most of the leading figures in the next generation of British social anthropology. Partly as a result of his rivalry with **Alfred**

Radcliffe-Brown, who was highly regarded as a theorist, Malinowski attempted to develop a social theory, which he half-playfully called 'the functional school of anthropology'. The basic idea was that human needs were universal, and that every 'culture' had to devise institutions to satisfy them. These institutions in turn required support systems, which were met by new institutions. Malinowski's explicitly theoretical contributions were received without enthusiasm, but a more sophisticated theory was implicit in his ethnographies. Human beings everywhere manipulate social institutions to serve their primary interests. If institutions and customs persist they must have a practical pay-off. Magical and religious practices meet emotional needs and help to order economic activities and political relations. Ethnographies should therefore focus on what people do rather than what they say they should do.

When he came into anthropology, Malinowski once remarked, the emphasis had been on the differences between peoples. 'I recognised their study as important, but underlying sameness I thought of greater importance & rather neglected. I still believe that the fundamental is more important than the freakish.' He conceived of a 'new humanism' based on philosophy and sociology, 'the science of your fellow human beings'. This would require the study of 'living man, living language, and living full-blooded facts'.

See also: Emile Durkheim, Alfred Radcliffe-Brown.

See also in *Fifty Key Sociologists: The Contemporary Theorists*: Talcott Parsons.

Major works

The Family among the Australian Aborigines. 1913. New York: Schocken Books, 1963.
The Ethnography of Malinowski: The Trobriand Islands 1915–1918. Ed. M. W. Young. London: Routledge, 1979.
Argonauts of the Western Pacific: An Account of Native Enterprise and Adventure in the Archipelagoes of Melanesian New Guinea. 1922. London: Routledge.
Crime and Custom in Savage Society. 1926. London: Routledge.
The Sexual Life of Savages. 1929. London: Routledge.
Coral Gardens and their Magic, 2 vols. 1935. London: Routledge.
A Scientific Theory of Culture and Other Essays. 1939–41. Chapel Hill, NC: University of North Carolina Press, 1944.

Malinowski's reflections on his Trobriand fieldwork can be found in *A Diary in the Strict Sense of the Term*, ed. Raymond Firth. Stanford, CA: Stanford University Press, 1989.

Further reading

Adam Kuper. 1996. *Anthropologists and Anthropology: The Modern British School*, London, Routledge, ch. 1.

George W. Stocking, Jr. 1995. *After Tylor: British Social Anthropology 1888–1951*. Madison, WI: Wisconsin University Press.

Michael Young. 2004. *Malinowski: Odyssey of an anthropologist 1884–1920*. New Haven, CT: Yale University Press.

ADAM KUPER

KARL MANNHEIM

Great figures in sociology are remembered for their original and influential contributions to the theory or method of social inquiry. Characteristic, too, are the range and scope of their work. Measured by these standards, Karl Mannheim arguably belongs to any survey of such distinguished sociologists. His studies of generations, economic ambition, competition, structures of thinking and similar topics in the sociology of culture, as well as his later work in political sociology, notably on the theme of planning, mark him out as an ingenious and innovative thinker. Above all, he is known for his methodological and substantive work, beginning with his seminal essay on conservative thought, in the sub-discipline he helped to establish as the 'sociology of knowledge'. Notwithstanding his other achievements, it is this approach to knowledge that qualifies Mannheim as a classic. Mannheim's most famous book is *Ideology and Utopia*. It first appeared in German in 1929 and then in an expanded and revised English version in 1936. It has remained in print ever since. In the last analysis, the most striking contributions to sociology are those that embody a compelling vision of sociology as a practice.

Mannheim was born in Budapest, Hungary, in 1893 and died in London, England, in 1947. As a student and young intellectual in Hungary, he was close to several individuals who later became prominent communists. Although that was not his own political affiliation, he was nevertheless forced to flee when the short-lived Soviet regime in Hungary was overthrown in 1919 and the new rulers persecuted anyone they distrusted. Between 1920 and 1933, he lived in Germany and taught at the University of Frankfurt. In the spring of 1933, soon after Hitler's rise to power, Mannheim lost his university professorship and was forced into exile because he was a foreigner and a Jew. Mannheim's repeated victimization by political upheavals is relevant to understanding his approach to political ideas. He knew first hand that political ideas are not empty talk: they can have consequences, even deadly ones.

As a writer, and even more as a teacher, Mannheim believed that one had to speak directly to people's experiences; that it was pointless to offer answers to questions that people have not been led by their lives to ask or recognize. With his sociology of knowledge, Mannheim sought to clarify – and to help overcome – at least three kinds of troubling experiences, all of which are as common today as they were in his time.

The first experience takes the form of a discrepancy between one's own situation, as lived subjectively in mind and body, and the supposedly objective 'meaning' ascribed to it by the publicly recognized and officially sanctioned ways of talking about things. Mannheim cited the cases of women and young people: there is an accepted definition of what it means to be a woman or to be a youth, but women and youths cannot apply those meanings to make sense of what is happening to them, what they are doing and what they are feeling. The existence of a generally accepted objective construction of meanings – often called a 'worldview' – caught Mannheim's attention early on, instructed by some of the intellectual mentors of his younger years, most notably the sociologist **Georg Simmel** and the literary and social theorist **Gyorgy Lukács**. While other sociologists are more likely to emphasize the extent to which such socially constituted constructions of reality shape and define our experiences, Mannheim focused on the experience of discrepancies between the 'objective' and the 'subjective,' which they variously saw as a source of profound and irremediable dissatisfaction (Simmel's 'tragedy of culture') or as a potential source of crisis and revolutionary overturn (Lukács' theory of 'alienation').

The second of the troubling experiences qualifies and to some extent undermines the first, in that one is often confronted with conflicting ways of assigning 'meanings'. There may be no single 'publicly recognized or officially sanctioned way'. And these multiple ways may be mutually incomprehensible, so that one group may not even understand what another group means. They 'talk past each other'. Mannheim emphasized such contested concepts as religion, superstition, science and education, but also such fundamental philosophical categories as time and space. After Mannheim arrived in Germany, which was embroiled in pervasive intellectual, political and social conflict, he concluded that most sectors in modern societies are characterized by a competition among incompatible models of meaning, not by a single integrated worldview. To designate these multiple constructions, he borrowed and revised the concept of ideology from Marxist theory. From Marxism, too, Mannheim adapted the notion that ideologies have to be understood as a 'function' of some distinctive social location, that there is a 'correspondence' between occupying a certain position in society and interpreting the world in a certain way. Ideologies are socially grounded: they are 'imputable' to a given social site. Mannheim avoided a causal vocabulary, and he does not claim that all individuals sharing a social location profess the same ideology. Yet he was confident that a 'fit' can be demonstrated and that the ideology can only be elucidated by reference to that experiential grounding.

Mannheim's adaptation differs from the Marxist theory in two important respects. First, he identified social locations additional to economic class position as the grounds of ideologies. His prime examples in *Ideology and Utopia* are the bureaucracy, to which he imputed a special kind of 'bureaucratic conservatism', as well as, within the strategic formation of 'the intellectuals', a deracinated segment that serves as social reference point for an understanding of fascist ideology. Generational and gender differences also enter, but only as sources for modifications or adaptations of ideological structures. As these examples suggest, Mannheim saw the primary ideologies competing in his time as taking the form of political ideologies, and he designated them by the names of prominent political tendencies and parties: socialism, liberalism, conservatism and, as noted, bureaucratic conservatism and fascism. Yet, unlike Max Weber, who was important to him in many respects, Mannheim did not consider ideologies with religious content or social constituencies, notwithstanding the influence of the Catholic religious party in Weimar political life. This remains a blind spot in his sociology.

In explaining the linkages between social locations and ideologies, Mannheim expressly avoided the notion that groups only talk about the world in a certain way because this promotes their economic interests. He acknowledged that this often happens, but he did not consider it to be the ultimate account of ideology. He explores instead the metaphorical language of 'perspective' and 'standpoint'. Things simply look different from different locations. Their peculiar socially grounded interpretations enable groups to orient themselves to the activities and problems peculiar to their location in social space and time, including their struggles for power. Ideologies make sense of the world they encounter.

Second, then, Mannheim differs from Marxism in rejecting its claim that a class may be ordained by history with a privileged point of view, because it is destined to shape the next stage in history. Not rarely, Marxists apply the label 'ideology' only to the views of their opponents and the term 'science' to their own. Mannheim expressly asserts that Marxism is as much an ideology as the 'liberalism' of the bourgeoisie or the 'conservatism' of the older dominant social groups hostile to modernity.

The third and most serious of the 'troubling experiences' mentioned above presupposes the other two. On the German political scene of the 1920s, Mannheim diagnosed a crisis of universal distrust. All political parties claimed that they could see through the arguments of all the others as nothing but the self-interested point of view of some class or social grouping, 'ideology' in the vulgar sense. Under these conditions, Mannheim concluded, there is no productive competition among ideologies. No one can persuade anyone of anything; they cannot even negotiate. And the Fascists, Mannheim observed at the time, were the most thoroughgoing advocates of the proposition that there was nothing to reason or to bargain about in politics, that the only thing was to have an ideology that could win. 'Ideology' and violence, on this view, are part of the same equation.

For Mannheim, in contrast, ideology is a partial but invaluable mode of knowing. Sociology of knowledge is a form of holistic 'therapy.' It is a strategy for having available social knowledge take a form that promotes the reasonable management of human affairs. Implicit is the possibility of achieving a 'synthesis,' which involved a 'total' vision, bringing together in a multi-dimensional whole the things that the various ideological perspectives are best situated to see. Socialists can see the mechanisms of economic exploitation, for example, while Liberals can see the dangers of oppressive state power. A 'synthesis' of perspectives would not eliminate all conflicts among groups, but it could provide a common reference point for calculating the costs and benefits of different alternatives, and a reference point as well for bargaining and deal-making. There would be new opportunities for responsible choices within a constitutional order of democratic competition, a culminating point of the analysis that reveals Mannheim as a successor to **Max Weber** in political thought.

How can such a 'synthesis' come about if all perspectives are partial? Mannheim's famous answer is that modern societies include a stratum of social actors who are in important ways 'detached' from the social ground – the 'intellectuals.' This formation, leaving aside the demoralized segment associated with fascism, is recruited from diverse social locations and engages in activities – notably of an intellectual kind – that keep its members from identifying with the groups and standpoints of their origins. Their formative experience of intense and advanced education produces a 'distance' from the ideologies at home in one or another primary social location. They have insight into ideology without the bitterness or frustration that accompanies the dismissive versions of that insight, which is typical of the political groups caught up in the 'crisis of distrust'. As the intellectuals-turned-sociologists develop and refine the sociology of knowledge, then, they can promote 'synthesis' and help to overcome the 'crisis', not by presuming to take command (as Fascists do) but by a combination of two things. First, they act as catalysts in the political process, offering interpretations that cool temperatures and promote bargaining. And second, they bring 'political education' to the newly enfranchised democratic masses, to counteract fanaticism and to infuse the people with a recognition that there are no saviours or saving visions, echoing Weber, as well as a sense of their own responsibility.

What can we say today about Mannheim's vision of sociology as practice? It is obvious that his proposals, although widely debated, did nothing to prevent the Nazi seizure of power. Translated into English, moreover, his work was stripped of its grand aims, even by those who valued it, and the sociology of knowledge was taken as a way of explaining political ideas or other forms of socially grounded knowledge, without any expectation that such explanations improve practical political knowledge or lessen political incoherence. Sociology of knowledge became part of sociology as a value-free, strictly explanatory 'science', rather than as a practice of diagnosing social problems and devising therapeutic interventions. Yet the idea of sociology as a kind of intervention in social life, conducted by and for actors, rather than simply a remote scientific explanation, as conducted by a totally disinterested spectator, never stays dead for long. Working through 'classics' like Mannheim's famous *Ideology and Utopia* encourages us to return to questions about the limits and responsibilities of social science. This is precisely what makes them 'classics'.

See also: Gyorgy Lukács, Karl Marx, Max Scheler, Max Weber.

See also in *Fifty Key Sociologists: The Contemporary Theorists*: Norbert Elias.

Major works

Structures of Thinking. 1922–4. London: Routledge & Kegan Paul, 1982.

Conservatism. 1925. London: Routledge & Kegan Paul, 1986, 2001.

Essays in the Sociology of Knowledge. 1923–30. London: Routledge & Kegan Paul, 1952.

Sociology as Political Education. 1930. New Brunswick, NJ: Transaction Publishers, 2001.

Ideology and Utopia. Rev. 1936. London: Routledge & Kegan Paul.

Man and Society in an Age of Reconstruction. 1935–7. London: Routledge & Kegan Paul, 1940.

Essays in Sociology and Social Psychology. 1936–40. London: Routledge & Kegan Paul, 1953.

Diagnosis of Our Times. 1939–43. London: Routledge & Kegan Paul, 1943.

A useful compilation of extracts from Mannheim can be found in *From Karl Mannheim* (2nd expanded edn), ed. Kurt H. Wolff. New Brunswick, NJ, and London: Transaction Publishers, 1993. A number of essays of varying quality and authenticity have been published as *Freedom, Power and Democratic Planning*. London: Routledge & Kegan Paul, 1951; *Essays in the Sociology of Culture*. London: Routledge & Kegan Paul, 1956; and *Systematic Sociology*, London: Routledge & Kegan Paul, 1957.

Further reading

David Kettler and Volker Meja. 1995. *Karl Mannheim and the Crisis of Liberalism: 'The Secret of these New Times'*. New Brunswick, NJ: Transaction Publishers.

Colin Loader and David Kettler. 2002. *Karl Mannheim's Sociology as Political Education*. New Brunswick, NJ: Transaction Publishers.

Volker Meja and Nico Stehr. 1990. *Knowledge and Politics. The Sociology of Knowledge Dispute*. London: Routledge & Kegan Paul.

DAVID KETTLER AND VOLKER MEJA

HERBERT MARCUSE

Philosopher, social theorist and political activist, Herbert Marcuse gained world renown during the 1960s as the 'father of the New Left'. The author of many books and articles, and for decades a popular university professor, Marcuse gained notoriety when he was perceived as both an influence on and defender of the 'New Left' in the United States and Europe. His theory of 'one-dimensional' society provided critical perspectives on contemporary capitalist and state communist societies, while his notion of 'the great refusal' won him renown as a theorist of revolutionary change and of 'liberation from the affluent society'. Consequently, he became one of the most influential intellectuals in the United States during the 1960s and into the 1970s.

Marcuse was born in Berlin in 1898 and after serving with the German army in the First World War he went to Freiburg to pursue his studies. After receiving his PhD in literature in 1922, and following a short career as a bookseller in Berlin, he returned to Freiburg in 1928 to study philosophy with Martin Heidegger, then one of the most influential thinkers in Germany. Marcuse's first published article, in 1928, attempted a synthesis of the philosophical perspectives of phenomenology, existentialism and Marxism, a synthesis that decades later would be carried out again by various 'existential' and 'phenomenological' Marxists, such as Jean-Paul Sartre and Maurice Merleau-Ponty, as well as the American students and intellectuals of the New Left.

Marcuse published the first major review of Marx's *Economic and Philosophical Manuscripts of 1844* when it first appeared in print in 1933. The review anticipated the tendency to revise interpretations of Marxism from the standpoint of the works of the early Marx. In the same year, Marcuse joined the Institut für Sozialforschung (Institute for Social Research) in Frankfurt and soon became deeply involved in its interdisciplinary projects, which included working out a model for radical social theory, developing a theory of the new stage of state and monopoly capitalism, and providing a systematic analysis and critique of German fascism. Marcuse deeply identified with the 'critical theory' of the Institute and throughout his life was close to Max Horkheimer, **Theodor Adorno** and others in the Institute's inner circle.

In 1934, Marcuse – a German Jew and a radical – fled from Nazism and emigrated to the United States, where he lived for the rest of his life. The Institute for Social Research was granted offices and an academic affiliation with Columbia University, where Marcuse worked during the 1930s and early 1940s. His first major work in English, *Reason and Revolution*, traced the genesis of the ideas of Hegel, Marx and modern social theory. It demonstrated the similarities between Hegel and Marx, and introduced many English-speaking readers to the Hegelian–Marxian tradition of dialectical thinking. In 1941, Marcuse joined the Office of Secret Services (OSS) and then worked in the State Department, becoming the head of the Central European bureau by the end of the Second World War. Marcuse always claimed that his service with the US government from 1941 through the early 1950s was motivated by a desire to struggle against fascism.

After this government service, he returned to intellectual work and published *Eros and Civilization*, in which he attempted an audacious synthesis of Marx and Freud and sketched the outlines of a non-repressive society. Marcuse argued that the current organization of society produced 'surplus repression' by imposing socially unnecessary labour, unnecessary restrictions on sexuality, and a social system organized around profit and exploitation. In the light of the diminution of scarcity and the prospects for increased abundance, Marcuse called for the end of socially unnecessary repression and the creation of a new society. His radical critique of existing society and its values, and his call for a non-repressive civilization, elicited a dispute with his former colleague Erich Fromm, who accused him of a 'nihilism' towards existing values and society and an irresponsible hedonism. Nevertheless, the text became a cult classic of the 1950s and was extremely popular in the 1960s, whose ethos and counterculture the work anticipated.

In 1958, Marcuse received a tenured position at Brandeis University and became one of the most popular and influential members of its faculty. During his period of government work, Marcuse had been a specialist in fascism and communism, and in 1958 he published a critical study of the Soviet Union under the title *Soviet Marxism*. This broke the taboo in his circles against speaking critically of the USSR and Soviet communism. While attempting to develop a many-sided analysis of the USSR, Marcuse focused his critique on Soviet bureaucracy, culture and values, and on the differences between the Marxian theory and the Soviet version of Marxism. Distancing himself from those who interpreted Soviet communism as a bureaucratic system incapable of reform and democratization, Marcuse pointed to potential 'liberalizing trends' that, indeed, eventually materialized in the 1980s under Gorbachev.

At the beginning of the 1960s, Marcuse published a wide-ranging critique of both advanced capitalist and communist societies in *One-Dimensional Man*. This book theorized the decline of revolutionary potential in capitalist societies and the development of new forms of social control. Marcuse argued that 'advanced industrial society' creates false needs that integrate individuals into the existing system of production and consumption. Mass media and culture, advertising, industrial management and contemporary modes of thought all reproduce the existing system and attempt to eliminate negativity, critique and opposition. The result was a 'one-dimensional' universe of thought and behaviour in which the very aptitude and ability for critical thinking and oppositional behaviour was withering away.

Not only had capitalism integrated the working class, the source of potential revolutionary opposition, but it had developed new techniques of stabilization through state policies and the development of new forms of social control. Thus Marcuse questioned two of the fundamental postulates of orthodox Marxism: the revolutionary proletariat and the inevitability of capitalist crisis. In contrast with the more extravagant demands of orthodox Marxism, Marcuse championed the non-integrated forces of minorities, outsiders and radical intellectuals, and he attempted to nourish oppositional thought and behaviour through promoting radical thinking and opposition.

One-Dimensional Man was severely criticized by orthodox Marxists and theorists of various political and theoretical commitments. Despite its pessimism, it influenced many in the New Left as it articulated their growing dissatisfaction with both capitalist societies and Soviet communist societies. Moreover, Marcuse himself continued to defend demands for revolutionary change and defended the new, emerging forces of radical opposition, thus winning the hatred of establishment forces and the respect of the new radicals.

One-Dimensional Man was followed by a series of books and articles that articulated New Left politics and critiques of capitalist societies. An essay on 'Repressive Tolerance' attacked liberalism and those who refused to take a stand during the controversies of the 1960s. It won Marcuse the reputation of being an intransigent radical and voice for the left. *An Essay on Liberation* celebrated all of the existing liberation movements from the Viet Cong to the hippies and exhilarated many radicals while further alienating establishment academics and those who opposed the movements of the 1960s. *Counterrevolution and Revolt*, by contrast, articulated the new realism that was setting in during the early 1960s when it was becoming clear that the most extravagant hopes of the decade were being dashed by a turn to the right and 'counter-revolution' against the 1960s.

Brandeis refused to renew his teaching contract in 1965 but Marcuse soon after received a position at the University of California at La Jolla, where he remained until his retirement in the 1970s. During this period of his greatest influence, Marcuse published many articles and gave lectures and advice to student radicals all over the world. He travelled widely and his work was often discussed in the mass media, so that he became one of the few American intellectuals to gain such attention. Never surrendering his revolutionary vision and commitments, Marcuse continued to his death to defend Marxian theory and libertarian socialism. He was a charismatic teacher, and Marcuse's students began to gain influential academic positions and to promote his ideas, making him a major force in US intellectual life long after his death in 1979.

Marcuse's work in philosophy and social theory generated fierce controversy and polemics, and most studies of his work are highly tendentious and frequently sectarian. Although much of the controversy involved his critiques of contemporary capitalist societies and defence of radical social change, in retrospect Marcuse left behind a complex and many-sided body of work comparable to the legacies of Ernst Bloch, **Gyorgy Lukács**, **Theodor Adorno** and Walter Benjamin. Marcuse's dialectic of liberation and domination distinguished his work. He developed a vision of the full development of the individual in a non-repressive society, along with a sharp critique of existing forms of domination and oppression. Though he was primarily a philosopher, Marcuse's work lacked the sustained empirical analysis in some versions of Marxist theory and the detailed conceptual analysis found in many versions of social and political theory. Yet he constantly showed how science, technology and theory itself had a political dimension and produced a solid body of ideological and political analysis of many of the dominant forms of society, culture and thought during the turbulent era in which he lived and in which he constantly struggled for a better world.

See also: Theodor Adorno, Sigmund Freud, Karl Marx.

See also in *Fifty Key Sociologists: The Contemporary Theorists*: Jürgen Habermas.

Major works

Negations. 1936–8. New York: Beacon Press, 1968.
Reason and Revolution. 1941. New York: Oxford University Press.
Eros and Civilization. 1955. Boston, MA: Beacon Press.
One Dimensional Man. 1964. Boston, MA: Beacon Press.
An Essay on Liberation. 1969. Boston, MA: Beacon Press.
Counterrevolution and Revolt. 1972. Boston, MA: Beacon Press.

Marcuse's unpublished papers are collected in the *Stadtsbibliothek* in Frankfurt, Germany, and several volumes of his unpublished work have been published in German by Zu Klampen, edited by Peter-Erwin Jansen, and in English by Routledge, edited by Douglas Kellner.

Further reading

John Abromeit and Mark Cobb, eds. 2003. *Herbert Marcuse: A Critical Reader*. London and New York: Routledge.
John Bokina and Timothy J. Lukes, eds. 1994. *Marcuse: New Perspectives*. Lawrence, KS: University of Kansas Press.

Douglas Kellner. 1984. *Herbert Marcuse and the Crisis of Marxism.* London and Berkeley, CA: Macmillan and University of California Press.

Robert Pippin, Andrew Feenberg and Charles P. Webel, eds. 1988. *Marcuse. Critical Theory and the Promise of Utopia.* South Hadley, MA: Bergin and Garvey.

DOUGLAS KELLNER

T. H. MARSHALL

Thomas Humphrey Marshall was one of the most influential British sociologists in the mid-twentieth century. Like so many of the earliest British sociologists, he came to sociology from another discipline and via the route of personal experience. Born in 1893 into a Blooms-bury family (his sister was the diarist Frances Partridge), he was edu-cated at Rugby and Trinity College, Cambridge, where he gained a first in history in 1914. Intending to enter the Foreign Office, he went to Germany to learn German that summer, and when war broke out he was interned as an enemy alien in the Ruhleben pris-oner of war camp near Berlin for the duration of the First World War.

This experience in his early twenties, far from his English upper-middle-class background, was formative. A prison camp composed of people from all strata of society, thrown together by the accident of war, provided an insight into social structure which had a consider-able influence. Returning to Cambridge after the war, he was elected a prize fellow by his college, Trinity, where he pursued historical studies, including writing a short life of James Watt. This was briefly interrupted by standing as Labour candidate for an unwinnable seat in the general election of 1922. In 1925 he was appointed tutor in social work at the London School of Economics and Political Science (LSE).

T. H. Marshall remained at LSE for the rest of his academic career, promoted to reader in 1930 and later to professor of social institu-tions, holding the headship of the Department of Social Science and Administration from 1944 to 1949 and the Martin White Professor-ship of Sociology from 1954 to 1956, when he departed to become director of the social sciences division of UNESCO from 1956 to 1960. Previously, he served in the Foreign Office research depart-ment from 1939 to 1944 and with the Allied Control Commission in Germany from 1949 to 1950. He was president of the International Sociological Association from 1959 to 1962.

91

He began developing his sociological interests at LSE during the 1930s, when he wrote on social stratification and social policy. Sociology at the School was small, and was dominated by the philosophical interests of **Leonard Hobhouse** and Morris Ginsberg. Marshall provided an alternative approach, which only flowered with the expansion of sociology teaching after the end of the Second World War and his supervision of PhD students such as David Lockwood and Ralf Dahrendorf.

Marshall's name is irrevocably part of the canon of sociology because of his formulation of the place of citizenship in modern society, first delivered as the Marshall Lectures in Cambridge in 1949. As David Lockwood observed on his eightieth birthday, this essay combined a concern with theoretical ideas and evidence, bringing academic sociology into symbiotic contact with practical concerns in 'the only work of post-war British sociology that in the boldness of its perspective and conceptualisation bears comparison with, and stands in a direct line of succession to, those classic texts that mark the origin of modern sociology. I refer, of course, to *Citizenship and social class* (1950)'.

Marshall's focus in 1949 was upon the rights and responsibilities of the citizen in industrial societies, set out in terms of a three-fold distinction between types of citizenship and incorporated in a generalized formulation of Weberian sweep. Though grounded in historical analysis of the British case, his categories were presented as ideal types which were tools of analysis rather than specific hypotheses of the historical sociologist. He distinguished between '*civil citizenship*', '*political citizenship*' and '*social citizenship*'. Civil citizenship involved the recognition of all members of society as equal before the law and the abolition of legal statuses such as slave or serf. Political citizenship involved the admission of all adult societal members as full participants in the political process, entitled to vote in elections and hold office. Social citizenship, which Marshall saw as a feature of the twentieth century, involved the extension of social rights to the whole of the population, through state intervention or the introduction of compulsory insurance schemes. This reflected his deep interest in social policy and interest in the social changes brought about by the extension of welfare provision.

The formulation raises a whole range of significant questions about contemporary society. What are the boundaries of a society? Which groups belong and which do not? Is 'citizenship' a more useful concept than the somewhat nebulous concept 'society'? What criteria of full citizenship are invoked? What entitlements to social benefits and services do different members of the society enjoy? What is the relationship between the actual distribution of rights and their ideal distribution? What is the balance between obligation and entitlement in contemporary society?

Marshall's aim was to bring together the discussion of obligations and entitlements with consideration of the stratified character of modern industrial society, particularly British society in the first half of the twentieth century. His concepts of citizenship provided the means to weave an analysis of social class into the discussion of the rights of the citizen. As Lockwood remarked:

> Citizenship does possess an inner logic, and the conflicting group interests that shape its institutional form at any one particular stage are themselves in turn changed and have their social force redirected as a consequence both of the practical working out of these arrangements and the principles dormant in them; principles that are as yet unrealised in social relationships and which have the potential for exacerbating as well as diminishing the impact of class.

The value of Marshall's formulation of citizenship has not gone uncontested since his death in 1981, and indeed it has been the subject of lively debate. His approach has been criticized for its neglect of women and the family; of people lacking in self-determination; of the very poor (the 'underclass'); of ethnic and racial minorities; and of other countries, where the generalizability of the Marshallian typology has been questioned. Its precise relation to historical development has been challenged. Nevertheless, his theory of citizenship remains an influential landmark in sociology as the twenty-first century opens.

See also: Leonard Hobhouse.

See also in *Fifty Key Sociologists: The Contemporary Theorists*: David Lockwood.

Major works

Citizenship and Social Class and Other Essays. (Essays of 1934–39.) Cambridge: Cambridge University Press, 1951.
Sociology at the Crossroads and Other Essays. (Essays of 1938–60.) London: Heinemann, 1963.
Class, Citizenship and Social Development. (Essays of 1937–60.) With intro. by S. M. Lipset, Garden City, NY: Doubleday, 1964.

Social Policy. 1970. London: Hutchinson.
'A British Sociological Career'. 1973. *International Social Science Journal*, vol. 25.
The Right To Welfare, and other Essays. (Essays of 1964–72.) London: Heinemann, 1981.

Further reading

Martin Bulmer and A. M. Rees, eds. 1996. *Citizenship Today: The Contemporary Relevance of T. H. Marshall.* London: UCL Press.
Albert H. Halsey. 'Marshall, Thomas Humphrey (1893–1981)'. 2004. *Oxford Dictionary of National Biography.* Oxford: Oxford University Press.
David Lockwood. 1874. 'For T. H. Marshall'. *Sociology*, vol. 8,

MARTIN BULMER

HARRIET MARTINEAU

Harriet Martineau is recognized as the first woman sociologist, as well as a historian, a journalist and a public educator. Martineau was an innovator and pioneer in conducting social research and in articulating a methodology for sociology, in formulating a macro-sociological paradigm for the study of whole societies, in analysing the repercussions of economic and social change, in communicating sociological knowledge to the general public, and in participating in the discourse of early social science. In a period when women were unable to attend British universities and were only slowly accepted into scientific circles, Harriet Martineau surpassed these barriers, conducted a great deal of research and published widely. Between the ages of nineteen and seventy-four, she published more than seventy books, dozens of articles in journals and other publications, and nearly 2,000 newspaper editorials, articles and letters. Her works included fictional portrayals of political economy, macrosociological studies of a number of societies, treatises on law, socialization and illness, journalistic essays and accounts, religious tracts, travelogues, novels, short stories, poetry and correspondence. The topics addressed in her writings included, among many subjects, human nature and development, education, socialization, religion, slavery, modern history, colonialism, work and industry, and the status of women.

Born in 1802, Harriet Martineau was the fourth of six children in a middle-class Unitarian manufacturer's family in Norwich, England. Women in Britain were not allowed to pursue higher education in the early decades of the nineteenth century; however, Martineau was well educated up to the university level. She studied languages, history, literature, philosophy and a wide range of subjects in the humanities and sciences. Her interest in books was precipitated by her intellect and curiosity, and by childhood illness and a loss of hearing by the age of twelve. By her late twenties she was quite deaf and began to use an ear trumpet that subsequently became a conversation piece and often a good opener in interview situations. Although she was engaged at the age of twenty-four, Martineau's fiancé became ill and soon died. She never married, preferring to focus on her career, given her passion for ideas and the limitations imposed by her deafness. She concluded that she was 'the happiest single woman in England'.

As a daughter of the Enlightenment, Martineau believed in societal progress, human perfectibility and the primacy of reason. She was influenced by German philosophy (Kant, Lessing, Hegel), French socialism (D'Eichtal, Saint-Simon, **Auguste Comte**), British political economy (Adam Smith, Thomas Malthus, Dugald Stewart, David Ricardo, James Mill), utilitarianism (Bentham, J. S. Mill), the literature of Austen, Bunyan, Milton, Shakespeare, Bacon, Goethe and the scientific work of David Hartley (theory of association) and Joseph Priestley (doctrine of philosophical necessity). Following the publication of approximately 100 articles, stories and poems in the Unitarian *Monthly Repository* while still in her twenties, Martineau engaged in a project of twenty-five novelettes published as *Illustrations of Political Economy* to illustrate the principles of political economy, based on her conviction that, as economy and society function according to inherent natural laws, the harmony and effectiveness of the emerging economic order and the well-being of all members of society required that all social classes have a thorough understanding of the workings of political economy. An outline of the principles illustrated accompanied each tale. *Illustrations of Taxation* and *Poor Laws and Paupers* followed. These writings, especially the political economy series, sold at the rate of 10,000 per month, guaranteeing Martineau's financial independence and firmly establishing her reputation as a writer and public educator.

Martineau set out in 1834 for America, where she would spend two years conducting a macrosociological study of American society. On the voyage she planned the work ahead by writing *How to Observe Morals and Manners*. Published in 1838, this was the first methodological treatise on the study of society, preceding Comte's complete *Positive Philosophy* and decades before **Durkheim**'s *Rules of* *the Sociological Method. How to Observe Morals and Manners* outlines basic principles of research, methods and sources for gathering data, techniques of interviewing, means of recording observations and data, and details of what to observe in a macro study of society – basic institutions, classes, popular culture and so on. Here and in later writings, Martineau used typological analysis to explain phenomena such as suicide and religion, as key indicators of culture and social behaviour.

Her two-year study of America is presented in *Society in America*, a comprehensive macrosociological analysis, and in *Retrospect of Western Travel*, an ethnographic study of selected persons, geographical places and cultural practices in America. Martineau's approach was that of immanent critique, an analysis that compares and assesses the normative structures, that is, the political and cultural principles and values of, in this case, American society, as articulated in documents, creeds, politics and social institutions, with the actual social practices and the behaviour of its members. The central issues of this young democracy were equality and justice, as she saw it. Contradicting America's commitment to the rights of the indivi-dual and to 'government by the consent of the governed' were the institution of slavery and all its practices and the subordinate, if not oppressed, status of women. After presenting and discussing her findings, she concludes: 'the civilization and the morals of the Americans fall far below their own principles'. The two issues would have to be resolved if this new society was to survive. Martineau's study of America can be compared with **Alexis de Tocqueville**'s *Democracy in America*. While they agree on a number of general points about the young democracy, their perspectives (those of a French male and a British woman) and analyses are quite different. Martineau was more systematic, thorough and empirical in her research, and her books on America are seen by many as more comprehensive and scientific.

Harriet Martineau integrated her life and her work through her travels, reading, research and writing. Even in periods of illness between 1839 and 1844 and in 1855 she continued to write, produ-cing such works as *Life in the Sickroom* and *Letters on Mesmerism*, which address the sociological aspects of illness as well as health and possible cures. In 1855, she wrote her *Autobiography*, which she had printed and stored for posthumous publication, thereby controlling her own story. She used convalescent time to write *The Hour and the Man*, about revolution in Haiti, a series of moralistic children's tales and a criticism of the game laws that functioned to benefit the upper classes and to disadvantage farmers and the poor. In 1846 Martineau travelled to the Middle East and spent seven months studying Egypt, Sinai, Palestine and Syria. Her observations and findings are reported in *Eastern Life: Present and Past*, which demonstrates that Judaism, Christianity and Islam are related and are derived from ancient Egyptian religion, evidenced by the legends, myths and practices depicted on ancient Egyptian monuments. Martineau was convinced, as a social scientist, that religion is one of the basic institutions of society, but that it had been changed considerably through the historicization of legends. She ultimately came to the conclusion that institutionalized religion is oppressive, especially for women and slaves in the American context, largely because it resists change and suppresses individuality and freedom. She was convinced that science provides a clearer path to truth, understanding, tolerance and knowledge. She believed that religion in the era of science would take on more rational and ethical forms such as those found in Unitarianism, Dissenting sects and secular culture.

Martineau's commitment to the importance of science in the modern world led her to collaborate with Henry George Atkinson in *Letters on the Laws of Man's Nature and Development*, a volume of exchanges about universal natural laws, the materiality of the mind and of human existence, the need for studying human behaviour and human affairs scientifically, and the necessity to use scientific knowledge in matters of legislation, education and the social order. The letters particularly emphasized the universality of cause and effect and the need for empirical evidence.

Martineau generally welcomed modern positivism, subscribing to its emphasis on the inherent unity of the sciences, the influence of natural laws on human existence, the importance of scientific methodologies and empirical knowledge, and the critical role of science in social change and progress in society. Since 1830, Martineau had been reading French sociology, including the writings of Saint-Simon. In 1853 she completed a translation and condensation into two volumes of Auguste Comte's six-volume *Cours de philosophie positive*, a schematic of the sciences and a sound methodological foundation, she thought, for the new science of sociology. Martineau's translation remains the standard English version for sociologists. She was particularly interested in the Law of Three Stages, which accounts for the transformation of knowledge as having evolved from the theological stage to a later philosophical or metaphysical stage and finally to the scientific stage. So convinced was she that she framed her own life story in her *Autobiography* in terms of the

Law of Three Stages. During this period, Martineau promoted the idea of social science and of sociology, partly through the National Association for the Promotion of Social Science, but made it clear that 'social science does not yet exist ... the true science of society is the establishment of the laws under which mankind lives in society'. She further asserts that 'the best practice must proceed from sound theory'.

It is important to point to Martineau's feminism, reflected in her studies of America, the Middle East and Ireland, and her many empirical investigations. Martineau initiated research in areas such as industrial sociology and the sociology of occupations, socialization, education, religion, health and illness, disability, political economy, colonialism, marriage and the family, race relations, and women and work, major subject areas of sociology. She was active in women's causes such as the reform of marriage and divorce laws, women's suffrage, children's rights, factory conditions and legislation, and the Contagious Diseases Acts. In these and other contexts and genres, Martineau addressed significant sociological problems, processes of social change and the intellectual debates of her time.

Martineau died in 1876. She influenced the ideas and sociological work of many who came after her, including Durkheim, **Veblen**, **Myrdal**, Charlotte Gilman, **Beatrice Webb** and **William Sumner**. Martineau's investigations and her theoretical work provide a critical lens for scrutinizing social practices in sociological, historical, ethnographic and statistical terms towards building a body of socially useful knowledge.

See also: Auguste Comte, Alexis de Tocqueville, Beatrice Webb.

Major works

Illustrations of Political Economy. 9 vols. 1832-4. London: Charles Fox.
Society in America. 3 vols. 1837. London: Saunders and Otley. Abridged edn, ed. with an intro. by S. M. Lipset. New York: Doubleday, 1962.
Retrospect of Western Travel. 3 vols. 1838. London: Saunders and Otley.
How to Observe Manners and Morals. 1838. London: Charles Knight. Sesquicentennial edn, with intro., appendices and index by Michael R. Hill. New Brunswick, NJ: Transaction, 1989.
Eastern Life: Present and Past. 1848. London: Edward Moxon.
Letters on the Laws and Man's Nature and Development. With Henry G. Atkinson. 1851. London: John Chapman.
The Positive Philosophy of Auguste Comte, freely translated and condensed by Harriet Martineau. 2 vols. 1853. London: John Chapman. Many later editions.

Further reading

Michael R. Hill and Susan Hoecker-Drysdale, eds. 2001. 2003. *Harriet Martineau: Theoretical and Methodological Perspectives*. New York: Routledge.

Susan Hoecker-Drysdale. 1992. *Harriet Martineau: First Woman Sociologist*. Oxford and New York: Berg Publishers.

Susan Hoecker-Drysdale. 2002. 'Harriet Martineau: The Theory and Practice of Early Critical Social Research'. In Mary Ann Romano, ed. *Lost Sociologists Rediscovered*. Lewiston, NY: The Edwin Mellen Press.

Susan Hoecker-Drysdale. 2003. 'Harriet Martineau'. In George Ritzer, ed. *The Blackwell Companion to Major Classical Theorists*. Malden, MA: Blackwell Publishing Ltd.

Susan Hoecker-Drysdale, ed. 2004. *Harriet Martineau: Studies of America, 1831-1868*. 8 vols. Bristol: Thoemmes Continuum.

Robert Nisbet. 1988. 'Tocqueville's Ideal Types'. In Abraham S. Eisenstadt, ed. *Reconsidering Tocqueville's Democracy in America*. New Brunswick, NJ: Rutgers University Press.

SUSAN HOECKER-DRYSDALE

KARL MARX

Karl Marx was born in Trier in 1818 and died in London in 1883. His father came from a rabbinical family but was a devotee of the Enlightenment who, as an official of the Prussian government, formally enrolled in the Lutheran Church. Marx studied law and philosophy, writing a thesis on Heraclitus. He participated in the debates and polemics of the Young Hegelian philosophers and his early notebooks seek to develop Hegel's account of the concept of alienation. By his mid-twenties Marx was already an active supporter of the democratic movement in Germany and edited one of its most influential newspapers, the *Neue Rheinische Zeitung*. He was impressed by the revolt of the Silesian weavers in 1844 and began to display an interest in both workers' organizations and socialist theory. Lenin saw Marx's distinctive ideas as stemming from three crucial sources, German philosophy, English political economy and French socialism. But Marx's engagement with these currents of thought typically took the form of critique.

Thus, while broadly accepting the Hegelian idea of history as the unfolding of ever-higher forms of freedom he sought to correct what he saw as the speculative character of Hegelianism by drawing on the idea of successive stages of historical development as it had been worked out by Scottish Enlightenment writers such as Ferguson and

Millar. Likewise, when Marx appropriated Hegel's notion of the dialectical relationship between master and servant he nevertheless sought to ground it in a precise account of the characteristics of wage labour. Marx immersed himself in the writings of the classical political economists, above all Adam Smith and David Ricardo, but he sought to correct what he saw as their reductionism and philistinism, using his impressive command of humanist, classical and Romantic literature to make his points. Finally he learned much from French socialists, especially Fourier and Proudhon, but thought them blind to the true lessons of the class struggle and of the French Revolution, as variously spelt out by Abbé Sièyes in 'What is the Third Estate?' and Buonarotti in 'The Conspiracy of Equals'.

Marx's emerging doctrine of historical materialism was first advanced in *The German Ideology*, especially in the section on Feuerbach, but undoubtedly it was to be embodied in its most striking and influential form in *The Communist Manifesto*, co-authored with Friedrich Engels and published in 1848, on the eve of the great revolutionary upheavals of that year. The *Manifesto* had been commissioned by a club of émigré German workers and sought openly to proclaim a worldview and a political programme, and thus to break with what its authors saw as the world of secrecy, fantasy and conspiracy of previous social organizations. The *Manifesto* integrated political economy, class analysis and socialist polemic into a sketch of human history. Whereas previous writers had seen successive historical stages emerging through some mysterious inner logic, Marx tied these stages to modes of production and insisted on the key role of class relations. The latter embraced both the struggle between exploiters and exploited and the rivalry between such different groups of exploiter as the slaveowner, the feudal serf-lord, the rentier, merchant and capitalist. The move from one socio-economic system to the next was rooted in an interaction between class struggle, on the one hand, and the intrinsic potential and limits of successive socio-economic systems, especially their ability to raise the productivity of labour and to advance the forces of production, on the other.

In the 1850s and after, Marx was to develop his ideas in voluminous writings, ranging from the brief 'Introduction to the Critique of Political Economy', the first volume of *Capital* (1867), and extensive drafts and notebooks which were posthumously to be published as volumes two and three of *Capital*, as *Theories of Surplus Value* and as the *Grundrisse* (Outline). The arguments developed in these writings make Marx the pre-eminent student of capitalism among the founders of social science, and the source of crucial insights into the origins and destiny of this remarkable socio-economic system. Sometimes, as in the *Manifesto*, it is as if Marx saw too far ahead, already anticipating the world of globalization without having fully registered the complex and contradictory role of national forms and religious worldviews in capitalist development. And furthermore Marx did not anticipate that his own ideas would be appealed to by communist regimes in large backward or semi-developed states in order to promote a non-capitalist modernization of their economies and societies.

Marx set himself apart from most other socialists of the time by his stress on the great achievements of capitalism and on the need for socialism to be based on the superior productivity and international division of labour which the bourgeoisie had brought about. Some economists of the time, such as Sismondi, saw capitalism as generating only misery and destructive competition. Marx readily granted that the advance of capitalism exacted a terrible human cost. What he called 'primitive capitalist accumulation' involved the slave trade, the expropriation of European peasantries, colonialism and war. It was also marked by repeated crisis and the accumulation of wealth at one pole and poverty at the other. But he also insisted that capitalism had applied technology to the process of production and made human labour vastly more productive than it had ever been before. In Marx's view it had produced the potential for a higher form of social co-operation, making possible the eradication of poverty and the emancipation of the producers.

While many socialist visionaries harked back to a lost golden age, Marx welcomed modernity and looked forward to a time when its full potential would be realized by the expropriation of the expropriators and the self-emancipation of the producers. As he and Engels memorably put it in the *Communist Manifesto*, the precondition for the free development of all was the free development of each.

Marx famously declared in his 'Theses on Feuerbach' that the point was not to interpret the world in different ways, but rather to change it. The *Manifesto* was written for the Communist League, a network of émigré German workers. In the 1860s he worked with English trade unionists to found and develop the International Working Men's Association. And over several decades he carried on an extensive correspondence not only with fellow socialist thinkers but with the founders of Social Democratic parties and the organizers of trade unions. He certainly believed that changing the world required understanding it and that the account he developed in *Capital* and other writings had an objective and scientific character. At one point he drew up a questionnaire, the '*Enquête ouvrière*', designed to allow him to learn the details of French workers' conditions of life and outlook. He also spent long days at the British Museum studying the British government's Blue Books as well as works of history and economics.

Marx's work impinges on general social theory, historical sociology, the sociology of class, economic sociology, social and economic history and political economy. Marxist currents have appeared in these disciplines as well as in interdisciplinary studies. While Durkheim, **Weber** and **Simmel** all have greatly influenced subsequent generations in social science, it is probably true to say that Marx's impact has been the most widespread, especially outside the academy, and that the work of these other theorists was itself in part stimulated by Marx's account of capitalism and class struggle.

Marx's theory of social class and class struggle is one of the most distinctive in his corpus but also one of the most criticized. Marx believed that sooner or later those who were exploited would be educated by struggle to learn their true interests and destiny. This claim has been much criticized for its supposed teleology and for counterposing a notion of stark class 'interests' as against the confused 'commodity fetishism' or 'false consciousness' of so many workers. Marx did distinguish between the class 'in itself' and the class 'for itself'. The latter was not narrowly focused on economic interest but rather on an emergent and potential collective orientation to society and history. In his writings on French class struggles in the period 1848–52 Marx exhibited a close interest in the collective morale and projects of class fractions and of how they are caught up in a large historical scheme. However, brilliant as they are, his contemporary pamphlets do not necessarily furnish a vindication of his wider theory of class.

Another problem is that Marx appears to stress exploitation as the source of poverty whereas in the modern world huge inequalities are instead rooted in exclusion. To some extent this exclusion might be held to be functional to capitalist exploitation because it establishes the pressure of what Marx termed a 'reserve army of labour', that is, a mass of unemployed workers who weaken the bargaining power of those in work. But the huge scope of poverty and exclusion in the modern world is greater than would be needed simply for these purposes. A further explanation of this phenomenon might be that many communities find it difficult to flourish in a capitalist way, that capitalist behaviour is not natural but needs to be learned and often runs counter to traditional values. Marx's insights into the logic of wage labour and generalized commodity production would help to illuminate such a social complex (see, for example, Mike Davis, *The Planet of Slums*). More generally, the mistakes, inadequacies or lacunae in Marx's account can be treated not as fatal flaws but simply as reasons to further the historical materialist account by remedying the problem with a new account of, say, nationalism and its 'imagined community', or organized religion as a dimension of 'hegemony', or the emergence of a 'labour aristocracy'.

Marx claimed that capitalism had produced a class, the proletariat, which would become the agent of its overthrow. Clearly this prediction was not borne out. Class politics of a sort did develop in many capitalist states, and labour movements emerged in many parts of the world, their leaders often influenced by Marx's ideas. But in the United States, for long the world's leading capitalist economy, no distinct political labour movement ever developed. Socialist revolutions occurred in countries that were not fully capitalist such as Russia, China, Vietnam and Cuba; militant and minority workers' organizations played some role in these attempts to overthrow capitalism but were controlled by, rather than controlling, the ruling party in the post-revolutionary state. Marx's notion that the rule of the bourgeoisie would be succeeded by the 'dictatorship of the proletariat' seemed to assume a sort of sociological reduction that failed to register the need for a political articulation of class power. While working-class parties and trade unions played a large role in the history of the twentieth century, it was not the leading role which Marx assigned to them. Non-proletarian class forces – the peasantry and petit bourgeoisie – were more important than Marx anticipated, as were nationalist objectives and ideologies. Towards the close of the twentieth century organized labour played a major role in challenging apartheid in South Africa, and dictatorship in South Korea and Brazil, but this was not the prelude to any challenge to capitalism; in Poland and Russia labour militancy eventually helped to bring down regimes that claimed to be communist.

By the late twentieth century the political influence of labour movements was in decline. However, social research still shows classes to explain much about the internal workings of capitalist societies, the life chances available to their members, patterns of health and life expectancy, the inclination to read this paper or support that political party. Marx famously defined class not in terms of differences in income but rather in terms of a common relationship with the ownership of the means of production. Modern workers were defined by the fact that they needed to sell their labour power if they were to feed, clothe and house themselves and their families. (Marx and Engels drew importance to the sphere of the reproduction of labour power; see, in particular, Engels' study of *The Origins of the Family and Private Property*.)

When Marx wrote that the value of labour power was determined by what was required to reproduce it, he took this to include cultural as well as physiological needs. He explains:

> In contrast to the slave, [wage] labour becomes more productive because more intense, since the slave works only under the spur of external fear but not for his existence. ... The free worker, however, is impelled by his wants. The consciousness (or better: the Idea) of free self-determination, of liberty, makes a much better worker of the one than of the other. The free worker is impelled by his wants. ... Of course, the conditions of his existence – and the limited amount of money he can earn – compel him to make his selection from a fairly restricted selection of goods. But some variation is possible as we can see from the fact that newspapers, for example, form part of the essential purchases of the urban English worker. He can save or hoard a little. Or else he can squander his money on drink. But even so he acts as a free agent; he must pay his own way; he is responsible to himself for the way he spends his wages.

In such formulations Marx saw 'commodity fetishism' and proletarian destiny wrestling for the worker's soul. Nevertheless, whatever refinement or sense of mission the workers might achieve, their condition was defined by a lack of sufficient means, so they had to sell their labour power.

The capitalist, on the other hand, had a different sort of problem. He had purchased the labour power of the worker but now he needed to bring it together with tools, raw materials and market opportunities. The capitalist could claim surplus value only if he could sell the product of labour for more than it cost him to acquire it. This was the problematic of the 'realization' of surplus value, which hence did not solely concern the different ways of extracting extra labour from the worker.

A century and a half after Marx developed his analysis of class its primacy is not difficult to challenge. Gender and ethnicity have always been very important in the allocation of life chances and they have recently become very important in stimulating movements for historical transformation. Workers themselves aspire to bourgeois goals. But class cleavages remain very marked – and often overlap with those based on sex and race – whether we look at access to education, life expectancy, social morality or political behaviour. Workers have often disappointed the sort of political hopes entertained by Marx, while doing so in a collective idiom that seems to reflect class situation and outlook.

The strength of Marx's account is its stress both on the totality of social relations and on their conditioning by history. Marx was interested in capitalists as well as workers and preoccupied with identifying the inner workings of the capitalist system. In Karl Marx's account of capitalism, those who control investment have to follow the dictates of the accumulation process and the working out of the law of value. The particular aims and idiosyncrasies of the individual capitalist have to be pursued within a structural context set by his (or her) ability to realize surplus value. In a famous passage Marx declares: 'Accumulate! Accumulate! That is Moses and the prophets!' For Marx the actions of the capitalist 'are a mere function of capital' and from this standpoint 'even his own private consumption counts as a robbery committed against the accumulation of his capital'. Evidently, in this account, the capitalist is powerfully constrained by context, by the need to extract and realize and reinvest surplus value in the circuit of accumulation. In an earlier passage Marx had given an account of the constraint of competition operating on the capitalist. This constraint prevents him from buying labour power too expensively just as it prevents him from selling goods too cheaply. But this should not be understood as enabling the capitalist simply to raise prices, or lower wages, in a crude imperative to maximize the rate of exploitation.

Thus the competitive context obliges the capitalist to reckon with the impact of innovation in the productive process. The capitalist making the innovation may find it advantageous to lower prices in order to capture more of the market:

> The law of the determination of value by labour time makes itself felt to the individual capitalist who applies the new method of production by obliging him to sell his goods under their social value; this same law acting as a coercive law of competition, forces his competitors to adopt the new method.

Marx sees this as a process whereby 'the immanent laws of capitalist production manifest themselves in the external movement of the individual capitals, assert themselves as the coercive laws of competition, and therefore enter into the consciousness of the individual capitalist as the motives which drive him forward'. Marx's discussion of factory legislation demonstrates another process whereby the outlawing of child labour or limitations on the length of the working day create conditions which are generally favourable to big capital and help to foster its control of wider areas of production.

When Marx speaks of the 'anarchy of the capitalist mode of production' he is emphasizing that it is not subordinate to the will of the individual capitalist – except insofar as the latter makes himself the bearer of the impersonal forces of accumulation. The immanent laws of capitalist competition and accumulation lead to big capitals gobbling up small capitals, big capitals undermining one another (if they can), and all capitals using up the productive force of both labourer and soil in the interests of self-preservation and self-expansion. While limits can be set on capital, it is in its nature continuously to resist external control if it can. So if, say, child labour is effectively prohibited in one jurisdiction, it may well crop up in another.

In Marx's conception of the functioning of the capitalist system the relentless growth of commodification and self-expansion of capital is the key process. The enterprise is directly commanded by the capitalist, but he is simply the bearer of a wider social mechanism. It would be too simple a conclusion to say that his or her personal qualities or inclinations are of no account. There will be many differences of capacity and judgement between individual capitalists. Some will readily grasp the scope for innovation or will understand that limitations on the working day will be favourable to their long-term interest. Others will fail to grasp the true possibilities of their situation. Marx was well aware that many dramatic social conflicts would be fought out before it was established which manner of proceeding was to prevail. Such conflicts, with their variable alliances, were not mere by-products of the working out of some higher logic. They were themselves an essential part of the mechanism whereby the supposedly 'iron laws' of accumulation worked themselves out (see, for example, Marx's critique of the so-called 'iron law of wages' in his debate with Weston in *Wages, Prices and Profit*). Furthermore, Marx was aware that in the more developed pattern of capitalist production there was an incipient separation of finance from operational management. Thus with the introduction of the joint stock company the supervision and co-ordination of the productive process becomes increasingly distinct; the work involved is, in Marx's terms, productive. He even declares that '[i]t has therefore become superfluous for this work of supervision to be performed by the capitalist'. But the process of capitalist production can only go forward if there is a continually replenished extraction and realization of surplus value. The interest which the capitalist promises to pay to those who extend credit to him is 'the surplus value inherently contained in the commodity of capital as a potentiality'. The industrial and commercial capitalists need access to credit, and what Marx calls 'fictitious capital', if they are to seize profitable opportunities. Often the direct profits they are making are not sufficient for this, especially where large-scale investments are required. In Marx's account industrialists looks to bankers to supply the credit they need. These bankers hold deposits on behalf of the mass of large and small producers. This potential loan capital includes both the reserves and cash balances of merchants and manufacturers but also the savings of all classes: 'Small sums which are incapable of functioning as money capital by themselves are combined into great masses and thus form a monetary power'. Thus in Marx's view 'it is the bankers as representatives of all lenders of money who confront the industrial and commercial capitalists'. The credit extended by the bankers is only, to begin with, 'fictitious capital' because, as yet, it only concerns 'the commodity of capital as a potentiality'. It is up to the capitalist to ensure that these credit resources are ploughed into a profitable venture. In advance nobody can be sure how matters will turn out and the possibility of a dead loss is always present. (The implications of this analysis were not widely registered and tended to be overlooked when national cartels were at their strongest.).

Who controls the commodification process, the banker or the industrial or commercial capitalist? In an immediate sense it may seem to be the banker since it is the banks who decide to favour investment in one concern or another, according to their judgement. But the scope for new types of commodification will originally have been demonstrated by the entrepreneur or venture capitalist. The profitable opportunity will only be seized if the industrial capitalist succeeds in realizing sales which are significantly greater than the sums he lays out. Time may be required to ascertain whether the project is successful or not. The banker may lack the requisite patience – but then he or she is in competition with other bankers. So once again there is a structural relationship, elements of antagonism, elements of cooperation and the likelihood of conflict over the division of the spoils. The banker controls access to what Marx called 'fictitious capital', the capitalist to profitable investment. Whether the one or the other has the upper hand at any one point will depend on a host of particular conditions. Over time patterns will emerge, and then, perhaps, change, reflecting a host of contingent conditions,

with the concatenation of the trade cycle, technological development, the class struggle, cultural mobilizations, wars, revolutions and
so on interacting in a far from predictable manner. The end result is
that more and more activities and processes are subordinated to the
commodity form by those in search of profit. The spread of 'fast
food' and the culture industries, the privatization of public services –
even private prisons and security companies – and the commerciali-
zation of the World Wide Web are carrying capitalist principles into
ever new areas.

Marx's analysis concerned the capitalist system as a whole and is
generally abstracted from the specific features of each capitalist state,
though Britain and the United States are often taken as cases which
exemplify the direction of capitalist development. The question of
uneven development is typified in his work by the fate of, respectively, Ireland, and the US South. The possibility of the emergence of
cartels and monopolies within each capitalist state is referred to but is
not central to the analysis. However, this is probably because such
developments were not so strong in the 1860s, when Marx was
writing *Capital*, as they were subsequently to be in the Gilded Age
of, roughly, 1873–1914. Marx does not shun the concept of monopoly itself since his account of the proletarian condition stresses that
the capitalists monopolize access to the means of production. Marx
had a few thoughts about the joint stock company, direct ancestor of
the modern corporation, but this economic form was then in its
infancy.

Marx wrote very little about the institutions of the post-capitalist
social order and what he did say about it diverged markedly from the
Soviet model. Indeed the Soviet regime of national autarchy was to
be much closer to the model set out in Fichte's 'Closed Economy
State' (1809). When Marx declared that the value of commodities
stemmed from the 'socially necessary labour time' that they embodied, and that socialism should be built on the achievements of
capitalism, he had in mind something very different from the Soviet-
style command economy. The command economies established by
most communist governments, notwithstanding privileges offered to
working-class cadres and successes in wartime, proved incapable of
the complex economic functioning required by a modern economy.
If a feasible alternative to capitalism is ever discovered, it will doubtless learn from the communist experience.

Marx wrote on many topics. While his economic writings were
sometimes dense, his philosophy, journalism and letters abound in
striking phrases and provocative thoughts. But at the centre of his

work, and of lasting importance for social science, in his account of capitalism. The reason that Marx's ideas are still alive is because of the huge insight he had into a socio-economic system that still shapes our world.

See also: Theodor Adorno, Antonio Gramsci, Gyorgy Lukács, Herbert Marcuse.

See also in *Fifty Key Sociologists: The Contemporary Theorists*: Louis Althusser, Jürgen Habermas, Ralph Miliband.

Major works

Critique of Hegel's Philosophy of Right. 1843. Cambridge: Cambridge University Press, 1970.
Economic and Philosophical Manuscripts. 1844. London: Lawrence and Wishart, 1959.
The Holy Family. 1845. London: Lawrence and Wishart, 1956.
The German Ideology. 1846. London: Lawrence and Wishart, 1970.
The Poverty of Philosophy. 1847. Chicago: C. H. Kerr, 1910.
Communist Manifesto. 1848. With Friedrich Engels. Harmondsworth: Penguin, 1967.
The Class Struggles in France. 1850. Moscow: Progress Publishers, 1968.
Eighteenth Brumaire of Louis Bonaparte. 1852. Moscow: Progress Publishers, no date.
Grundrisse. 1858. Harmondsworth: Penguin, 1973.
A Contribution to the Critique of Political Economy. 1859. London: Lawrence and Wishart, 1971.
Theories of Surplus Value. 1862–3. London: Lawrence and Wishart, 1969–72.
Capital, 3 vols. 1864–78. Harmondsworth: Penguin, 1976–81.
The Civil War in France. 1871. Beijing: Foreign Languages Publishing House, 1970.

Further reading

Robin Blackburn, ed. 1991. *After the Fall*. London: Verso.
Gerry A. Cohen. 2000. *Karl Marx's Theory of History*. 2nd edn. Cambridge: Cambridge University Press.
Rodney Hilton, ed. 1978. *The Transition from Feudalism to Capitalism*. London: Verso.
Ernest Mandel. 1971. *The Formation of the Economic Thought of Karl Marx*. London: New Left Books.
Edmund Wilson. 1940. *To the Finland Station*. London: Collins, 1960.

ROBIN BLACKBURN

MARCEL MAUSS

Father of French ethnography, Marcel Mauss has had a profound influence on the human and social sciences and has left behind an incredibly rich intellectual legacy. He is automatically linked with his uncle and teacher, **Emile Durkheim**: some would say that he was 'in the shadow of Durkheim' when describing his scholarly output produced in direct cooperation with him.

Born to a family of merchants and rabbis at Epinal in 1872, Mauss studied philosophy at Bordeaux under Durkheim. After gaining his *agrégation* (teaching exam) in philosophy in 1895, he gave up the standard career path of secondary teaching to which this led, turning his attention instead to the sociology of religion. During his studies at the Ecole Pratique des Hautes Etudes and a trip to Holland and England, he gained a solid grounding in philology, the history of religions, and ethnology. Mauss was also politically active from his university days, supporting Dreyfus and the socialists. He worked with the Mouvement Social and he took part in founding the new Société de librairie et d'édition with Lucien Herr and Charles Andler. Once he became a professor, Mauss was involved in the co-operative movement and the Socialist Party and he published numerous articles in *L'Humanité*, of which he had been one of the founders.

Marcel Mauss produced his first major work together with his friend and colleague Henri Hubert under the title 'Sacrifice: Its Nature and Functions'. The essay appeared in *L'Année sociologique*, founded by Durkheim in 1898: in charge of the section on religious sociology, Mauss was one of its leading contributors. At the Ecole Pratique des Hautes Etudes, where he succeeded Léon Marillier in 1901, Mauss was responsible for teaching the history of the religion of primitive peoples. Frequently comparative and backed up with detailed evidence, the research undertaken by Mauss was set out as part of a programme that had as its subject the ritual expressions of religious life and as its purpose the development of a theory of the sacred. His work quickly went beyond the boundaries of the sociology of religion to deal with the theory of knowledge, as can be seen from the essay written with Durkheim, entitled *Primitive Classification*. Concerning sociology, the supporters of Durkheim were quick to point out that it was a collective psychology with the purpose of studying collective representation.

The main debate in Durkheim's first books at the end of the nineteenth century revolved around the conflict between the individual and society and one of the problems faced by sociology since its inception has been its specific nature and its relation to other disciplines, particularly to psychology. This debate not only pitted Durkheim against his opponents, such as **Gabriel Tarde**, it also divided his colleagues, as can be seen from the initial volumes of L'Année sociologique. Célestin Bouglé, who, like his friend Paul Lapie, was undecided regarding the theoretical framework proposed by Durkheim, recognized the role of the individual and sought to go beyond the conflict between the individual and society, talking of interaction, association between individuals and communication of conscious awareness.

The intention of softening the dogmatic tone of Durkheim can also be seen in the work of Mauss. In a text entitled 'Sociology', co-authored with Paul Fauconnet in 1901 for La Grande Encyclopédie, he stressed the psychological aspect of social life, beliefs and communal feelings. 'The very core of social life is a collection of representations', he wrote, adding that, '[i]n this sense then, it could be said that sociology is a kind of psychology'. He clearly meant a psychology different from that of the individual. Together with Henri Hubert, Mauss published in L'Année sociologique of 1902 the important A General Theory of Magic, demonstrating that here the laws of collective psychology transgress the laws of individual psychology: 'It is belief that creates the magician ... and the effects he unleashes', they wrote. The use of the concept of mana, as the source idea of magic, stirred up a long-lasting controversy.

Mauss had volunteered and served as an interpreter during the First World War, which resulted, directly and indirectly, in the tragic deaths of Durkheim, his son André and several contributors to L'Année sociologique. After the war, Mauss undertook the difficult task of replacing his uncle. He attempted to relaunch L'Année sociologique, but only two volumes appeared, in 1925 and 1927. He also kept up his intense political activity, undertaking the editing of an important work on the state and, after publishing his 'Observations sur la violence' in Vie socialiste, he planned a book on Bolshevism. Then, encouraged by the current exoticism that was attracting a new public to ethnology, Mauss worked together with Lucien Lévi-Bruhl and Paul Rivet to set up the Institut d'Ethnologie in Paris in 1925. The Institute attracted many students and researchers – Jeanne Cuisinier, Alfred Métraux, Marcel Griaule, Georges Dumézil, Denise Paulme, Michel Leiris, Germaine Dieterlen, Louis Dumont, André-Georges Haudricourt, Jacques Soustelle and Germaine Tillion – who led many field studies, particularly in Africa, and organized the first important ethnological expeditions.

A man of tremendous intellectual curiosity and exceptional erudition, Mauss undertook research in a large number of areas: from magic to body technique via the idea of the individual, he rectified the anti-psychological attitude of his uncle, setting up new real and practical relationships between psychology and sociology in an article that he published in 1924 in *Journal de psychologie*. The following year he published in the new series of *L'Année sociologique* his essay on *The Gift*.

Durkheim's nephew had never before been so interested in concerning himself with work undertaken by psychologists, and he took part in the projects of the Société de Psychologie, becoming its president in 1923. His friends included Charles Blondel, Georges Dumas and, above all, Ignace Meyerson, the managing editor of the *Journal de psychologie normale et pathologique*. 'Sociology, psychology, physiology, everything should be combined', wrote Mauss. The intention was thus to take as a subject 'the entire, actual human being' and to analyse 'the phenomenon as a whole'. In 1936 then, again in the *Journal de psychologie*, he published a study on the 'Effet physique chez l'individu de l'idée de mort suggérée par la collectivité' (The physical effect upon the individual of the collectively suggested idea of death). Mental confusion, inhibitions, delusions and hallucinations were all phenomena in which Mauss had a keen interest, but which, contrary to the opinions of psychologists, he did not perceive as pathological symptoms.

Marcel Mauss was elected to the Collège de France in 1930 and he became head of sociology. The texts he published in this period include 'Body Techniques', which appeared in 1934 in the *Journal de psychologie*, and an essay on the self in the *Journal of the Royal Anthropological Institute*. His last academic presentation was in 1941 and consisted of the paper 'Les techniques et la technologie'. Marcel Mauss died on 11 February 1950, aged sixty-seven. Many of his writings had appeared as essays, and they were first collected together by Claude Lévi-Strauss in 1950 and published as *Sociologie et anthropologie*, then in 1969 Victor Karady produced a larger three volumes entitled *Œuvres*. His extensive political writings were collected together by Marcel Fournier in 1997. The political work of Mauss consists of a large number of reflections and invaluable 'reflections' where he combined and expressed, as he recognized himself, the fervour of the scholar and the politician. He had no doubt at the end of *The Gift* about the worth of ancient moral values, such as charity, and he put forward a morality based upon solidarity and reciprocity.

See also: Emile Durkheim, Maurice Halbwachs.

See also in *Fifty Key Sociologists: The Contemporary Theorists*: Pierre Bourdieu.

Major works

Sacrifice: Its Nature and Functions. 1899. With Henri Hubert. Chicago: University of Chicago Press, 1964.
'Sociology'. 1901. With Paul Fauconnet. In Mike Gane, ed. *The Nature of Sociology.* Oxford: Berghahn Books, 2005.
A General Theory of Magic. 1902. With Henri Hubert. London: Routledge & Kegan Paul, 1972.
Primitive Classification. 1903. With Emile Durkheim. Chicago: University of Chicago Press, 1963
Seasonal Variations of the Eskimo: A Study in Social Morphology. 1906. With Henri Beuchat. London: Routledge & Kegan Paul, 1979.
The Gift. The Form and Reason for Exchange in Archaic Societies. 1925. London: Cohen and West, 1954.
'Body Techniques'. 1934. In Ben Brewster, ed. *Sociology and Psychology.* London: Routledge & Kegan Paul, 1979.

Further reading

Marcel Fournier. 2005. *Marcel Mauss: A Biography.* Princeton, NJ: Princeton University Press.
Claude Lévi-Strauss. 1950. *Introduction to the Work of Marcel Mauss.* London: Routledge & Kegan Paul, 1987.

MARCEL FOURNIER

GEORGE HERBERT MEAD

Chicago pragmatist, social psychologist, pedagogist and founder of symbolic interaction, George Herbert Mead is a central figure in sociology. His processual model of human development, his central role in creating a unique American philosophical standpoint (pragmatism), his training of approximately half of all doctoral sociologists in the world prior to his death in 1931 and his connection of behaviour and action combine to make him a founding figure in the discipline.

Both of Mead's parents were educators who espoused Protestant and liberal values. They came from established New England families with the social responsibilities and benefits associated with that status. Mead's father, Hiram Mead, held the chair of sacred rhetoric and pastoral theology at Oberlin College from 1869 until his death in

1881. His mother, Elizabeth Storrs Billings Mead, was the first president of Mount Holyoke College from 1893 to 1900. Their only son, George Herbert Mead, was born on 27 February 1863.

Mead entered Oberlin's Preparatory Department in 1876 and Oberlin College in 1879, graduating from the latter in 1883. After a series of makeshift jobs, he experienced a depression that lasted for many years. Mead entered Harvard University in 1887, where he studied with Josiah Royce, the Christian neo-Hegelian philosopher. Mead switched from a philosophy major to physiological psychology before finishing his degree and beginning doctoral work in Germany.

In Germany, Mead studied first in Leipzig under Wilhelm Wundt, the physiological and theoretical psychologist, in the winter of 1888–9. He transferred after one semester to the University of Berlin, where he studied under the psychologists Wilhelm Dilthey, Hermann Ebbinghaus and Friedrich Paulsen, and the socialist Gustav Schmoller. In late 1891 John Dewey, the eminent philosopher and educator who became his life-long friend and colleague, offered Mead a position to teach philosophy at the University of Michigan in Ann Arbor. Mead quickly accepted the post and left Berlin without completing his doctorate.

Mead's long depression was resolved finally through his marriage to Helen Castle in 1891 and his new life in Ann Arbor. He was swept into the intellectual excitement of this department and his new professional and personal relationship with Dewey. In 1894, Dewey was offered the chair of the Department of Philosophy and Psychology at the University of Chicago and he argued strongly and successfully that Mead should be hired too.

Mead lived within a vibrant world of friends, family, students, colleagues, community activists and civic ties in Chicago, which became his home for the rest of his life. William James, an eminent pragmatist from Harvard University, named the school of thought established by Mead and Dewey 'Chicago pragmatism'. This Chicago approach, emphasizing process and interpersonal relations, provided a naturalistic and evolutionary interpretation of intellectual activity as problem-oriented and based on scientific methods. It stressed the democratic reconstruction of society through education and other institutions. This complex and exciting group, the 'world of Chicago pragmatism', inspired Mead's life and ideas, including his seminal social philosophy based on social interaction and community.

Mead's early work, prior to 1920, focused on the importance of comparative psychology, the child, emotions, childhood education and the connections between ideas and their impact on everyday life.

Three books capture his thought and work during these years from 1894 until 1920. By 1910 he had written a book of essays that showed his evolving approach from a biological and individual model to a more social and rational one that connected the individual and the group. This book was in the final stages of publication, but for some unknown reason the project was never completed. The book was issued for the first time as *Essays in Social Psychology* in 2001. Similarly, the concept of 'play' was central to Mead's thought during these early years when he emphasized the importance of childhood, emotions and public schooling in a series of articles, largely written prior to 1910 and unpublished. He connected these issues, moreover, to the importance of play in a democracy, making childhood an important time to become a member of a just community. They were collected and published in 1999 in the book *Play, School, and Society*. A third book that also stresses Mead's early writings is *The Individual and the Social Self*, eventually published in 1982. It relies on course notes from Mead's classes in social psychology at the University of Chicago in 1914 and 1927, with an emphasis on the first set of student records.

These books reveal that Mead was progressively moving from a physiological, individual and emotional model of the person in society, with an emphasis on childhood, towards a model where the self is explained as a product of social interaction and humanly generated meanings. After 1920, Mead increasingly emphasized adulthood – although his model of the emergence and formation of the self was a fundamental intellectual innovation to explain how humans became symbol-generating and social. It is unclear if this shift in his thought should be interpreted as connected to his earlier work, and in what ways, or if it should be seen as the result of a significant change from one model to a different one.

Determining the relationship between his work before and after 1920 is complicated by the fact that his most important books published prior to 1982 were all posthumously produced by his students. None of these students, moreover, specialized in sociology and their academic careers were spent in philosophy.

His philosophic approach to time and the construction of the act are foundations for his sociology, although sociologists tend to ignore these aspects of his thought. His model of the dynamic nature of the present as continually emerging and connecting the past and future in the contemporary moment draws on a view of time developed by Albert Einstein. Mead's book *The Philosophy of the Present* was pieced together by Arthur Murphy from a series of speeches Mead developed in 1930 while travelling on a train to present them as the Paul Carus Lectures in Berkeley, California. *The Philosophy of the Act* was produced by Charles Morris from unpublished papers on the association between physical action and thought as an interconnected experience. This book focuses on the process of movement and thought and is the most disjointed text of the posthumous books. Mead's monumental analysis of social thought as a movement during the nineteenth century is an exciting foundation for the history of ideas as shaped by events and human action. *Movements of Thought in the Nineteenth Century* was based on the stenographic notes created for Alvin Carus in Mead's course with this title. Although this is a major analysis of intellectual and popular changes as massive alterations in social consciousness, its impact and legacy remain largely unexplored.

Most sociologists stress the importance of *Mind, Self and Society*, edited in 1934 by Charles Morris from Carus' stenographic transcriptions of Mead's course on 'social psychology'. These notes were combined with others from 1927 (and, perhaps, 1928) to create this seminal volume. Here Mead presented his model of the genesis of the self and the other. He proposed that society and the self were mutually dependent and dynamic. They are created through human gestures, especially vocal gestures and symbols generated and maintained through social relationships. The mind, consciousness, intelligence and the ability to take the role of the other also emerged from this process. The concepts developed in this book created a distinct type of social psychology called 'symbolic interactionism'.

Another group of scholars emphasize Mead's feminism and efforts on behalf of women's suffrage, access to higher education and civil rights. This approach to his thought and politics is called 'feminist pragmatism'. His perspective here emerged from the influence of the remarkable women in his family, especially his erudite mother and life-long companion Helen Castle, as well as from his friendships with notable women at Chicago's Hull-House, the social settlement founded by the Nobel Laureate **Jane Addams**. The world of Chicago pragmatism was also a living example of combining the home, the academy, politics, family, friends, intellectual labour and social justice.

Although Mead published over 120 articles in his lifetime, the first four major works, the books published between 1932 and 1938, were compilations from students' notes and fragments of papers never intended for public scrutiny. The amazingly loyal and dutiful students who collected and edited these books had studied with him during the 1920s and before his death in 1931. They relied on his most mature ideas as expressed in the classroom. They did not understand or attend to his early interests in children, emotions, politics and urban life. These philosophers did not draw on Mead's early writings, his many published articles or the connection of Mead's ideas to sociology. Despite the limitations of these posthumous publications, Mead's fame relies on these books, and his professional reputation grew significantly after his death.

Mead's influence continues to increase through the activities of a group based on his ideas, the Society for the Study of Symbolic Interaction. These social psychologists hold two conferences annually and publish a journal, *Symbolic Interaction*, that encourages the development, application and interpretation of Mead's corpus. The relatively recent addition of books based on Mead's early work promises to raise significant new questions. Few scholars of postmodernism turn to Mead to examine the fluid nature of reality, the self and society. If they did, they would find Mead has an alternative explanation of the world as socially created that continues to be both exciting and optimistic.

See also: Jane Addams, Charles Cooley.

See also in *Fifty Key Sociologists: The Contemporary Theorists*: Howard S. Becker, Erving Goffman.

Major works

The Individual and the Social Self. 1910. Ed. and intro. by David L. Miller. Chicago: University of Chicago Press, 1982.

Play, School, and Society. 1910. Ed. and intro. by Mary Jo Deegan. New York: Peter Lang Press, 1999.

Essays in Social Psychology. 1910. Ed. and intro. by Mary Jo Deegan. New Brunswick, NJ: Transaction Books, 2001.

The Philosophy of the Present. 1932. Ed. and intro. by Arthur E. Murphy, pref. remarks by John Dewey. Chicago: University of Chicago Press.

Mind, Self and Society. 1934. Ed. and intro. by Charles Morris. Chicago: University of Chicago Press.

Movements of Thought in the Nineteenth Century. 1936. Ed. and intro. by Merritt H. Moore. Chicago: University of Chicago Press.

The Philosophy of the Act. 1938. Ed. and intro. by Charles W. Morris, in collaboration with John M. Brewster, Albert M. Dunham and David L. Miller. Chicago: University of Chicago Press.

MARY JO DEEGAN

LEWIS MORGAN

Lewis Henry Morgan is considered by many to be the founder of American anthropology, if not the discipline as a whole, and is the theorist of 'early society' upon whom **Marx** and Engels relied when considering the origins and development of society. Born on 21 November 1818 near Aurora, New York, Morgan was not a university-educated scholar, but rather was trained as a practising attorney. He became a successful businessman, involved in railway and industrial financing and in politics, serving as a New York State Assemblyman (1861–8) and Senator (1868–9). He died in 1881.

Morgan came to the research that ultimately led to his foundational contributions to the social sciences through a circuitous route. In the late 1840s, he joined a literary club, comprised of fellow alumni of the preparatory school he attended, which modelled itself on Greek and Roman motifs. Soon after, the club sought to remodel itself after the structure of the Iroquois confederacy, members of which lived on a nearby reservation. By chance, Morgan encountered a member of that Nation and thus began his serious scholarly research into the social life and, particularly, the kinship organization of societies. So consuming was this focus to become that Morgan neglected his legal practice as he sought to pull together his Iroquois research. His work with the Iroquois was innovative in a number of regards. For example, he undertook extensive field research, with the assistance of a young Seneca man, Ely Parker, and he used his research to assist the Seneca in their legal actions against attempted appropriations of their land. The major fruit of this labour was the groundbreaking publication *League of the Ho-dé-no-sau-nee or Iroquois*, arguably one of the earliest full-fledged ethnographies based on fieldwork.

At the end of the 1850s, after becoming moderately wealthy through his law practice, business interests and investments, Morgan turned his attention again to ethnological research. A chance realization on a business trip – that the neighbouring Ojibwa groups used a system of kinship similar to that he identified among the Iroquois – offered an opportunity to develop his work on the links between kinship and social organization, and allowed him to begin exploring the connections between different groups based on the similarities in their kinship systems. Following the philological practices of the day, and with funding from the Smithsonian Institution and the Department of State, Morgan developed a questionnaire soliciting kinship terms and distributed it to missionaries, diplomats, explorers and scientists in Europe and North America as well as in parts of Asia and the Pacific Islands. In all, he received responses covering about 140 cultures. From his tabulations of the survey data, Morgan concluded that kinship organization could be divided into two fundamental types. These were the 'descriptive' system, which, as in English kinship terminology, distinguishes between direct lineal ancestor (father and mother) and 'collaterals' (uncle and aunt); and the 'classificatory' system, in which a term (such as father and mother) refers both to direct ancestors and to some collaterals. This work resulted in the publication, in 1871, of *Systems of Consanguinity and Affinity of the Human Family*. This tome, which sought to explain the history and development of society through the detailed study of variations in kinship terminologies, is widely acknowledged as establishing the comparative study of kinship and its role in human history and society as a primary focus for the discipline of anthropology.

Ancient Society was Morgan's third foundational contribution to the social sciences. This traced a single trajectory of progress and development, placing societies at various points along the way. Beginning with societies based on matrilineal descent and then moving to those based on patrilineal descent and thus viewed by Morgan as more like our own, he classified societies into three levels: 'savagery', 'barbarism' and 'civilization'. He based his typology on such features as technological inventions and discoveries, government structure, kinship system and the rise of private property. Following an approach typical of cultural evolutionary theory in his day (and of some strains in ours), *Ancient Society* suggests that human development is cumulative, with contemporary technology, government systems and property relations developing out of earlier, 'simpler' systems, and presupposes that earlier evolutionary stages can be adequately represented through the examination of the life-ways of contemporary societies tautologically described as 'primitive'.

To fully appreciate Morgan's stance in presenting this sequence, it is important to remember that, at the time he wrote *Ancient Society*, this theory of social evolution was considered politically progressive for, as the use of the term 'human family' in *Systems* indicates, it presupposes that humans are of one kind and that the seed of human potential is thus found in every person in every culture and in every time period, so that every society, under the right circumstances, could eventually become civilized. As such, it provided a robust counter-argument to the so-called 'theory of polygenesis', which sought to establish that there could be no universal development of culture, as different 'races' had been 'created' at different times and for different purposes. This latter proposition was advanced by political conservatives to justify their support for slavery and for the systematic discrimination against former slaves.

Ancient Society had a direct and lasting influence on the development of the Marxist theory of evolution. The data it provided were sufficiently crucial to Marx that he transcribed large excerpts in a series of ethnological notebooks. In them, Marx recorded information relating to the origins of civilization and of the state of particular significance to his reflections on the origins and early development of society. After Marx's death, Engels came across these notes and made them the basis of his *The Origins of the Family, Private Property and the State*. Accepting much of Morgan's evidence and his general thesis that matrilineality preceded patrilineality, Engels' main contribution was to make connections between the historical data and the contemporary forms of family, political systems and forms of property under capitalism.

As the works discussed here attest, Morgan's contributions to the development of social theory in the nineteenth century are monumental. The legacy of the directions he took as an ethnographer and as a social theorist resound in the work of scholars today. Perhaps the most eloquent homage to his lasting contribution is found in the fact that Claude Lévi-Strauss's *The Elementary Structures of Kinship*, arguably the single most important contribution to kinship and social theory written in the last century, is dedicated to Morgan's memory.

See also: Karl Marx.

See also in *Fifty Key Sociologists: The Contemporary Theorists*: Claude Lévi-Strauss.

Major works

League of the Iroquois. 1851. New York: Corinth, 1962.
Systems of Consanguinity and Affinity of the Human Family. 1871. Smithsonian Contributions to Knowledge, vol. 17. Washington, DC: Smithsonian Institution.
Ancient Society, or Researches in the Lines of Human Progress from Savagery through Barbarism to Civilization. 1877. Tucson, AZ: University of Arizona Press, 1985.

Further reading

Friedrich Engels. 1884. *Origins of the Family, Private Property and the State*. London: Penguin, 1986.

Meyer Fortes. 1969. *Kinship and the Social Order: The Legacy of Lewis Henry Morgan*. Chicago: Aldine.

Lawrence Krader, ed. 1972. *The Ethnological Notebooks of Karl Marx: Studies of Morgan*. Assen: Van Gorcum.

Claude Lévi-Strauss. 1947. *The Elementary Structures of Kinship*, Boston, MA: Beacon Press, 1969.

Carl Resek. 1960. *Lewis Henry Morgan, American Scholar*. Chicago: University of Chicago Press.

Thomas R. Trautmann. 1987. *Lewis Henry Morgan and the Invention of Kinship*, Berkeley, CA: University of California Press.

MICHAEL ASCH AND ROBERT L. A. HANCOCK

GAETANO MOSCA

A pioneer of political sociology, Mosca contributed key elements to both elitist and pluralist accounts of democracy. Born in Palermo in 1858 to a professional middle-class family, Mosca studied law at the local university and graduated in 1882. All these biographical elements – from his birth in southern Italy to his legal training – exerted an influence on his sociological ideas.

Mosca's main contribution was contained in three books in which he progressively elaborated his theory of the political class. The first version of his thesis was published in 1884 as *On the Theory of Governments and Parliamentary Government: Historical and Social Studies*. This youthful work laid out the main elements of his theory, adopted an organizational plan followed by the later books and outlined his basic methodological approach. His central argument criticized the Aristotelian division of polities into tyrannies, aristocracies and democracies. In fact, these political forms were but variations of the permanent division of all political systems into rulers and ruled. Whereas the Aristotelian categories defined the rulers as one, some or the many, respectively, Mosca argued that in all three cases a small political class prevailed. He attributed the predominance of elites to two 'indisputable properties of the social nature of man': first, 'a superiority of moral character' and, second, and more originally, the fact 'that an organized minority, that acts in a co-ordinated manner, always triumphs over a disorganized majority, which has neither will, nor impulse, nor action in common'.

Having stated his thesis, Mosca proceeded to its demonstration. His statements of his method were crudely positivistic. Mosca contended that the accumulation of facts alone would suffice to confirm his ideas. However, though he drew material from all periods of history, he allowed that the cultural and material conditions of societies varied over time, with these variations influencing their politics. Indeed, he noted both the diverse 'moral qualities' elites might have to possess and the various kinds of organization they might need to deploy in different historical periods and types of society. Mosca argued that in modern industrial societies there was a far greater accumulation of power by governments than ever before. Tax revenues, a standing army and a bureaucracy that entered into every aspect of public life meant the contemporary political elite had unprecedented influence. The qualities determining their selection were novel too, involving technical skills rather than military prowess or mere wealth.

Mosca's analysis turned here from description to prescription. He claimed the most suitable political elite for his times to be the educated, moderately well-off professional middle class to which he himself belonged. However, this belief raised the question of why this group did not dominate. Mosca blamed democracy. The democratic system favoured a type of political elite that was otherwise unsuited to modern industrial societies, so that they were far more poorly governed than they should be.

Mosca believed all elites need a 'political formula' to justify their rule. Rule could not be maintained by force alone. This formula changed according to the level of culture and social and economic conditions of a given society, and so differed over history. To retain power, elites had to change their justificatory formula accordingly, otherwise a new elite employing a more suitable formula would supplant them. Though the prevailing socio-economic circumstances constrained the sorts of formula to which elites could appeal, it did not determine any one as the only formula available. Elites always had the power to choose the one that best suited their characteristics and circumstances. Democracy was simply the political formula most suited to a mass society where popular demands had to be addressed. However, it had no basis in reality. Rather than a mechanism of majority rule, it was merely a means whereby a minority imposed their rule. Worse, it actually corrupted the elite.

Mosca observed how 'whoever has assisted at an election knows perfectly well that the electors do not elect the Deputy, but usually the Deputy has himself elected by the electors' or, more accurately, 'his friends have him elected'. Drawing on his experience of the corrupt electoral practices prevalent in his native Sicily, he noted three main ways in which the electorate were manipulated: first, incumbents used the bureaucracy to favour their side; second, what he called 'grand electors' – the wealthy and socially powerful – could influence their dependents to support their favoured candidate; finally, unions and workers' associations could similarly deliver votes to particular political parties. The result of this corrupt system was that only corrupt politicians rose to the fore. The 'precious qualities' of 'independence of character, boldness and impartiality' were replaced by 'moral cowardice, lack of a sense of justice, cunning, intrigue'.

In this first book, Mosca largely despaired of reforming democracy. A more democratic system would merely enhance the opportunities for manipulation of the electorate by a corrupt and cynical elite and he opposed such measures as extending the franchise. However, he accepted that any viable solutions would have to be formally consistent with the prevailing democratic political formula. Somehow, he believed, space had to be made for the educated, professional middle class to hold more sway. The subsequent revisions of Mosca's thesis were largely devoted to this task, with his methodology, general theory of elite rule, and his idea of the 'political formula' remaining largely unchanged.

These revisions came mainly in the two editions of his *Elements of Political Science*, published in 1896 and 1923. Prior to publishing the first, he had seen parliamentary life first hand, acting as a *Revisore* at the Chamber of Deputies from 1886. The major innovation in this book was his notion of 'juridical defence'. He now adapted his conception of the elite to include those out of power as well as those in power, arguing that a key element in any ruling class was its capacity to renew itself from the wider pool of 'outs'. However, the existence of ins and outs served a broader purpose, preventing 'ins' from being too self-interested – at least overtly. 'Juridical defence' consisted of the organizational mechanisms, such as the separation of powers, whereby this 'moral discipline' was institutionalized. Though he still hoped his independent meritocracy would benefit from such arrangements, it remained unclear exactly how or why. In fact, his main criticisms now turned from the prevailing elite to the rising socialist elite. He argued that socialism was but another misleading 'political formula' that in reality would strengthen rather than diminish the power of the ruling class by abolishing a key separation between political and economic power. The second edition of his book left the first unchanged but added a second volume.

In 1896 Mosca secured a post teaching constitutional law at Turin University, where he was later to meet and influence Robert Michels. In 1908 he also became a deputy in the parliament, serving as undersecretary in the Colonial Office from 1914–16 and becoming a senator in 1919. Though a conservative liberal and strongly anti-socialist, this experience nonetheless reconciled him to parliamentary democracy. Unlike many conservative liberal politicians with whom he otherwise agreed, he consistently opposed the Fascists, who came to power in 1922. He now argued that 'real' as opposed to 'ideal' democracy could be beneficial in uniting the diverse interests within society and reconciling them to the public good. In an early version of later pluralist theory, he argued the key was to ensure a variety of social groups competed within the system. The key was to balance 'autocratic' and 'liberal' principles in the form of government with 'aristocratic' and 'democratic' tendencies in the recruitment of elites. The former tendency helped preserve continuity; the latter renewed the elite from below. Unfortunately, his reconciliation with parliamentary democracy more or less coincided with its demise in Italy and he died in 1941 before the Fascist regime fell.

See also: Oliver Cox, Ludwig Gumplowicz, Vilfredo Pareto.

See also in *Fifty Key Sociologists: The Contemporary Theorists*: C. Wright Mills.

Major works

Sulla teorica dei governi e sul governo rappresentivo: studi storici e sociali. 1884. Palermo: Tip. dello Statuto.
Elementi di scienza politica. 1886. 1923. Partially translated into English as *The Ruling Class*, ed. A Livingstone, trans. H. D. Kahn. New York and London: McGraw Hill, 1939.

Further reading

Ettore Albertoni. 1987. *Mosca and the Theory of Elitism*. Oxford: Basil Blackwell.
Richard Bellamy. 1987. *Modern Italian Social Theory*. Cambridge: Polity Press.
Joseph V. Femia. 1998. *The Machiavellian Legacy: Essays in Italian Political Thought*. Basingstoke: Macmillan.
James Meisel. 1958. *The Myth of the Ruling Class: Gaetano Mosca and the Elite*, Ann Arbor, MI: University of Michigan Press.

RICHARD BELLAMY

GUNNAR MYRDAL

Though an economist by training and profession, the Swedish social scientist, government advisor and politician Gunnar Myrdal made an important contribution to sociology in several areas: through his theoretical work on the problem of values in socio-economic theory and research; through his contribution, in collaboration with his wife Alva Myrdal, to the development of welfare-state theory and policy; and through his intellectual leadership over two major research investigations into the economic, social and institutional conditions that fuel racism, poverty and underdevelopment. Throughout his career, Myrdal moved between academic research and politically engaged activities on behalf of governments and international organizations, guided by the firm conviction that the two spheres of work were mutually interdependent.

Born in rural Sweden in 1898, Myrdal early developed an interest in the role of political values and social expectations in the fluctuating economic life of industrial modernity. In his theoretically groundbreaking doctorate he critically exposed the hidden value premises in orthodox economic theory. At his inaugural installation as professor at Stockholm University in 1933, he argued for the necessity of governmental economic planning to avoid the socially, and politically, disastrous effects of uncontrolled financial markets to which the poor had neither access nor claims. Such long-term planning, a concept with which he remained associated throughout his life, should treat public investment in social policy, education and employment as productive and 'prophylactic' rather than merely ameliorative interventions. This would require a strengthened public sector sensitive both to the needs of the economy and to popular demands for social and economic justice. In the early 1930s, when world depression was at its height, Myrdal became an active member of the Swedish Social Democratic Party. In a popular and influential publication he and his political activist and feminist wife Alva presented an intellectual manifesto outlining the political and economic rationale for family- and women-friendly welfare-state policy. In this they utilized sociological theories and empirical approaches, as well as the art of journalistic exposure of social misery, both learned on joint study visits to the US. Unlike similar welfare developments at the time in Germany, their welfare-state vision was based on a close co-operation between citizens, the labour movement and other reform-oriented democratic popular organizations, including those for women's rights. As members of several government investigative commissions underpinning the Social Democratic reform programme in the 1930s, the Myrdals gained considerable influence over the development of the Swedish model of welfare-state policy and growing international fame.

In 1937, Myrdal received an invitation from the Carnegie Corporation to direct one of the largest research projects ever funded, on the position in the United States of its black citizens. (His wife Alva also became the recipient of financial support for writing a subsequently highly influential book on Swedish family and welfare policy.) The project brought together a large number of social researchers from across the racial divide, and was theoretically influenced by the work of, amongst others, the sociologists William I. Thomas and **W. E. B. DuBois**. In all, 20,000 pages of economic and sociological evidence were collected, culminating in the two-volume work *An American Dilemma: The Negro Problem and Modern Democracy*. Shocked by the cruelty of the racism he observed in a nation hypocritically proclaiming a value creed of freedom and equality, his final report came to focus on white racism and its consequences in 'vicious circles' of prejudice and discrimination. Sociologically the work was groundbreaking in several ways: in its combination of large-scale quantitative as well as qualitative economic and social indicators as evidence of discrimination and its consequences; in its emphasis on the role and power of political, legal and economic institutions, at all levels in society, in the day-to-day subversion of constitutional rights; and in its insistence that social science research needs to engage not just with the facts of a situation, but also with the social and political values that form part of its context, including the researcher's own.

Politically, the most important legacy of Myrdal's project was its contribution as evidence to the 1954 US Supreme Court decision that outlawed educational segregation. In addressing the weaknesses of a nation as an outsider, like **de Tocqueville** before him, Myrdal faced criticism and suspicion, especially regarding his views on the role of government in the 'social engineering' of progressive change. The major long-term contribution of the project to sociology lies in Myrdal's explicit articulation of the role of values in social research (summarized in a methodological appendix). Alongside **Weber**'s contribution to the same topic, this is still of major relevance to contemporary debates on the nature of sociology as a science.

After the war, and a brief return to active politics in Sweden, Myrdal in 1947 took up a post as executive secretary of the UN Commission for Economic Reconstruction, a return to more international economic concerns in conflict-torn Europe. But plans for a new research project, aiming yet again to address fundamental questions about poverty and inequality, were not long in formulating themselves. This time Myrdal took on the urgent issue of third world economic development, again with the support of Alva, who was Sweden's ambassador to India from 1956. Funded by Twentieth Century Fund, the outcome of this ten-year project was published as *Asian Drama: An Inquiry into the Poverty of Nations*, again a magisterial work involving a large number of researchers and much evidence. In this he continued to pursue the themes of the need for central social and economic planning, for public investment in agricultural, social and educational reform, and for 'grass root' democratic participation as the only means whereby the cosy relationship between national elites and financial interests could be broken. His research approach was, again, a mixture of historical analysis of past trends, theoretical analysis and detailed empirical descriptions of individual social and economic circumstances, all framed by a critical approach to economic and political institutions more interested in serving the powerful than the powerless.

In 1974, Myrdal received the Nobel Price in Economics, together with Friedrich von Hayek, for pioneering work on monetary and market theory, and on the relationship between economic, social and institutional conditions. Up until his death in 1987, Myrdal's writings continued to reflect his rebelliously critical spirit. His continuing passion for a socially more fair, decent and rationally planned world is reflected in sharp critiques of state bureaucratization, both west and east of the Iron Curtain, as well as of the nuclear arms race and the failure of the US to tackle racism and discrimination.

See also: W. E. B. DuBois, Max Weber.

Major works

Population: A Problem for Democracy. 1940. Cambridge, MA: Harvard University Press.

An American Dilemma: The Negro Problem and American Democracy. 1944. New York: Harper and Brothers. 3rd edn 1996. New Brunswick, NJ: Transaction.

The Political Element in the Development of Economic Theory. 1953. London: Routledge & Kegan Paul.

Beyond the Welfare State: Economic Planning in the Welfare States and Its International Implications. 1957. London: University Paperbacks.

Value in Social Theory: A Selection of Essays on Methodology. 1958. London: Routledge & Kegan Paul.

Asian Drama. An Inquiry into the Poverty of Nations. 1968. London: Allen Lane, The Penguin Press.

Objectivity in Social Research. 1970. London: Duckworth.

Further reading

Walter A. Jackson. 1990. *Gunnar Myrdal and America's Conscience: Social Engineering and Radical Liberalism, 1938–1987.* Chapel Hill, NC: University of North Carolina Press.

Allan Carlson. 1990. *The Swedish Experiment in Family Politics: The Myrdals and the Inter-war Population Crisis.* New Brunswick, NJ, and London: Transaction Publishers.

David W. Southern. 1987. *Gunnar Myrdal and Black–White Relations: The Use and Abuse of 'An American Dilemma', 1944–1969.* Baton Rouge, LA: Louisiana State University Press.

E. STINA LYON

VILFREDO PARETO

Pareto made important contributions to economics as well as political sociology. Economists think of him as a classic liberal who pioneered the application of rational choice theory to welfare economics. By contrast, though an acknowledged founding father of political sociology, and particularly of elite theory, his reputation in this field is as an illiberal anti-democrat who explored the irrational in politics. In fact, he remained more or less true to his early ideals, but came to attribute their not being realized to the failings of democratic politics.

Pareto was born in Paris in 1848, the year of liberal revolutions, the son of a temporarily exiled Italian radical. He followed his father into engineering, graduating in 1869 and subsequently going to work for the Florence branch of the Rome Railway Company. During this period he became engaged in political debates as an ardent supporter of universal suffrage, republicanism, free trade and disarmament. An admirer of **Herbert Spencer** and J. S. Mill, he became a champion of liberal reform of the corrupt Italian political system. A regular polemicist in the local and national press, he began to make his name as a free-market political economist. Pareto viewed economic and political liberalism as logical entailments of the rational-actor model of human agency. He believed that since a free market and a limited state were in the public interest, their ultimate success ought to be assured. However, this optimism appeared to be increasingly confounded during the 1880s and 1890s. Rather than pursuing liberal policies, successive governments had practised what he termed 'bourgeois socialism', employing protectionism and state monopolies to benefit certain industrial and agricultural supporters.

Pareto condemned Marxism as utopian and unworkable, but was initially sympathetic to 'popular socialism' as an understandable reaction to the behaviour of the governing class. So long as liberal politicians pursued 'bourgeois socialism', he argued, they were in no position to criticize workers for espousing analogous views that merely happened to favour their class interests, albeit only in the short term. The rise of socialism could only be halted if the bourgeoisie returned to genuinely liberal ways and demonstrated to the workers the advantages of the market. Instead, though, they increasingly tried to buy them off by resorting to state welfare and similar measures. As a result, popular socialism was gradually being added to, and in some respects supplanting, bourgeois socialism, creating ever more inefficiencies and opportunities for corruption. Since he still maintained that the free market provided the optimal economic system, defending this thesis in a number of important works following his appointment as professor of political economy in Lausanne in 1893, the explanation for this development could not lie in either changes in the nature of capitalism or flaws in liberal political economy. Increasingly, he came to believe the answer resided in the psychological appeal of 'non-logical' irrational ideas to the masses and the ability of elites to exploit them to win power

Pareto's political sociology, which he began to develop from the 1900s, simply elaborated this diagnosis of the nature of Italian transformist politics. He first outlined his theory in his analysis of *Socialist Systems* published in 1902. Elite theory clearly emerges from this work as both an alternative to Marxism and a critique and explanation of its appeal. Class struggle is replaced by the circulation of elites, the proletariat with the mass, and a future without domination declared illusory because exploitative rule by an elite occurs under all systems, private property being but one source of power and authority. He likened socialism's attraction to millenarian religion: as emotional rather than intellectual. Notions such as the 'general will', the 'common good' or 'popular sovereignty' were in themselves incoherent. They simply offered a spurious legitimacy for the replacement of a capitalist by a socialist elite.

Subsequent writings, culminating in the massive *Treatise of General Sociology* of 1916, outlined the socio-psychological mechanisms involved. Pareto argued that humans were moved by a number of basic emotional 'residues'. These could then be manipulated by certain sorts of argumentation, which he called 'derivations'. Though he enumerated some fifty-two residues, the most important were the 'instinct of combinations' and the 'persistence of aggregates'. Adapting

Machiavelli, Pareto divided political elites into 'foxes' and 'lions', depending on which of these two residues they operated upon. The first favoured the 'cunning' of those who ruled through consent; the second was a conservative tendency that was more inclined to employ force. These two types of political elite obtained power by recruiting support from coalitions of much more heterogeneous social and economic groups possessing the parallel characteristics associated with innovative 'speculators' and investing 'rentiers', respectively. Pareto argued that there was a cyclical 'circulation' of elites which went hand in hand with socio-economic cycles. Thus, foxes wooed speculators by either tacitly or actively helping them to 'despoil' the rentiers – be they small petit-bourgeois savers or major shareholders. Initially, rising prosperity would be accompanied by a calling into question of traditional morality and a consumer boom. However, both the government and the populace would begin to go into debt due to over-consumption based on credit, whilst a scarcity of capital and a lack of productive investment would lead the economy to contract. The need for restraint and saving would become apparent, and a more conservative government of lions would come to the fore backed by a rentier economic class. Eventually, though, the economy would start to stagnate and people would tire of leonine austerity, thereby precipitating the rise of foxes and speculators again and the start of a new cycle.

Pareto claimed to be describing a universal phenomenon, and he mainly employed examples drawn from ancient history to demonstrate his theory's objectivity. However, the Italian context emerged as all important once he applied it to democracy in both the final chapters of the *Treatise* and the various articles written after the First World War. The latter were collected in his final book of 1921 as *The Transformation of Democracy*. Italy, he argued, was in the grip of a pluto-democracy. Parliamentary democracy offered the perfect instrument for foxish politicians to build up a clientalistic network of 'speculators'. To a certain degree, workers had common cause with the plutocrats. If the one desired increased wages and social benefits, the other wanted bigger bonuses and state subsidies. Both wished to expropriate the rentiers' surplus and raise taxes for an expanding state. However, at a certain point their paths were bound to diverge. He now feared democracy was likely to get the upper hand over plutocracy. Clientalism encouraged centripetal tendencies that dispersed state power, creating what he regarded as a new feudalism of warring barons, exemplified by the conflict between organized labour and fascists. Yet economic and social instability was encouraging centrifugal forces calling for a return to authority. Initially, he had anticipated a socialist seizure of power on the Bolshevik model, but he was equally happy to greet the rise of Mussolini as confirming 'splendidly the predictions of my Sociology and many of my articles'. In fact, Pareto's theory was but an *ex post facto* elaboration of his jaundiced interpretation of the Italian situation, whereby he re-described these events in terms of the categories of his theory and then read them back into all other past events as universal laws of human behaviour. However, though anti-democratic, he was not a fascist. He regarded the state as an instrument of 'spoilation' whoever ran it. Had he not died in 1923, he would undoubtedly have regarded Mussolini's regime as an archetypal 'demagogic plutocracy'. His difficulty was that he had ruled out the very possibility of realizing the regime he most desired – a free-market economy combined with a liberal state.

See also: Gaetano Mosca, Lester Ward.

See also in *Fifty Key Sociologists: The Contemporary Theorists*: George Homans, C. Wright Mills, Talcott Parsons.

Major works

The Mind and Society, 4 vols. 1916. Trans. of the *Treatise*. New York: Jonathan Cape, 1935.
The Transformation of Democracy. 1921. Ed. C. H. Powers, trans. R. Girola. New Brunswick, NJ: Transaction Books, 1984.
Extracts from Pareto's other works can be found in *The Other Pareto*. Ed. P. Bucolo, trans. P. and G. Bucolo. London: Scolar Press, 1980.

Further reading

Richard Bellamy. 1987. *Modern Italian Social Theory*. Cambridge: Polity Press.
Joseph Femia. 1998. *The Machiavellian Legacy: Essays in Italian Political Thought*. Basingstoke: Macmillan.
Samuel Finer. 1968. 'Pareto and Pluto-Democracy: The Retreat to Galapagos'. *American Political Science Review* 62.

RICHARD BELLAMY

ALFRED RADCLIFFE-BROWN

Born in 1881, Alfred Reginald Brown (he later adopted the additional surname Radcliffe) graduated in 1905 as part of the first cohort of the first undergraduate programme in Britain to include substantial teaching in anthropology. This was established at Cambridge University by two natural scientists, William H. R. Rivers and Alfred C. Haddon, whose aim was to introduce scientific rigour into the speculative evolutionist anthropology of the Victorians. In about 1910, Radcliffe-Brown adopted **Durkheim**'s sociological theory and abandoned the historical reconstructions of his teachers. Together with **Bronislaw Malinowski**, he established the modern discipline of social anthropology with its two pillars of intensive ethnographic fieldwork and structural or functionalist analysis in the Durkheimian tradition.

Radcliffe-Brown was very conscious of his role as a disciplinary pioneer. Many of his key publications were originally delivered as public lectures and were designed to set out and illustrate his projected 'comparative sociology'. And he carried the new discipline all over the world. He occupied the first chair in social anthropology in the British Empire, at Cape Town University, held foundation chairs in social anthropology at the University of Sydney and at Oxford, and served as ambassador for social anthropology at the University of Chicago and at universities in Brazil, China and Egypt.

Admired rather than liked, often accused of arrogance and coldness, Radcliffe-Brown affected an Edwardian upper-class style (symbolized by his monocle) but was raised in modest circumstances by a widowed mother, and had to leave King Edward's School in Birmingham, where he held a scholarship, at the age of fifteen. After working as a librarian for some years he studied briefly at Birmingham University, and was then awarded an exhibition to Trinity College, Cambridge, where he read for the mental and moral sciences tripos. Between 1906 and 1908 he did ethnographic fieldwork in the Andaman Islands. In 1910 he began two years of field research in Australia, working particularly on the complex systems of kinship and marriage of the aborigines, and over the next two decades he published a series of papers on Australian kinship, culminating in a long essay, 'The Social Organization of Australian Tribes', which was to be one of the central points of reference for debates on kinship for a generation.

Like Rivers, Radcliffe-Brown's objective was to make social anthropology an empirical science, which would proceed inductively from observation to classification and generalization. The social anthropologist begins by studying 'any convenient locality of a suitable size', focusing on 'the network of relations connecting the inhabitants amongst themselves and with the people of other regions'. The daily life of individuals provides the raw material, but the ethnographer is really interested in delineating an abstract figure, the 'person', the social role, which is defined by usages and norms. From the 'network of relations' the ethnographer abstracts an enduring web of customs and institutions. The chief dies, the daughter marries and leaves home, children are born, but the institutions of the chieftaincy, the household, the family endure. These stable features – persons, groups, institutions and norms – constitute the 'structural form' of the society. The structural form is generally in a state of equilibrium, its parts working harmoniously together. The analogy he favoured was with the structure of a biological organism.

Radcliffe-Brown once suggested that a social usage or norm 'is not established by the anthropologist ... it is characterized by what people say about rules in a given society and what they do about them'. However, he generally implied that just as the ethnographer should penetrate behind the flux of social process to abstract the enduring features, the social form, so the scientific observer should go beyond what people told him in order to divine the true, inward purpose of rituals and customs. An informant may say that a sacrifice feeds the ancestors, but the real purpose – and so the true meaning – of the rite is the contribution it makes to keeping up the social form, the structure of the society. So ancestor worship sustains the values of patriarchy and whips up the sentiments on which family life depends. The 'function' is the effect 'of an institution, custom or belief, or of some regular social activity, such as a funeral ceremony, or the trial and punishment of a criminal', upon 'the complex whole of social structure and the process of social life'.

In order to specify the function, the ethnographer begins by comparing similar customs or beliefs in a society. For instance, the Andaman Islanders insisted on ceremonial weeping on various set occasions – when people meet after a long separation, at peace-making ceremonies, after a death, at a marriage and at various stages of an initiation ceremony. These all mark situations in which social relationships have been interrupted and are about to be renewed. Evidently ceremonial weeping is an aspect of the ritualization of the passage of an individual from one social personality to another. This suggests that its function is to mark these transitions, to advertise the new status of the participants and to reconcile people to the changes in their lives.

This is, however, just a first approximation. The next step is to carry the comparison further, to other societies. Radcliffe-Brown insisted that generalizations had to be based on systematic comparison.

He himself engaged in comparisons within a culture area, aboriginal Australia, where he identified a limited range of types of kinship system, all of them based ultimately on similar principles. More ambitiously, a universal typology could be constructed, of kinship systems, or political systems, or religions. The final goal was to establish laws of society, which would, in effect, be statements about the universal functions of kinship, or religion, or education.

Radcliffe-Brown worked on the same lines as **Marcel Mauss**, Durkheim's nephew, who was also applying Durkheim's ideas to ethnographic materials. Their positivist programme – observe, abstract, compare, generalize – is unfashionable, yet the Durkheimian legacy is still very much alive, particularly in the study of religions, and the essays of Mauss remain influential. It is therefore perhaps surprising that Radcliffe-Brown's theoretical writings fell out of favour in the 1970s (he had died in 1955) – perhaps terminally. Some of his more specific theories are potentially as suggestive as any of those of Mauss. A good example is his theory of joking relationships. Elaborate and apparently transgressive 'joking' tends to occur where people are united as members of the same category or group in one context but are opposed as members of rival groups in another context. These inconsistencies are neutralized by elaborate rituals of distancing ('avoidance') or by formal laughter. Another instance is Radcliffe-Brown's mature theory of totemism, as a system of classification that domesticates nature, absorbing it into the social system. Almost as if to compensate for the neglect of his most ambitious work, Radcliffe-Brown has been recognized as an ancestor of 'social network' theory, although in fact he contributed little more than the term itself.

See also: Emile Durkheim, Bronislaw Malinowski, Edward Evans-Pritchard.

See also in *Fifty Key Sociologists: The Contemporary Theorists*: Mary Douglas.

Major works

The Andaman Islanders. 1922. New York: Free Press, 1964.
'The Social Organisation of the Australian Tribes'. 1930–1. *Oceania* 1 and 2.
A Natural Science of Society. 1937. Glencoe, IL: Free Press, 1957.
Structure and Function in Primitive Society. 1935–40. London: Cohen and West, 1952.

Radcliffe-Brown's numerous essays are his most important contributions, and a convenient anthology is Adam Kuper, ed. 1977. *The Social Anthropology of Radcliffe-Brown*.

Further reading

Adam Kuper. 1996. *Anthropologists and Anthropology: The Modern British School,* London: Routledge: ch. 2.
George W. Stocking, Jr. 1995. *After Tylor: British Social Anthropology 1888–1951.* London: Athlone Press: ch. 7.

ADAM KUPER

SEEBOHM ROWNTREE

Rowntree is now best remembered for his development of a 'scientific' measure of poverty based on the insufficiency of family income to meet basic needs. However, he also researched land values and agriculture and was active and innovative in the areas of industrial relations and management. His later works have been seen as pioneering the study of recreation.

Benjamin Seebohm Rowntree was born into the Quaker, chocolate-producing family of Rowntree's of York in 1871. He studied chemistry briefly in Manchester, and at the age of eighteen he returned to the Rowntree cocoa company to work alongside his father and older brother. He remained actively involved in the company for most of the rest of his life. Joseph Rowntree, Seebohm's father, had built up the cocoa works from its origins as a small business primarily concerned with the production of a temperance drink to a major sweet and chocolate business. Joseph Rowntree was a committed Quaker with wide interests, Liberal convictions, a strong social conscience and an active concern with improving the welfare of his workforce, economically, socially and intellectually. Seebohm Rowntree inherited many of the same interests and concerns. His management roles at the cocoa works, his religious conviction and his social conscience continued to underpin his interests and research activity until his death in 1954.

In 1899 Seebohm Rowntree embarked upon a social investigation that was to have a profound influence on the development of social research and the conception of poverty. Influenced by **Charles Booth**'s study of poverty in London, he undertook a comprehensive survey of working-class households in York. In a house-to-house inquiry of 11,560 families, he investigated living conditions and means in the working-class population. As Hennock has pointed out, he followed Booth in identifying as poor those living in 'obvious want and squalor'. However, he distinguished between those in 'primary poverty', who were poor because income simply could not meet the family's most basic needs, and those in 'secondary poverty', where incomes were higher and therefore some degree of wasteful expenditure could be inferred. He focused on the causes of poverty only for those in primary poverty, and consideration of secondary poverty was to lapse in his later work. In order to establish who was living in 'primary poverty' he constructed an estimate of the 'minimum necessary expenditure for the maintenance of merely physical health' for families of different composition. This estimate was based around nutritional needs to be met in the cheapest possible way, with allowances for the plainest clothing and for a minimal amount of fuel, light and sundries such as soap. As he noted, '[e]xpenditure needful for the development of the mortal, moral, and social sides of human nature will not be taken into account at this stage of the inquiry'. He did not discount the moral and social needs of the working classes. On the contrary, both his writings and his innovations at the Rowntree cocoa works attest to his belief in their vital importance. However, he was concerned to establish that the poverty he enumerated could not be reduced by greater 'thrift', the watchword of contemporary thinking on poverty as a social problem. He compared this 'poverty line' with actual incomes and found that over 15 per cent of the working-class population (and 10 per cent of the total population) of York were living below it. Rowntree identified low wages as being responsible for over half of primary poverty, with large families responsible for a further fifth. His investigation thus demonstrated that poverty was not simply the fate of the unlucky (such as widows) or the improvident.

The study was published in 1901 as *Poverty: A Study of Town Life*. Accessibly written, its conclusions were surprising and controversial, and it was widely read, quickly going into a second edition. Its approach met with support from reformers and resistance from those committed to seeing poverty as an individual issue of personal responsibility. He also recognized the importance of the life course and the duration of poverty in families' and individuals' welfare and distress. His account of alternating periods of want and relative comfort throughout an individual's life captured important longitudinal aspects of poverty and continues to be regularly cited in contemporary longitudinal research.

Poverty was also of methodological importance. Rowntree's approach to comparing incomes and needs stimulated many comparable studies in other urban environments. The statistician Arthur Bowley exploited the approach to undertake a comparative study across a number of towns, sampling households in place of the comprehensive coverage preferred by Rowntree. When Rowntree repeated his poverty survey of York in 1936 (see *Poverty and Progress*), he continued to survey all working-class households. However, by sampling from his survey returns, he was, reluctantly, forced to admit the potential of sampling as a viable alternative to population coverage. His third survey of York in 1950 thus used a 1 in 9 sample. Rowntree's methodological insights appear to have been primarily intuitive rather than reflecting mathematical sophistication or being influenced by statistical developments, despite his interest in the power of numbers and in their persuasive quality.

While the primary poverty line had been constructed as an illustrative rather than as a meaningful subsistence minimum, Rowntree himself saw its potential for developing a real minimum that could take some account of actual spending, such as that on tea and sick clubs. He outlined such a minimum, arguing for it as the basis for a minimum wage (a major concern of his) in his work on *The Human Needs of Labour*. This work influenced William Beveridge's 1942 report on *Social Insurance and Allied Services* (the Beveridge Report). Rowntree was in close communication with Beveridge throughout 1942, and Beveridge used Rowntree's minimum to establish rates of National Insurance payments.

Poverty established Rowntree as a meticulous and thoughtful social researcher, with skills applicable to a range of fields. His subsequent researches, many carried out at the instigation of the Liberal leader David Lloyd George, with whom he had a close working relationship throughout the 1910s and 1920s, covered land values and (with Viscount Astor) a series of studies of agriculture. In the 1920s and 1930s he also became increasingly concerned about unemployment and pursued research into it. He discovered that insurance payments did not adversely affect motivation, as had been claimed. He also proposed national rather than local solutions to the entrenched unemployment of depressed areas.

Alongside his social research, Rowntree remained active as labour director at the cocoa works. He continued his father's example of innovation and concern for the welfare of his workforce, introducing old-age pensions, family allowances and profit sharing, promoting democratic procedures and systems for hearing grievances and working closely with the unions. He also took these interests into the national arena. During the First World War he was responsible for industrial welfare in a post at the Ministry of Munitions. Good industrial relations were a key concern of his (expressed in *The Human Factor in Business*) and he regarded industry as properly an alliance between management and workers for the good of the community as a whole.

He was directly involved in two major conciliation efforts following strikes in 1919 and 1926. In 1919 he also initiated the first of a series of management schools, afterwards the long-running Oxford Management Schools.

In 1951, towards the end of his life, he published his third survey of poverty in York (*Poverty and the Welfare State*) and a work on leisure use and recreation, *English Life and Leisure*. Both have been criticized for their methods and the new poverty study was shown to be overly optimistic in its estimate of the role of the welfare state in reducing poverty. Nevertheless, as the final instalment of Rowntree's poverty studies, *Poverty and the Welfare State* reflects the changes that had taken place in standards of living, state welfare and conceptions of poverty since 1899. *English Life and Leisure*, by contrast, is the first full expression of Rowntree's life-long interest in the social and moral conduct of the population. Between them they represent many of his prevailing interests and concerns, his approach to social research and his ability to identify and take up the challenge of investigating critical sociological questions for the future. Moreover, they convey the same optimism for the future that impelled him throughout his life.

See also: Charles Booth.

See also in *Fifty Key Sociologists: The Contemporary Theorists*: William Julius Wilson.

Major works

Poverty: A Study of Town Life. 1901. London: Longmans, Green & co.
Unemployment. 1911. London: Macmillan.
How The Labourer Lives. 1913. With May Kendall. London: Thomas Nelson.
The Human Needs of Labour. 1918. London: Thomas Nelson.
The Human Factor in Business. 1921. London: Longmans, Green & co.
Poverty and Progress. 1941. London: Longmans, Green & co.
Poverty and the Welfare State. 1951. With G. Russell Lavers. London: Longmans, Green & co.
English Life and Leisure. 1951. With G. Russell Lavers. London: Longmans, Green & co.

Further reading

Anthony B. Atkinson, J. Corlyon, A. K. Maynard, H. Sutherland and C. G. Trinder. 1981. 'Poverty in York: A Re-Analysis of Rowntree's 1950 Survey'. *Bulletin of Economic Research* 33.

Asa Briggs. 1961. *Social Thought and Social Action: A Study of the Work of Seebohm Rowntree, 1871–1954.* London: Longmans, Green Rowntree, (Benjamin) Seebohm'. *The Dictionary of National Biography.*

Ernest P. Hennock. 1991. 'Concepts of Poverty in the British Social Surveys from Charles Booth to Arthur Bowley'. In Martin Bulmer, K. Bales and K. Kish Sklar, eds. *The Social Survey in Historical Perspective.* Cambridge: Cambridge University Press.

Stephen Jenkins and Alan Maynard. 1981. 'The Rowntree Surveys: Poverty in York since 1899'. In C. Feinstein, ed. *York 1831–1981: 150 Years of Scientific Endeavour and Social Change.* York: Ebor Press/The British Association for the Advancement of Science.

John H. Veit-Wilson. 1986. 'Paradigms of Poverty: A Rehabilitation of B. S. Rowntree'. *Journal of Social Policy* 15.

LUCINDA PLATT

FERDINAND DE SAUSSURE

Ferdinand de Saussure, born in 1857, is best remembered for his *Course in General Linguistics*, published shortly after his death in 1913. The book was based on notes of a lecture course delivered at the University of Geneva from 1907 to 1911. Although Saussure himself left few textual traces of the course, the book was produced from the notes gathered together by students who attended the lectures. Equally, because the course varied considerably on the three occasions it was delivered, the book cannot be said to represent Saussure's considered theory of language. Nonetheless, the *Course in General Linguistics* is a revolutionary work that lays claim not only to furnishing linguistics with an authentic object of analysis, but also to developing a distinctively structuralist approach to the human and social sciences. The work of structuralists and poststructuralists such as Claude Lévi-Strauss, Jacques Lacan, Roland Barthes, Louis Althusser, Jacques Derrida and Ernesto Laclau is unthinkable without Saussure's seminal contribution.

Saussure's theory of language introduces four basic conceptual oppositions. First, he privileged the *synchronic* over the *diachronic* study of language, the former consisting of a system of related terms without reference to time, while the latter explores the evolutionary development of language. This does not mean, however, that Saussure ignores the transformation of language, as it is only if language is viewed as a complete system 'frozen in time' that linguistic change can be accounted for at all. Without the synchronic perspective, there

139

would be no means for charting deviations from the norm. Second, Saussure asserts that 'language is a system of signs expressing ideas' – a *langue* – that consists of the linguistic rules that are presupposed if people are to communicate meaningfully. Importantly, *langue* is rigorously contrasted with 'speech' or *parole*, where the latter refers to individual acts of speaking. Saussure thus contrasts both the social and individual aspects of language, and demarcates what he regards as the essential from the merely contingent and accidental. In other words, each individual use of language (each 'speech-event') is only possible if speakers and writers share an underlying system of language.

The third basic conceptual opposition arises from the basic unit of language for Saussure: the linguistic sign. Signs unite a sound–image (signifier) and a concept (signified). Thus the sign *dog* consists of a signifier that sounds like *d-o-g* (and appears in the written form as *dog*) and the concept of a 'dog', which the signifier designates. A key principle of Saussure's theory concerns the 'arbitrary nature of the sign', by which he means that there is no natural relationship between signifier and signified. In other words, there is no necessary reason why the sign *dog* is associated with the concept of a 'dog': it is simply a function and convention of the language we use. This does not mean that language simply names or denotes objects in the world, as this nominalist conception of language would assume that language simply consists of words that refer to objects in the world. Such a view implies a fixed, though ultimately arbitrary, connection between words as names, the concepts they represent and the objects they stand for in the world. For Saussure, however, meaning and signification are entirely immanent to language itself. Even signifieds do not pre-date words, but depend on language systems for their meaning. Given this, Saussure claims that the words in languages – or rather the rules of language – articulate their own sets of concepts and objects, rather than serving as labels for pre-given objects. Language is 'a system of interdependent terms in which the value of each term results solely from the simultaneous presence of the others'. This *relational* and *differential* conception of language means that the term 'mother' derives its meaning not by virtue of its reference to a type of object, but because it is different from 'father', 'grandmother', 'daughter' and other related terms.

To explain the paradox that words stand for ideas but have also to be related to other words in order to acquire their meaning, Saussure introduced the concept of *linguistic value*. He compares language to a game of chess, arguing that a certain piece in chess, say the knight, has no significance and meaning outside the context of the game: it is only within the game that 'it becomes a real, concrete element . . . endowed with value'. Moreover, the particular material character-istics of the piece, whether it be plastic or wooden, or whether it resembles a man on a horse or not, do not matter. Its value and function are simply determined by the rules of chess and the formal relations it has with the other pieces in the game. Linguistic value is similarly shaped. On the one hand, a word represents an idea but, on the other hand, a word must be contrasted to other words that stand in opposition to it. This means that the value of a word is not determined merely by the idea that it represents, but by the contrasts inherent in the system of elements that constitute language (*langue*).

These reflections culminate in Saussure's theoretical principle that in language there are only 'differences without positive terms'. Here, language should not be seen as having ideas or sounds that exist prior to the linguistic system, 'but only conceptual and phonic differences that have issued from the system. The idea or phonic substance that a sign contains is of less importance than the other signs that surround it'. This stress on language as a pure system of differences, however, is immediately qualified, as Saussure argued that it holds only if the signifier and signified are considered separately. When united into the sign it *is* possible to speak of a positive entity functioning within a system of values:

> When we compare signs – positive terms – with each other, we can no longer speak of difference; the expression would not be fitting, for it applies only to the comparing of two sound-images, e.g. *father* and *mother*, or two ideas, e.g. the idea 'father' and the idea 'mother'; two signs, each having a signified and signifier, are not different but only distinct. The entire mechanism of language . . . is based on oppositions of this kind and on the phonic and conceptual differences they imply.

In sum, Saussure's purely formal and relational theory of language claims that the *identity* of any element is a product of the *differences* and *oppositions* established by the underlying structures of the lin-guistic system.

According to Saussure, therefore, languages comprise systems of differences and relationships, in which the differences between sig-nifiers and signifieds produce linguistic identities, and the relation-ships between signs combine to form sequences of words, such as phrases and sentences. In this regard, Saussure introduces his fourth and final conceptual division between the *syntagmatic* and *associative* 'orders of values' in language. These two orders capture the way words may be combined into linear sequences (phrases and sentences), or the way absent words may be substituted for those present in a linguistic sequence. In the sentence 'The cat sat on the mat', each of the terms acquires its meaning in relation to what precedes and follows it. This is the syntagmatic ordering of language. However, others can substitute for each of these terms. 'Cat' can be replaced with 'rat', 'bat' or 'gnat'. Similarly, 'mat' could be replaced with 'carpet', 'table' or 'floor'. This is what Saussure calls the associative ordering of language and it is derived from the way in which signs are connected with one another in the memory.

These principles of associative and syntagmatic ordering are manifest at all levels of language, ranging from the combination and association of different phonemes into words to the ordering of words into sentences and discourse. Thus Saussure analyses relations *within* and *between* different levels of language while still employing the same basic principles. When allied to Saussure's advocacy of semiology, in which it would be 'possible to conceive of a science *which studies the role of signs as part of social life*', this enabled the development of a unique structuralist methodology in the social sciences. It is evident in the work of Claude Lévi-Strauss, who argues that social relations in 'primitive' societies could be treated *as if* they were linguistic structures or symbolic orders, as well as in Roland Barthes' treatment of phenomena as diverse as social formations, political ideologies, myths, family relationships, texts and wrestling matches as systems of related elements. Saussure's influence is also central for Jacques Lacan's structuralist interpretation of Freud, though Lacan emphasized the continuous 'sliding of the signified under the signifier', thus problematizing the fixity of meaning and paving the way for a poststructuralist approach to social relations. The latter has been taken up by theorists such as Jacques Derrida, Julia Kristeva, Ernesto Laclau and Slavoj Žižek.

See also: Emile Durkheim.

See also in *Fifty Key Sociologists: The Contemporary Theorists*: Louis Althusser, Roland Barthes, Claude Lévi-Strauss.

Major works

Course in General Linguistics. 1916. Originally lectures of 1907–11. London: Fontana, 1974.

Further reading

Jonathan Culler. 1976. *Saussure*. London: Fontana.
Roy Harris. 1988. *Language, Saussure and Wittgenstein: How to Play Games with Words*. London: Routledge.
David Howarth. 2000. *Discourse*. Buckingham: Open University.

DAVID HOWARTH

MAX SCHELER

Max Scheler was a great sociologist in spite of himself. His love was philosophy, but his philosophical inquiry led him to the recognition that the actual state of the knowledge he sought was subject to social causation, and that its future depended on the ability to limit and to guide the effects of this confrontation between the ideal truths he treasured and the real factors he could not disregard. The creativity of his sociological imagination was so vigorous that his efforts attracted students and generated a research programme in the sociology of culture – and especially the sociology of knowledge – that was by no means constrained within the limits of the philosophical context he postulated. While Scheler's philosophical project doubtless remains interesting, his sociological legacy has been historically abstracted from it without serious loss of substance.

Max Scheler was born in Munich in 1874 and he died in 1928, at the age of fifty-four, in Frankfurt am Main. His life and career were unconventional for an academic and very much influenced by the rapid changes through which he lived. Born of a Lutheran father and orthodox Jewish mother, he converted to Catholicism as an adolescent, but he never ended his unorthodox spiritual search and occasionally offended clerical authorities. He studied medicine at Munich and Berlin, where he also attended classes in philosophy and sociology by Wilhelm Dilthey and **Georg Simmel**. In keeping with the freedom of movement granted German students, he went to Jena for his doctoral degree, working under the philosophical writer Rudolf Eucken, who received the Nobel Prize for Literature in 1908. Scheler returned to Munich, where he completed the advanced studies that entitled him to conduct classes and seminars to fee-paying students. During this time, partly as teacher but later as an independent scholar living on his family income, Scheler immersed himself in the philosophical work of Edmund Husserl, the leader of the phenomenological school. He was active as publicist during the First World

War, eagerly supporting the German cause while inveighing against the nationalist slogans of most of his fellow propagandists.

In 1919, Scheler was called to a chair in philosophy and sociology at the new municipal university of Cologne. The mayor of Cologne, Konrad Adenauer, later the first chancellor of the Federal Republic of Germany, had led the conversion of the local commercial academy into a municipal university and fostered the creation of an institute for the scientific study of what was called the 'social question', to be staffed by a tripartite allocation among the primary interests of the three 'Weimar' parties, social policy for his own Catholic Centre Party, economic policy for the Liberals, and social legislation for the Social Democrats. In practice, the institute was shaped rather by two key appointments: the market-oriented economist and formal sociologist Leopold von Wiese, promoted by the Liberals; and the moral philosopher Scheler, as candidate of the Catholics. In this setting, Scheler attracted not a few students whose primary interests were in social research rather than in the philosophical issues uppermost in Scheler's mind.

These institutional details are of interest because they help to explain the autonomous development of Scheler's sociological insights out of his interaction with his students, just as they may also suggest some experiential grounds for the importance of just such institutional issues in Scheler's sociology of knowledge. Scheler's well-received public lecture on 'Science and Social Structure' at the 1924 annual meeting of German sociologists, as well as the ensuing publications by himself and a number of his students, led to his selection as successor to the sociologist Franz Oppenheimer at Frankfurt in 1928. Scheler died before he could assume the position and was replaced, in 1930, by **Karl Mannheim**, who also inherited his book series devoted to the interface between sociology and philosophy and who made *Ideology and Utopia* the first book in the series. Yet it would be misleading to treat the two best-known originators of the sociology of knowledge as representing steps in a line of succession. Like other classical masters, Scheler is poorly understood as a mere precursor.

For reasons arising out of his philosophical attempts to ground and establish truths relating to human salvation and the ultimate meanings and values of things, Scheler devoted great efforts to understanding the structures, sources and dynamics of those forms of knowledge, notably science, that threatened to deprive the more highly valued forms of their necessary social space and energies. It was never his view that the knowledge celebrated by positivism was without sufficient grounds or false: the question was about its threatened rise to a monopoly position, which he took to be a function of sociological developments. The issue is epitomized in Scheler's rejection of **Comte**'s positivist thesis of a universal historical sequence of the three stages of religion, metaphysics and science. All three forms of knowledge, according to Scheler, are in principle available to humankind at all times. If one predominates, it is due to social circumstances which can be understood and in some measure counteracted: the predominance cannot be taken as the valid judgement of a historical tribunal or natural law. An indication of the richly varied sociological research to which this philosophical problem definition took Scheler and his students is provided by the density of microsociological reference in the partial characterization of the discipline offered by Scheler in *Die Wissensformen und die Gesellschaft* (1926):

> The sociology of knowledge ... must trace the laws and rhythms of the downward flow of knowledge from the top of society (i.e., the intellectual elites) and determine the manner of its distribution over the various groups and strata ... as well as the ways in which this distribution is organized by society – partly by institutions for the dissemination of knowledge such as schools and newspapers, and partly by barriers to it, such as mysteries, indexes, censorship, and the prohibition of certain kinds of knowledge for some castes, estates, or classes.

Illustrative in another respect is Scheler's hope that a regulative policy to counter a spiritually fatal domination of humankind by the technological drive behind science would centre on a transnational European university exempt from commercial or national-political constraints.

See also: Gyorgy Lukács, Karl Mannheim.

Major works

The Nature of Sympathy. 1913. London: Routledge & Kegan Paul, 1970.
Ressentiment. 1915. New York: The Free Press, 1961.
Problems of a Sociology of Knowledge. 1926. London: Routledge & Kegan Paul, 1980.

The complete German editions of Scheler's sociology and philosophy can be found in *Gesammelte Werke*, 15 vols. Bonn: Bouvier Verlag, 1985.

Further reading

Manfred Frings. 1997. *The Mind of Max Scheler*, Milwaukee, WI: Marquette.
Werner Stark. 1955. *The Sociology of Knowledge*. London: Routledge & Kegan Paul.
John R. Staude. 1967. *Max Scheler*. New York: The Free Press.

VOLKER MEJA AND DAVID KETTLER

ALFRED SCHUTZ

The circumstances under which Schutz became an influential figure in contemporary sociology and social philosophy were rather unusual. Trained in law and economics, circumstances forced him to choose a career in banking rather than in academic scholarship. Even when he began teaching part time, after his emigration to the USA, he did so at an institution which played no role in mainstream American academic life. At the time of his death he was not well known beyond a limited group of intimate intellectual friends and students.

Alfred Schutz was born in Vienna on 13 April 1899 of Jewish parentage, though his father had died before his birth. His family name was Schütz, but after his emigration to the United States of America he briefly spelled his name Schuetz before eventually settling on Schutz (in publications that appear in German the original spelling continues to be used). His mother married her late husband's brother, a bank executive, and Alfred was brought up as his son. Schutz attended a Viennese secondary school with a classical curriculum, but his schooling ended early because of the First World War. During the war he graduated a year early, at the age of seventeen and with a special examination, in order to join the Austro-Hungarian army, in which he served as a junior artillery officer in battles on the Piave river in northern Italy. He was eighteen when the Empire collapsed. Being on furlough in Vienna at the time, he avoided being taken prisoner of war and was soon able to begin his studies.

In 1921, Schutz received his LLD from the University of Vienna. His teachers included the legal theorist Hans Kelsen, a foremost exponent of legal positivism, and the economic theorist Ludwig von Mises, the most prominent third-generation representative of the Austrian school of marginal utility theory and whose conception of economics as a science of individual human action became one of the sources of rational choice theory.

As a student, Schutz joined a circle discussing economics and the philosophy of science, another devoted to literature and still another to music, and he continued to participate in these after entering business life. An older student, the mathematician and philosopher Felix Kaufmann, became his friend and formed a link to the well-known Viennese philosophical circle that included Rudolf Carnap. Schutz also formed friendships with several members of a circle of von Mises' students that, among others, included Friedrich von Hayek and Oscar Morgenstern. The political philosopher Eric Voegelin, the economist Fritz Machlup (later director of the Princeton International Finance Section) and the lawyer and musicologist Emanuel Winternitz (who in later years became curator of the musical instruments collection at the Metropolitan Museum of Art in New York City) became life-long friends. These friendships were based on intense intellectual companionship and critical discussion of numerous topics. The friends saw each other less frequently after emigration to various places in the USA, but they continued their discussions and commented on one another's publications and plans by correspondence.

During his student days in Vienna, Schutz began an intensive study of **Max Weber**'s sociology. He searched for a solution to the problems which had been left unanswered when Weber rested his 'interpretive' sociology upon an analysis of the meaning which actors on the social scene associate with their actions. Study of Henri Bergson and of Edmund Husserl helped Schutz in analysing the temporal structures of consciousness (of retention and protention, memory and planning) as elementary conditions for the constitution of meaning in subjective experience and in social interaction. The result of his efforts was a book, *Der sinnhafte Aufbau der sozialen Welt* (The meaningful construction or structure of the social world), a title which stands in programmatic opposition to Rudolf Carnap's *The Logical Structure* (or Construction) *of the World*. Schutz's book appeared in Vienna in 1932, when Hitler was about to assume power in Germany and when Austria, six years before its annexation by Germany, was ruled by a right-wing clerical government. It went almost unnoticed at the time. Its importance was discovered only slowly after an American translation was published in 1967 and when it could be seen that it foreshadowed his groundbreaking later analyses of the structures of the life-world.

In the 1930s, legal and banking matters took Schutz often to Paris. There he met Aron Gurwitsch, a scholar with a physical science background who became one of the foremost phenomenologists.

Their friendship, too, continued in the USA. Another friend of the Vienna period was the Japanese Tomoo Otaka. This may partly explain the strong interest in Schutz in Japanese sociology. It led to the establishment of a Schutz Archive at Waseda University in Tokyo, modelled on the Social Science Archives at the University of Constance in Germany. The latter contains important Schutz materials along with materials from Albert Salomon and Carl Mayer, colleagues of Schutz at the University in Exile, as well as copies of the G. H. Mead and Paul Lazarsfeld archives.

After many complications, some fraught with considerable danger, Schutz and his family succeeded in emigrating in 1939 and settled in New York City, where Schutz could continue in his profession. (For details of his emigration and his successful though not always happy career, see the comprehensive biography by Michael Barber.) In America, he was able to help many European refugees from Nazism. In 1943 he also began teaching part time at the University in Exile, an institution founded by Alvin Johnson to receive a large number of important European economists, political scientists, psychologists and philosophers who were fleeing from Nazism and Fascism. It became the Graduate Faculty of Political and Social Science of the New School for Social Research, but it did not develop into a major American university, in spite of the excellence and renown of the faculty. The influence which its members had on American and international psychology, economics, philosophy and sociology was primarily through their publications and only later through the work of their students.

Although Schutz had published several important articles in social theory, their influence was not immediately felt. Neither his meeting and correspondence with Talcott Parsons, whose theory of action he had constructively criticized, nor his intensive study of the American pragmatist philosophy of Charles Peirce, William James, John Dewey and **George Herbert Mead**, which had at least a surface effect on his writings, led to an entry into the mainstream of American sociology. At the time of his death in 1959, only a handful of social scientists in America and in Europe would have considered him a major figure in modern sociology. However, the last decades of the twentieth century brought a heightened appreciation of Schutz's work. It became clear that Schutz had initiated changes in certain basic assumptions in social theory and in social philosophy.

Max Weber's neo-Kantian premises about the relation between the social world and social science, about 'ideal-types' and reality, did not provide a satisfactory explanation of how 'meaning' determines social action. Schutz saw early that a theory of relevance was required in order to show how natural and social objects acquire typical meanings in the differing temporal conditions of subjective experience and social interaction, how such typical meanings form social stocks of knowledge and how these provide the framework within which subjective experience and social interaction become meaningful to the individual. He developed a theory of topical, interpretive and motivational relevance, planning to integrate it into a comprehensive description of the universal structures of the human life-world. That, in turn, was to provide a firm foundation for comparative analyses of historical social realities. Schutz was certain that only such a description of the human constitution of social reality could resolve the basic methodological question of all the social sciences: what are they about? What is their subject matter?

Schutz was forty when he arrived in America. He had twenty more years to live. After his first book he published more than thirty essays and articles, most of them in English. The topics with which he dealt include language, signs and symbols, typification, intersubjectivity, 'multiple realities', the relation between common sense and scientific analyses of human action and the methodology of the social sciences. Some of them contain critical discussions of William James, Edmund Husserl, **Max Scheler**, and Jean-Paul Sartre. Despite the early uncertainties of this final period in his life, the demands of profession and family, his continued devotion to music, his teaching at the Graduate Faculty of the New School since 1943 and, eventually, his ill health, these essays, scattered through many journals, show that he continued his intensive investigation into the foundations of social science. (He drafted an incomplete book during the 1950s and his *Collected Papers*, covering a similar area, were published posthumously.)

The basic pattern of Schutz's thought was established in the *Sinnhafter Aufbau*. The formulation of the theory of relevance and the account of the links between everyday life and the levels of reality transcending it, the analysis of the objectivating activities of the human mind, of the role of signs and symbols in bridging the gaps between various levels of reality and their function in intersubjective communication, addressed problems raised and partly dealt with in that book. In addition to the ongoing discussion with his old friends, especially with Eric Voegelin, Fritz Machlup and Aron Gurwitsch, these analyses were also enriched by his encounter with American pragmatism. Discussions with his students, especially Maurice Natanson (the editor of the memorial volume for Alfred Schutz), and other theorists, among them Harold Garfinkel, were important in helping him formulate his thought for different audiences.

Schutz planned to write a second book in which the results of these further analyses would complete what he had begun a quarter of a century earlier. The project was sketched out, the place that earlier publications and unpublished manuscripts were to occupy in the final work was carefully laid out, the problems that remained were identified. Illness prevented Schutz from carrying out the project and Schutz's widow Ilse asked Thomas Luckmann, a former student of Schutz, then professor at the Graduate Faculty of the New School, to step in. Luckmann accepted and wrote the two volumes of *The Structures of the Life-World* in German, the language in which Schutz had planned to write it.

Unsurprisingly, the profound influence of Schutz is to be seen in *The Social Construction of Reality*, written by Peter Berger, another student of Schutz, and Thomas Luckmann, as well as in the latter's theory and investigation of communicative genres and, in a rather different way, in Garfinkel's ethnomethodology and its offshoot, conversation analysis. However, it is probably too early to trace the less obvious importance of Schutz's work in the writings of others, not only in sociology but also in other social sciences and in the humanities.

There is much Schutz scholarship, an early impetus for which was provided by Schutz's widow, who was instrumental in the posthumous publication of the *Collected Papers* and the translation into many languages of Schutz's publications. After Ilse Schutz's death, Schutz's daughter Evelyn Schutz Lang continued with these activities. The University of Constance Social Science Archives and the Schutz Archives at Waseda University provide opportunities for research in Schutz's writings. A third archive exists in the Beinecke Library at Yale University in New Haven, Connecticut. A complete edition of his published and unpublished writings is underway at the University Publishers in Constance.

See also: George Herbert Mead, Max Scheler, Max Weber.

See also in *Fifty Key Sociologists: The Contemporary Theorists*: Harold Garfinkel.

Major works

Life Forms and Meaning Structure. Written 1924–7. London: Routledge & Kegan Paul, 1972.

The Phenomenology of the Social World. 1932. Evanston, IL: Northwestern University Press, 1967.

Reflections on the Problem of Relevance. Written 1947–59. Ed. Richard Zaner. New Haven, CT, and London: Yale University Press, 1970.

Collected Papers I, The Problem of Social Reality. 1962. Ed. Maurice Natanson. The Hague: Martinus Nijhoff, 1962.

Collected Papers II, Studies in Social Theory. 1964. Ed. A. Brodersen. The Hague: Martinus Nijhoff, 1964.

Collected Papers III, Studies in Phenomenological Philosophy. 1966. Ed. Ilse Schutz. The Hague: Martinus Nijhoff, 1966.

Collected Papers IV. 1996. Ed. Helmut Wagner and George Psathas, with F. Kersten. Dordrecht: Kluwer Academic Publishers, 1996.

Structures of the Life-World, Volumes 1 and 2. 1974 and 1989. With Thomas Luckmann. Evanston, IL: Northwestern University Press.

Further reading

Michael Barber. 2004. *The Participating Citizen: A Biography of Alfred Schutz.* Albany, NY: State University of New York Press.

Peter Berger and Thomas Luckmann. 1966. *The Social Construction of Reality.* Harmondsworth: Allen Lane, 1971.

Maurice Natanson, ed. 1970. *Phenomenology and Social Reality: Essays in Memory of Alfred Schutz.* The Hague: Martinus Nijhof.

Helmut Wagner. 1983. *Alfred Schutz: An Intellectual Biography.* Chicago: University of Chicago Press.

THOMAS LUCKMANN

GEORG SIMMEL

'The most brilliant man in Europe', wrote Santayana to William James; many of Europe's finest intellectuals thought likewise; and the founding generation of American sociologists swore by him. An urbane Berliner – 'The Metropolis and Mental Life' essay of 1903 remains a genial essay on metropolitan culture – Georg Simmel came to symbolize intellectual modernity in a milieu stifled by Wilhelmian pomp, Prussian bureaucracy and professorial rigidities, yet pulsating with intellectual and political counter-currents. Through prolific writings, virtuoso lecturing and cultivated salons hosted with his wife Gertrud, herself an accomplished philosophical writer, Simmel magnetized Berlin's intellectual elite in the two decades preceding the First World War.

Simmel was born in 1858 and his parents stemmed from the Jewish community of Wroclaw (Breslau). Before they married and moved to

Berlin his mother converted to Protestantism; his father, while travelling in Paris on business, converted to Catholicism. Georg,
youngest of seven offspring, was baptized in his mother's faith. Often
described as Jewish in intellectual style and physical mannerisms,
Simmel expressed little affinity with his ancestral traditions, though
he once told the Jewish philosopher Martin Buber, 'We really are a
remarkable people.'

Despite Simmel's Protestant affiliation, expressed anti-Semitism
helped keep him from a regular academic post for most of his career.
So did his imputed 'aestheticism' and a breadth of interests that
bespoke dilettantism to Germany's academic establishment. To be
sure, Simmel had wide-ranging aesthetic as well as philosophic
interests (he studied piano and violin, wrote on music, befriended
leading artists, including the poet Rainer Maria Rilke and French
sculptor Auguste Rodin, and wrote about the theatre, Michelangelo
and Rembrandt). Nonetheless, he achieved conventional academic
credentials at the University of Berlin under such luminaries as
Mommsen, Treitschke, Droysen, Grimm, Lazarus and Bastian, and
established himself as a credible philosopher with a dissertation on
Kant in 1881. Specialists came to credit him with seminal contributions in a number of fields, including epistemology, ethics, aesthetics,
jurisprudence and metaphysics, as well as sociology. In Germany
Simmel was known chiefly as a neo-Kantian, a philosopher of culture
or a philosopher of life, and as such his influence on major German
thinkers of the twentieth century – including Ernst Cassirer, Edmund
Husserl, **Max Weber**, **Max Scheler**, Martin Heidegger, **Alfred
Schutz**, Albert Schweitzer, Ernst Bloch, **Georg Lukács**, Siegfried
Kracauer and Max Horkheimer – has been amply documented.

Outside Germany, Simmel was and is known chiefly for his work
as a seminal sociologist, indeed one of the pantheon of founding
fathers of modern sociology along with **Emile Durkheim** and Max
Weber. His sociological writings were appropriated primarily in the
United States, through a lineage of aficionados associated principally
with the Universities of Chicago and Columbia: **Albion Small**,
Robert E. Park, Louis Wirth, Everett Hughes, Robert Merton and
Lewis Coser. (He would have been known even better had Talcott
Parsons not deliberately excluded him from his canon of classical
founders.) These writings consisted mainly of two contrasting streams
of thought, one evolutionary, the other analytic. The evolutionary
approach appeared in his first major work on social differentiation, to
date only partially translated. This work grew from an early interest
in Darwin and **Spencer** and depicts developmental patterns over

time as diverse modes of individuation: from collective responsibility to individual liability; from small homogeneous groups to large internally diversified groups; from common culture to individualized thinking; and from compulsory social ties based on kinship and neighbourhood to voluntary and individuated associations.

It was Simmel's analytic work that proved most consequential for sociology. (Parsons did credit Simmel for being the first to have proposed that sociology be an independent analytic science.) Developed over about a dozen years starting in the mid-1890s, this work started with a programmatic essay, 'The Problem of Sociology', which would orient most of his sociological investigations. It enunciated the principle that sociology should distinctively analyse the diverse forms of social interaction, forms such as exchange, conflict, super- and subordination, secrecy and honour. For this view of the field he is often labelled a 'formal sociologist'. Comfortable with the ambiguity of his core concept of social forms, subsequent analysis has shown the concept to be a rough rubric for diverse phenomena known more familiarly as social relations, social processes, social types, collectivities, dynamic patterns and structural variables. This work culminated with a masterly collection of 1908, published as *Soziologie* and subtitled 'essays on the forms of association'. Each of these essays explored the nature, properties and variants of selected patterns of social interaction. Simmel identified these patterns, or 'forms', through what has been called an eidetic methodology, the intuitive grasp for formal essences. Most of the essays have stimulated research traditions in such areas as social distance, social conflict, secrecy and secret societies, strangers, interaction in small groups and urbanism. Especially well known are the discussions of the ways social conflict produces group cohesion; the analysis of the effect of group size on modes of interaction; and the depiction of social types like 'the stranger', 'the poor', 'the mediator' and 'the renegade'. Its most striking features include the attempt to apply the Kantian notion of *a priori* categories to the domain of social interaction and the direction of sociological attention to the phenomenology of everyday interaction. Simmel's delineation of what persons experience in sociable gatherings, when exchanging letters or in relationships coloured by jealousy or gratitude has helped inspire scholars to create what became known as the 'sociology of everyday life'.

Simmel's most profound work, *The Philosophy of Money*, first published in 1900 but translated into English only in 1978, conjoins an abstract analytic focus (exchange, social types) with a quasi-evolutionary account of the effects of a monetary economy on modern society. It begins with a tightly argued formulation of a 'relativistic' metaphysics and epistemology, and goes on to develop a speculative interpretation of the effects of a money economy on modern culture. These effects include an accentuation of the human capacity for rational calculation and an enormous expansion of the domain of human freedom, and at the same time a pervasive moral deracination and the manufacture of cultural products which are alienated from the absorptive capacities of human consumers.

A dominant feature of all Simmel's writings – evolutionary, abstract and philosophical – is a pronounced affinity for dualistic constructions. This feature of Simmel's thought has been associated with his affinity for Spinoza and a deep acquaintance with legal reasoning and its heavy use of logical dualities. Virtually every form he identified appeared as a combination of opposites: the stranger as a combination of nearness and remoteness; adornment as a combination of self-interest and altruism; fashion as a fusion of wishes for individuation and assimilation; conflict as a mixture of associative and antagonistic impulses; domination as a blend of compulsion and freedom; secrecy as a combination of disclosure and concealment. Diachronic patterns were envisioned as involving an accentuation of opposed tendencies: public matters becoming more public and private matters more private; social circles becoming more inclusive, while individuals become more differentiated; honorific customs becoming more formalized as law and yet more personalized as morality; values becoming more objectified, while individuals gain more room for expressing subjectivity. Perhaps Simmel's most profound insight concerns the essence of modernity – that it consists not of this or that dominant tendency, but in an amplification of opposed tendencies.

Simmel's impact has sprung up at diverse times and unexpected venues. His ideas have fertilized the work of Robert Park on crowds versus publics, the race relations cycle and social marginality; Karen Horney on psychoanalytic feminism; Louis Wirth on urbanism; Everett Hughes on professions; Erving Goffman on deference and demeanour; Emory Bogardus and others on social distance; J. L. Moreno on sociometry; Stanford Lyman on secret societies; David Riesman on sociability; Lewis Coser on social conflict; Theodore Mills on the social psychology of small groups; Theodore Caplow on coalitions in triads; Alvin Gouldner and Peter Blau on exchange; Edward Laumann and Ron Breiger on network theory; Charles Kadushin on social circles; and Robert Merton on reference groups. On the other hand, no crisply formulated hypotheses do justice to the richness of his texts, every page of which contains numerous insights, stunning historical allusions and stimuli for further thought.

In later years, Simmel's interest focused on problems of modern culture and then, under the impact of Bergson but with a renewed interest in Goethe, Schopenhauer and Nietzsche as well, shifted to articulating a philosophy of life. In *View of Life: Four Metaphysical Chapters*, he argued that an essential characteristic of human life is the propensity to create novel forms and then to attack those forms as obstructions to the life process; and that death should be regarded not as the termination of life but as an integral dimension of life itself.

Despite this record of achievement and the constant support of leading German academics like Weber, Rickert, and Husserl, Simmel was consistently denied a regular appointment in the German university system; only in 1914, four years before his death in 1918, did a professorship materialize at the University of Strasbourg, where he taught for a semester until war closed down the lecture halls. The war fired his German nationalism: Simmel lapsed into uncharacteristic sentimentality about its energizing potential and publicly abetted the German war effort. Yet the civilized philosopher in him was not wholly subdued. In the *Berliner Tageblatt* of 7 March 1915 he dared to publish a luminous article on 'The Idea of Europe', in which he scorned 'the blindness and criminal frivolity of a handful of Europeans' for sparking off a war which entailed 'the suicidal destruction of existing European values' and tried to discern some way in which the idea of Europe might yet survive as a 'locus of spiritual values which the contemporary cultured man reveres'.

See also: Gyorgy Lukács, Ferdinand Tönnies, Max Weber.

See also in *Fifty Key Sociologists: The Contemporary Theorists*: Erving Goffman, Alvin W. Gouldner, Robert Merton.

Major works

Über soziale Differenzierung. 1890. Leipzig: Duncker und Humblot.
The Problems of the Philosophy of History. 1905. Trans. of the 2nd edn. New York: Free Press, 1977.
Philosophy of Money. 1907. London: Routledge & Kegan Paul, 1978.
The Sociology of Georg Simmel. 1908. New York: Free Press, 1950.
Conflict and the Web of Group Affiliations. 1908. Glencoe, IL: Free Press, 1955.
Rembrandt: An Essay in the Philosophy of Art. 1916. London: Routledge, 2005.
Georg Simmel: On Women, Sexuality and Love. (Essays of 1890–1918.) New Haven, CT: Yale University Press, 1984.

Simmel on Culture. (Essays of 1892–1918.) London: Sage, 1997.
Essays on Religion. (Essays of 1898–1918.) New Haven, CT: Yale University Press, 1997.
Essays on Interpretation in Social Science. (Essays of 1904–18.) Totowa, NJ: Rowman and Littlefield, 1980.
On Individuality and Social Forms. (Essays and extracts of 1907–18.) Chicago, IL: University of Chicago Press, 1971.

Further reading

David Frisby, ed. 1994. *Georg Simmel: Critical Assessments*. 3 vols. New York: Routledge.
Gary Backhaus. 1998. 'Simmel as an Eidetic Social Scientist'. *Sociological Theory* 16: 3.
Donald N. Levine, Ellwood B. Carter and Eleanor Miller Gorman. 1976. 'Simmel's Influence on American Sociology', Parts I and II. *American Journal of Sociology* 81: 4 and 5.
Donald N. Levine. 1985. *The Flight from Ambiguity: Essays in Social and Cultural Theory*. Chicago, IL: University of Chicago Press: chs 5, 6 and 9.
Donald N. Levine. 1991. 'Simmel and Parsons Reconsidered'. *American Journal of Sociology* 95(5).
Donald N. Levine. 1997. 'Simmel Reappraised: Old Images, New Scholarship'. In Charles Camic, ed. *Reclaiming the Sociological Classics*. Oxford, Blackwell, 1997.

DONALD N. LEVINE

ALBION SMALL

Albion Small was notable for several reasons. First, he was one of the founders of American sociology. Second, in 1892 he was named chair of the Sociology Department at the University of Chicago, the first officially established sociology department in any university. Third, Small, along with his co-author George E. Vincent, published in 1894 the first textbook of sociology by an American author. Fourth, in 1895 Small was named editor of the *American Journal of Sociology*, sociology's first academic journal. For these reasons, Small played a crucial administrative role as gatekeeper in the early stages of the development of sociology in America.

Albion Woodbury Small was born in 1854, the son of a Baptist minister. When he entered Colby College in Waterville, Maine, in 1872, he followed his father in pursuing a course of divinity training. After graduating in 1876, Small entered the Newton Theological Institution in Massachusetts, where he studied until 1879. His enthusiasm for the ministry waned considerably with his father's improving economic standing and, with his father's blessing, he could afford to pursue secular studies in Germany.

In Germany Small took courses in history and national economy, first at the University of Berlin and then at Leipzig. While at Berlin Small met **Georg Simmel**, who was studying philosophy there, and the two developed an intellectual and social relationship. Small's studies in Germany were cut short, however, in 1881 when he was offered, and accepted, a position at his *alma mater*, Colby College. Small remained at Colby for seven years, primarily teaching courses in history and political science. After a brief sabbatical at Johns Hopkins University in 1888–9, he returned to Colby once again and was elected president of that institution. Small remained in the presidency for three years.

While at Colby Small began to put his interests in sociology to work, both as an administrator who encouraged faculty to offer sociology courses and also occasionally teaching his own sociology courses. The first such sociology course was offered at Colby in 1890. In that same year Frank Blackmar, who had been a fellow student with Small at Johns Hopkins University, offered a sociology course at the University of Kansas. These were the first sociology courses offered at American universities since those offered by **William Sumner** at Yale in 1875 or 1876.

Small believed strongly in the idea that if sociology was to advance as a legitimate scientific discipline, it must get away from grandiose and cosmological social theories. **Comte**, **Spencer** and **Ward** had already done this work for sociology, and it was now time to emphasize specialization, where specialists in more narrow subfields could bring their expertise to bear on pressing issues in sociological theory and research. According to Small, then, the 'era of sociology' had arrived.

Small also believed that American scholars were especially well equipped to subordinate their specialized knowledge to the broader project of developing this burgeoning science of society. Based in large part on the spirit of American pragmatism and the need to complement ideas with empirical data in the service of reform and social restoration, scholars from many walks of life and diverse academic training would be prepared to co-ordinate their specialized knowledge towards this greater goal. According to Small, journals such as the *American Journal of Sociology* would play an essential role in contributing to the ultimate betterment of humanity through science.

In his roles as sociology chair at Chicago and as editor of the *American Journal of Sociology*, Small was predisposed towards the values of efficiency and pragmatic control. Chris Bernert, among others, has argued that Small was at heart a follower of the cameralists, the earliest formulators of administrative efficiency in Europe. Indeed, Small even published in 1909 a study on the subject (*The Cameralists*) which helped him formulate one of the early statements (alongside those of **Emile Durkheim** and Charles Ellwood) of the nature of sociological methodology.

Probably Small's most important work was *General Sociology*, published in 1905. At the time, a handful of prominent sociologists including Georg Simmel, Emile Durkheim, **Gabriel Tarde**, Lester Ward, **Ludwig Gumplowicz**, Franklin Giddings and Gustav Ratzenhofer had propounded general sociological doctrines, but each was deficient as a final strategy for sociological analysis. Rather than rejecting their thought outright, though, Small took from these and other theorists what was most useful for the purposes of fashioning his own programme of general sociology. For example, in his chapter on the individual, Small accepted Lester Ward's idea that desires were the engine of human behaviour while the intellect guided or directed its course (much like a cybernetic system). Rather than relying on Ward's typology of social forces or his overly abstract notion of telesis, however, Small remained at the level of the individual and attempted to work out more concretely the limited set of factors lying behind actual human conduct. Small also changed Ward's terminology, replacing 'desires' with 'interests' or 'sentiments', in the tradition of Adam Smith.

Small identified six basic factors motivating all human conduct. Human beings act for the sake of health, wealth, sociability, knowledge, beauty, rightness or some combination of these. Although this was an intriguing idea, and garnered some attention over the years as a candidate theory in the field of general sociology, it never really caught on. Small died in 1926. For all his attempts at original thought, Small was and still is remembered – rightly or wrongly – more for his role as administrator and gatekeeper for early American sociology, as well as for his occasionally brilliant commentaries on historical trends and predictions for the field of sociology.

See also: Ludwig Gumplowicz, Lester Ward.

Major works

An Introduction to the Study of Society. 1894. With George E. Vincent. New York: American Book Co.

'The Era of Sociology'. 1895. *American Journal of Sociology* 1.

General Sociology. 1905 Chicago: University of Chicago Press.
Adam Smith and Modern Sociology: A Study in the Methodology of the Social Sciences. 1907. Chicago: University of Chicago Press.
The Cameralists. 1909. Chicago: University of Chicago Press.
'Fifty Years of Sociology in the United States 1865–1916'. 1916. *American Journal of Sociology* 21.

Further reading

Chris Bernert. 1982. 'From Cameralism to Sociology with Albion Small'. *Journal of the History of Sociology* 4.
Roscoe Hinckle. 1980. *Founding Theory of American Sociology, 1881–1915.* London: Routledge & Kegan Paul.

JAMES J. CHRISS

WERNER SOMBART

Werner Friedrich Wilhelm Carl Sombart is recognized from his numerous publications over more than fifty years as having made social scientific contributions variously in economics, sociology, political science and law. However, present-day standards in assessing his work would regard his greatest contributions as having been his analyses of the nature of capitalism as an economic system and his concern with understanding all the causes and consequences of capitalism.

Sombart, though not sunk wholly into oblivion, has a precarious posthumous reputation, largely because his own political views changed through his life from an earlier sympathy with Marxism (though not a formal supporter of the Sozial-Demokratische Partei Deutschlands [SPD]), through progressive disenchantment from the left (as is to be seen in the nature of the revisions of successive editions of his books related to this issue), to the point at the end of his life when he became converted to most of the tenets of National Socialism. Still, he was never wholly accepted by this regime, although he himself had enthusiastically endorsed the *Führerprinzip* for having dealt with the chaos of Germany's Weimar years. Sombart's movement towards this position was impelled by his increasingly vituperative rejection of the socialist movement, specifically the Russian and the attempted German Revolutions, but his contemporary defenders do claim that he was sceptical in some of his later writing of National Socialism's biological and race theories.

159

Sombart was born on 19 January 1863 in Ermsleben, Germany, the youngest son of the politician, industrialist and landowner Anton Ludwig Sombart. The family was of Huguenot origin and Sombart's father was a National Liberal member of the Prussian House of Representatives and later the Reichstag, as well as a founder in 1872 of the Verein für Sozialpolitik (Association for Social Policy), to whose proceedings his son later voluminously contributed. From 1882 Sombart studied jurisprudence in the Universities of Pisa and of Berlin, then afterwards in Rome he studied variously law, political science, economics, history and philosophy. From 1888 to 1890 he was company lawyer of the Bremen Chamber of Commerce. Then, by virtue of support from within the Prussian Ministry of Education, Sombart was in 1890 able to secure a post, against the vote of its faculty, as adjunct professor at the University of Breslau (now Wroclaw) till 1906, then as professor at the new Berlin Commercial University, before finally in 1917, with government support but against the wishes of numerous academic staff, being named as full professor of economics at the University of Berlin. He became an emeritus professor in 1931 but continued some teaching activities till 1940. Sombart's earlier reputation as a *Kathedersozialist* ('academic socialist') clearly haunted his progress through his professional career. However, it had been his earlier sympathy for Marxism that had led to his involvement in the Verein. He was co-opted on to its committee in 1892, became its deputy chair in 1930 and chair in 1932. Also, from 1903 he was a co-editor of the highly influential journal *Archiv für Sozialwissenschaft und Sozialpolitik*.

Sombart's writings were eclectic in approach and content. Even in his earliest work he had shown familiarity with – and willingness to use in order to illustrate his arguments – the substantial bodies of statistical material that were increasingly available to social analysts, using data as diverse as on workers' family budgets and railway accident casualties. Among Sombart's writings on numerous topics, those that repay most current interest concern the workers' movement and capitalism, subjects that he had earlier in his theoretical trajectory thought mutually related. His *Socialism and the Social Movement in the Nineteenth Century* had set out this thesis when first published in 1896, moving through to its tenth edition in 1924, titled *Der proletarische Sozialismus ('Marxismus')*, with his denunciation of socialism in the light of the Russian and German revolutionary experiences. He later produced, as the work's final edition, an equally rebarbative *Deutscher Sozialismus* in 1934. His principal work, among many, on capitalism was *Der moderne Kapitalismus*, whose first edition appeared in two volumes in 1902 and whose six-volume revision appeared from 1916 to 1927; this sought to be a history of capitalism in Europe from its beginnings to the present. Still, Sombart was animated by **Max Weber**'s thesis on the relationship between religion and the rise of capitalism and, with this theoretical quest, was to argue instead that particular features of Judaism and of the mindset of the bourgeoisie were specifically conducive to the rise of capitalism – these being themes of his *The Jews and Modern Capitalism* and *The Quintessence of Capitalism* (translated from *Der Bourgeois*). His speculations that social-psychological features of Jews, value systems in Judaism and the laws of Jewish conduct were factors in Jews' role in capitalism were greeted with criticism, even at the time. In his analyses of capitalism Sombart wrote also about luxury and capitalism and about war and capitalism. Displaying his disillusion with the growth of capitalism, his *Die Deutsche Volkswirtschaft im neunzehnten Jahrhundert* was equally a thorough analysis of all aspects of the German economy, from the stock exchange, transport and industry to the nature of social classes; the work went through numerous editions.

Sombart's linguistic affinity was, like that of his contemporary Robert Michels, most associated with Italian; in the light of his time there as a student and his writings on Italian issues, he was early seen in Germany as an Italian expert. His various works were widely translated, but perhaps the most thorough translation coverage was into Italian. However, Sombart was also attuned to English. With Max Weber and others, he had visited the United States in 1904 and produced at the time a major bibliography of work on American capitalism and America's workers' movement. He had been rather less mesmerized than Weber had been with the extrovert features of American capitalism – though concluding, with some ambivalence, that affluence was the principal reason for the failure in America of an indigenous working-class movement on the European model. This argument was set out in his *Why Is There No Socialism in the United States?*, a publication that was little more than a short monograph appearing in 1906. Yet it is perhaps the work of his that remains the most accessible to English-language readers, and it undoubtedly counts as one of the classic writings in the extensive debate about 'American exceptionalism' with regard to the labour movement. Indeed, the issue is sometimes referred to simply as 'the Sombart question', in deference to the title of his monograph.

Sombart's best sociological insights came from his empirical and historical work on capitalism, particularly his suggestions about class-consciousness and his analyses of the class structures of capitalism. His attempts to write explicitly about sociology (for example in his

Soziologie of 1923) are now considered as of little importance among his works, and his 1915 *Händler und Helden* is regarded solely as inspired by a need to be seen as offering intellectual support for the German war effort. His economic and historical work on capitalism is how he most deserves to be remembered, by sociologists as well as economists. Sombart died in Berlin on 18 May 1941.

See also: Max Weber.

Major works

Socialism and the Social Movement in the Nineteenth Century. 1896. English trans. of the 6th edn. London: J. M. Dent, 1909.
Der moderne Kapitalismus. 1902. Berlin: Duncker und Humblot. This appeared in numerous later editions.
Die deutsche Volkswirtschaft im neunzehnten Jahrhundert. 1903. Berlin: G. Bondi, 1921.
Why Is There No Socialism in the United States? 1906. London: Macmillan, 1976.
The Jews and Modern Capitalism. 1911. London: T. Fisher Unwin, 1913.
The Quintessence of Capitalism. 1913. London: T. Fisher Unwin, 1915.
Luxury and Capitalism. 1913. Ann Arbor, MI: University of Michigan Press, 1967.
Händler und Helden: patriotische Besinnungen. 1915. Berlin: Duncker und Humblot.
Soziologie. 1923. Berlin: Pan-Verlag R. Heise.
Der proletarische Sozialismus ('Marxismus'). 1924. Jena: G. Fischer.
*A New Social Philosophy (Deutscher Sozialismus).*1934. Oxford: Oxford University Press, 1937.

Further reading

Friedrich Lenger. 1995. *Werner Sombart, 1863–1941: eine Biographie.* Munich: Verlag C. H. Beck.
Arthur Mitzman. 1973. *Sociology and Estrangement: Three Sociologists of Imperial Germany.* New York: Alfred A. Knopf.
Nico Stehr and Reiner Grundmann, eds. 2001. *Economic Life in the Modern Age.* New Brunswick, NJ: Transaction Publishers.

CHRISTOPHER T. HUSBANDS

PITIRIM SOROKIN

Pitirim Sorokin was one of the most adventurous, outspoken and original practitioners of the sociological craft. His life was not only one of scholarship, but one of boldness, risk-taking and adventure. Sorokin's origins in the Komi people of Russia instilled in him a life-long integralist perspective that took reality to be the synergistic intertwining of empirical, logical and spiritual truths. Life was a unity, and these three dimensions of humanness were not only his personal and sociological foundation and orientation to the world, but also the foundation on which humans constructed their natural cultural, social and historical worlds.

Born in 1889, the young Sorokin grew to early manhood in a Komi society widely known for its high levels of intellectual achievement. He learned to think critically and argue convincingly with the village literati, Orthodox priest and often very exacting and rigorous teachers. It was on this solid foundation that he left his northern homeland to pursue further study in St Petersburg. He first attended night schools to affirm his basic skills and later studied at the Psycho-Neurological Institute under the renowned behaviourists V. M. Bekhterev and Ivan Pavlov. From there he went to the University of St Petersburg. It was also in St Petersburg that Sorokin began a long and dangerous engagement with the movement to overthrow the Czar. By the age of seventeen he finished his basic formal education and, as a neophyte political activist, served his first term in a Czarist prison.

His activism intertwined with his educational aspirations in St. Petersburg and it was there that he earned a PhD in sociology and a master's in criminal law. A combination of devoted involvements in political efforts to overthrow the Czar brought him to the attention of Alexander Kerensky, to whom he later served as vice-president in the first of the post-Czarist governments. When the Bolsheviks overthrew the Kerensky government, Sorokin was imprisoned three times by Vladimir Lenin, and in September 1922 he avoided execution by accepting 'voluntary exile' to Czechoslovakia. There he and his wife Elena began new lives, and Pitirim was free from the constant threats of prison and execution. Shortly following their arrival Pitirim accepted an invitation from two influential American sociologists, Edward C. Hayes and Edward. A. Ross. They expressed their desire and an invitation that he come to the United States and give a series of lectures on the Russian Revolution, among other things. On arriving in America the Sorokins first went to Vassar College as guests of the then president, Henry Noble McCracken, whom Sorokin had met in Prague. It was there that he prepared his lectures, worked on his English and finalized the logistics for his tour.

The tour went well, and Sorokin accepted an offer as an assistant professor of sociology at the University of Minnesota. He now had a stable foundation and proceeded to publish a number of major sociological works: *Leaves from a Russian Diary, The Sociology of Revolution, Social Mobility* and *Contemporary Sociological Theories*. To these were added two works in rural sociology: *Principles of Urban–Rural Sociology*, co-authored with Carle Zimmermann, and the first of three volumes of *A Systematic Source-Book in Rural Sociology* (also with Carle Zimmermann and the addition of Charles J. Galpin). Sorokin established himself as a pioneering, groundbreaking scholar by the originality and breadth of the first three of these works. The then president of Harvard University was at that time looking for a chairman for a planned formalization of a department of sociology. In his quest he read *Contemporary Sociological Theories* and was impressed by the depth and breadth of the book. As a result, Sorokin was invited to Cambridge to give a short series of lectures and seminars and he was later offered a chairmanship and professorship at the university. After a short period of six years, Sorokin had risen from émigré scholar to one of the most prestigious positions in American sociology.

Once at Harvard, Sorokin was intensely motivated to produce a unique and definitive contribution to sociology. In the four volumes of *Social and Cultural Dynamics* he developed a theory of social order and change that spanned more than 2,000 years of human cultural development, and concluded with a set of prophetic insights into the then emerging crisis of the modern era. These volumes embodied a fine-grained, longitudinal analysis of historical changes in major cultural institutions and forms of social organization. The dominant cultural types were sensate, ideational and idealistic. The foundation on which Sorokin differentiated among cultural types was grounded on the epistemic principle by which they reckoned reality. The empirical sensate cultures were based on the truths revealed by the senses, rational idealistic culture on the truths of reason and logic, and the supersensory ideational culture on the truths of faith found in the moral, religious and ethical dimensions of human society. These forms of culture and their principles for reckoning truth were brought together in the Sorokinian concept of integralism and the integral culture. Integralism embodies the fusion of the three defining cultural principles into an integrated system for reckoning obdurate social reality and providing the epistemic basis for the integral cultural form of human social organization.

Unhappily, contemporary sociology was not ready for such a work. Sorokin had been prescient or fortunate by delaying the fourth volume of *Dynamics* until 1941. This provided an opportunity to respond to his critics and also publish a capstone volume. Many, if not most, sociologists would view *Dynamics* and the books that followed – *Crisis of Our Age* and *Man and Society in Calamity* – as marking Sorokin's shift from scientific sociology to an emphasis on social criticism and reconstruction. It was these works, though, that brought Sorokin together with the philanthropist Eli Lilly and resulted in the founding of the Harvard Research Center for Creative Altruism. Sorokin and Lilly agreed that the current political and economic realities led not only to the rise of crime and violence within the US but also to an increase in threats of global violence and clashes between the superpowers. Only a massive alteration of social dynamics would save humanity from these internal threats and the hazards of nuclear destruction. The centre was dedicated to developing altruistic techniques that would minimize violence in social relationships extending from primary groups to nation–states.

These new lines of research and publication moved Sorokin to the margins of the sociological establishment. He might have stayed there had it not been for a casual luncheon conversation between Otis and Beverly Duncan and Albert J. Reiss at the University of Michigan. They observed that after losing the 1952 presidential election of the American Sociological Association (ASA) to **Florian Znaniecki** Sorokin had not received the traditional second nomination. They contacted seven other prominent members of the ASA and, on the suggestion of Robert K. Merton, organized a Committee of Correspondence. There was a tremendous response to the idea and it rippled outward with great success. The results were unequivocal: Sorokin had won by a substantial margin. Thus, when Pitirim A. Sorokin died in 1968 it was with all the recognition of an accomplished and respected scholar.

See also: Auguste Comte.

See also in *Fifty Key Sociologists: The Contemporary Theorists*: George Homans.

Major works

Social Mobility. 1927. New York: Harper and Brothers.
Sociological Theories: Through the First Quarter of the Twentieth Century. 1928. New York: Harper and Row.
Principles of Rural–Urban Sociology. 1929. With Carle C. Zimmerman. New York: Henry Holt and Co.
A Systematic Source-Book in Rural Sociology. 3 vols. 1930. With Carle C. Zimmerman and Charles J. Galpin. Minneapolis, MN: University of Minneapolis Press, 1930, 1931 and 1932.

Social and Cultural Dynamics, vols 1–3. 1937. New York: American Book Co.
Social and Cultural Dynamics, vol. 4. 1941. New York: American Book
 Company.
The Reconstruction of Humanity. 1948. Boston, MA: Beacon Press.
'Integralism Is My Philosophy'. 1957. In Whit Burnett, ed. *This Is My Phi-
 losophy*. New York: Harper Brothers.
Society, Culture, and Personality: Their Structure and Dynamics. 1962. New
 York: Cooper Square Publishing Inc.
A Long Journey: The Autobiography of Pitirim A. Sorokin. 1963. New Haven,
 CT: College and University Press.
'Sociology of My Mental Life'. 1963. In Philip J. Allen, ed. *Pitirim A. Sor-
 okin in Review*. Durham, NC: Duke University Press.
Extracts from Sorokin's work can be found in Barry V. Johnston, ed. 1998.
 Pitirim A. Sorokin: On the Practice of Sociology. Chicago: University of Chi-
 cago Press, Heritage of Sociology Series.

Further reading

Barry V. Johnston. 1986. 'Sorokin and Parsons at Harvard: Institutional
 Conflict and the Rise of a Hegemonic Tradition'. *Journal of the History of
 the Behavioral Sciences* 22.
Barry V. Johnston. 1987. 'Pitirim A. Sorokin and the American Sociological
 Association: The Politics of a Professional Society'. *Journal of the History of
 the Behavioral Sciences* 23.
Barry V. Johnston. 1995. *Pitirim A. Sorokin: An Intellectual Biography*. Lawr-
 ence, KS: University Press of Kansas.
Edward Tiryakian. 1963. *Sociological Theory, Values, and Sociocultural Change:
 Essays in Honor of Pitirim Sorokin*. New York: The Free Press of Glencoe.

BARRY V. JOHNSTON

HERBERT SPENCER

In the middle of the twentieth century, Talcott Parsons echoed the
question raised by a political theorist and asked, 'Who now reads
Spencer?' The thought of Spencer, he held, was so outmoded that it
was of antiquarian interest at best. In his later work, however, Parsons
moved ever closer to the functionalist and evolutionary ideas that had
initially alienated him from Spencer. Since then, numerous system
theorists have rediscovered Spencer's insights and have come to realize that his ideas, though presented in the language of an earlier age,
are still of contemporary relevance.

Herbert Spencer was born into a nonconformist family in Derby in
1820. His father, a schoolteacher, was active in literary and diocesan

circles and encouraged free thinking in his son. Herbert was taught principally by his uncle, who shared his father's outlook, and Spencer developed an early interest in the study of butterflies and moths and an aptitude for mathematics and physics. Through a family connection he obtained employment as a draughtsman and civil engineer, working for the London and Birmingham Railway. He remained in the railway industry until the 1840s, by which time he had discovered Lyell's geological ideas and had become totally convinced of the long evolutionary history of the earth. Seeking a way of pursuing his intellectual interests, he found a job as sub-editor at *The Economist* – a job that allowed him to spend time on his own work (which included inventing the first paper clip). A legacy from his uncle in 1853 eventually gave him the freedom to concentrate on full-time scientific work.

Although he was an individualist in philosophy and politics, his first book was a critique of utilitarianism and individualisms that sought to establish the reality and autonomy of social phenomena. His first attempt at a work of human science, nevertheless, was a study in psychology that engaged with the works of John Mill and William Whewell. He had by this time discovered the positivism of **Auguste Comte**, largely through **Harriet Martineau**'s abridgement, and he admired the encyclopaedic view of science that Comte had taken. Spencer set himself the task of providing a 'synthetic philosophy' of evolution and, in 1857, he mapped out what was to be his life's work. He aimed to produce, in sequence, a set of general principles and then the principles of biology, psychology, sociology and ethics. Though he adjusted his plan in various ways, he did, indeed, achieve his intellectual goal by the time of his death. Though he was not a follower of Comte – and he vociferously underlined the distinctiveness of his own views – Spencer had been attracted to Comte's advocacy of sociology and he took it on himself to develop this in his own way. His organizing principle, the idea of evolution, he had derived from his wide reading in geology and biology, and Spencer was the first person to introduce the word 'evolution' in anything like its contemporary meaning.

His work on the larger synthetic philosophy, into which his earlier psychology was eventually incorporated, was carried out with the help of a number of research assistants who gathered the ethnographic data that he used as raw material for his theoretical work in sociology. These data were published in a series of massive volumes, publication of these continuing after his death under terms set out in his will. The *Principles of Sociology* were complemented by a short summary of scientific method entitled *The Study of Sociology*.

Spencer saw all phenomena as, ultimately, combinations of matter. Planets, mountains, animals, minds and societies are simply different arrangements of the same material. Reality consists of the constant motion of material, with forces of attraction and repulsion building aggregates of matter in varying states of equilibrium and disequilibrium. This continual transformation of matter shows a particular direction, towards increasingly coherent aggregations, and this is what Spencer termed 'evolution'. He saw his task as documenting the evolution of phenomena of all these different kinds.

He identified three levels in the organization of matter: the inorganic, the organic and the super-organic. Physics and chemistry deal with purely inanimate matter, but biology and psychology are concerned with living, organic phenomena. Minds, bodies and the ecological interrelations of bodies all exhibit this organic form of interdependence. Sociology, however, deals with phenomena that go beyond the organic level of organization and involve very different forms of interconnection. The bonds that link organic phenomena are direct physical connections through which causative energies and forces can flow. Super-organic bonds, however, consist of linguistic communication, of interpersonal influence through emotional and intellectual expression.

A society is, for Spencer, a particular kind of organism, though he explicitly rejects the suggestion that it is strictly equivalent to a purely organic entity. It is an organism, or system, insofar as it has properties of its own, irreducible to any properties of its individual parts. It is rooted in a collective mentality or spirit, and this differs fundamentally from the individual mentality studied by psychology. In the case of a society, there is no centralized 'social sensorium' with a consciousness of its own. Rather, the stable and persistent structures that result from the interactions of many individuals are recurrent patterns of interdependence that are sustained by sentiments and ideas that individuals hold in common and from which they derive their typical character or motivation.

The super-organic aggregation of matter in motion is conditioned by the physical environment (by climate, geology and ecology) and by the biological and psychological qualities of individuals, but it shows an autonomous level of social causation in which the interplay of social forces produces a directional change. Social evolution is a product of 'integration' or 'compounding'. However, societies, like other organisms, also increase in complexity as they grow in size, and as they do so their parts become ever more specialized and mutually dependent. Thus, processes of integration are complemented by processes of 'differentiation'.

All large societies have grown from small bands of hunter-gatherers, such as those that Spencer identified as still existing among the Kalahari Bushmen, the Australian aborigines and the inhabitants of the Andaman Islands. Such bands grow through their compounding into federations such as those of the Comanche, Dakota and Iroquois. Federations, in turn, grow into 'doubly compounded' societies such as those of the Egyptian kingdom and classical Greece. The 'triply compounded' civilizations and nations of the contemporary world are the most complex forms of society. At each stage of social evolution, the integration of individuals and groups becomes more extensive and their dependence on each other becomes greater.

At the same time, societies become more differentiated, which Spencer saw as involving the two distinct processes of stratification and functional specialization. Stratification is the process through which a 'ruling agency' – a ruling class or elite – is separated out from the mass of the society. Early forms of stratification are sexual, institutionalizing inequalities between dominant men and subordinate women. As societies are further compounded, sexual differentiation is combined with differences in economic and political resources and class structures become more complex. Functional specialization is the differentiation of societies into distinct systems or spheres of activity concerned with particular tasks. Domestic, ceremonial, political, economic, ecclesiastical, professional and industrial institutions comprise the principal functional spheres in any fully differentiated society. These are, however, interrelated into larger functional systems or 'organs', each having a greater or lesser degree of cohesion and stability.

The principal organs that develop as societies evolve are the 'sustaining system' and the 'regulating system', which are linked through an intervening 'distributive system'. The sustaining system of a society comprises those parts that are concerned with productive activities and that are shaped by the local and regional distribution of resources across space. The regulatory system consists of those parts concerned with government and inter-societal relations, ranging from the markets and monetary systems that regulate industrial and distributive activities to the centralized state and military apparatuses that regulate whole societies.

In large complex societies, the regulatory system tends to predominate. They are, as a result, 'militant' societies in which centralized and often despotic leaders can rule through a rigid hierarchy of subordinates and officials and a sharp stratification of rulers from all other members of the society. More complex modern societies, on the other hand, show a predominance of the sustaining system and are, therefore, 'industrial' societies. Individual members have rights as 'citizens' and this limits the power of the central government. Industrial societies are dependent almost exclusively on the integration that results from the contractual relations entered into by free citizens and that result in a stratification between employers and workers. The contrast between militant and industrial societies is largely, but not exclusively, a contrast between pre-modern and modern societies. Spencer recognized, however, that modern societies may develop militant tendencies if governments begin to interfere in the running of the economy. As a political liberal, he held that industrial activity is better regulated through the market and the monetary system than through the establishment of centralized agencies of planning and control.

Spencer had a massive international influence, with followers developing his ideas in the United States, France, Germany, Italy, Spain and Japan, as well as in Britain itself. Even the 'functionalist' theories that eclipsed social evolutionism for many years owed a great deal to Spencer's recognition of the autonomy of social phenomena and the functional interdependence of the differentiated elements of any society. It is hardly surprising that, as Parsons began to develop his functionalist theory he also began to read Spencer and reintroduce evolutionary ideas to sociological analysis.

See also: Leonard Hobhouse, William Sumner.

See also in *Fifty Key Sociologists: The Contemporary Theorists*: Talcott Parsons, Niklas Luhmann.

Major works

Social Statics. 1850. London: Chapman.
First Principles. 1862. 2 vols. London: Williams and Norgate.
Principles of Biology. 1864–7. 2 vols. London: Williams and Norgate.
Principles of Psychology. 1870–2. 2 vols. London: Williams and Norgate.
Principles of Sociology. 1873–93. 3 vols. London: Williams and Norgate.
The Study of Sociology. 1873. London: Kegan Paul, Trench, 1889.
Principles of Ethics. 1874–93. 2 vols. London: Williams and Norgate.
The Man Versus the State. 1884. London: Williams and Norgate.
Autobiography. 1904. 2 vols. London: Williams and Norgate.

Spencer also produced the continuing ethnographic series of *Descriptive Sociology* from 1874.

Further reading

John D. Y. Peel. 1971. *Herbert Spencer, The Evolution of a Sociologist*. London: Heinemann.
Jonathan H. Turner. 1985. *Herbert Spencer: A Renewed Appreciation*. Beverly Hills, CA: Sage.

JOHN SCOTT

WILLIAM SUMNER

William Graham Sumner, a founding father of American sociology, was the first person to offer a course in sociology in any university. In seeking to develop a science of society along the lines of his predecessors **Auguste Comte** and **Herbert Spencer**, Sumner resisted the use of the term 'sociology' because it was too close etymologically to the term 'socialism', which he opposed on both ideological and political grounds. Sumner preferred instead to refer to the fledgling science of society as 'societology', a term which, of course, never caught on.

Born in 1840, Sumner was admitted to Yale University in 1859 and studied philosophy, history, mathematics, Greek and Latin. After graduation and further study in England and Germany, Sumner returned to New Haven and was eventually ordained a priest in 1869.

His career as a priest, however, was short lived. In 1872, Sumner accepted the position of chair of political and social science at Yale University, where he remained until his death in 1910. His first twenty years were spent teaching economics, but by the early 1890s he had abandoned his undergraduate courses in economics altogether for the fledgling 'science of society' – sociology – that was now showing promise of becoming a legitimate discipline. As an orthodox Spencerian, Sumner defended *laissez-faire* government, most famously in his 1883 book *What Social Classes Owe to Each Other*. In this book, Sumner argued that the social classes owe each other nothing, cementing his position as a leading Gilded Age social Darwinist.

By 1875 or 1876 – accounts vary – Sumner was teaching courses in sociology at Yale. In these classes Sumner used Herbert Spencer's 1873 *Study of Sociology* as the major text, which did not sit well with Yale president Noah Porter's opposition to the teaching of evolution at Yale. Employing the defence of academic freedom, however, Sumner won the dispute and was allowed to continue using Spencer.

By far Sumner's most famous and enduring work is *Folkways*, published in 1906. Sumner ranged far and wide in this book, on topics as varied as cannibalism, abortion, infanticide, incest, slavery, prostitution and sports, all with an eye towards ascertaining why in certain times and places these and other acts have been either tolerated or condemned.

Sumner suggests that early human beings lived a brutish existence where the instinctual urge for survival guided them in their quest for all things needed to sustain life. In this primitive fight to survive, human beings relied on clumsy trial and error. Since human beings live in groups – first very small in size, then growing larger as food technologies and production increase – members of groups learn from one another the best approaches for coping with their situation. As Sumner explained:

> Thus ways of doing were selected, which were expedient. They answered the purpose better than other ways, or with less toil and pain. Along the course on which efforts were compelled to go, habit, routine, and skill were developed. The struggle to maintain existence was carried on, not individually, but in groups. Each profited by the other's experience; hence there was concurrence towards that which proved to be most expedient.

In any given human group, then, all members adopt the same way to do things for the purposes at hand. Over time these ways turn into customs, and these customary ways of doing things get passed on to the young through tradition, imitation and authority. The sum total of these informal ways of doing things, these customs that provide for all the needs of members of the group, Sumner calls 'folkways'. Folkways are a societal force to the extent that the frequent repetition of acts by all members of the group produces habits, and these habitual ways of acting produce a strain on everyone else to conform to them. The folkways are 'one of the chief forces by which a society is made to be what it is'.

Since the folkways evolve over a long period of time, being passed down from generation to generation, it is not difficult to see why in such human groups it is the older and more experienced members that accrue the greatest authority and respect. Because primitive societies have not yet developed technologies for the mass production of food, their populations tend to be small and differences within the group (tribes, sects and so on) tend to break along kinship or family lines. In such a society there are strong and abiding attachments developed within each distinct family or tribe, along with a concomitant lack of trust or even open hostility towards all those who are not members of the immediate family. Because of this, the folkways tend to produce strong in-group sympathies as well as strong out-group hostilities.

It is here that Sumner introduced another concept that has become a central idea in sociology and across the social sciences. 'Ethnocentrism' is the tendency for groups to judge other groups by their own standards. There is also a tendency to assume that one's own folkways are the best way of doing things, thereby characterizing the ways, means, attitudes and behaviours of members of other groups as somehow deficient, strange or even threatening. Ethnocentrism, then, contributes to the heightening of tensions between distinct sects or factions within a society.

Over time, the informal ways of knowing and acting, informed and guided by the folkways, start becoming formalized or codified as 'truths', raising the folkways to a new plane that Sumner called the 'mores'. Although folkways provide guides for behaviour, because they are tacit or unstated, their violation brings only mild punishment or sanctions. Violations of the mores, on the other hand, are seen as serious and tend to elicit harsh punishments. A large class of mores consists of taboos, namely things that ought *not* to be done. Anything seen as injurious to the group can become taboo, whether it is eating the wrong types of food, carrying out war, having sex with the wrong persons (incest, for example), making the gods or ghosts angry and so on.

As societies advance even further, for example moving away from a reliance on self-help in settling disputes to the development of formal agents of control specializing in order maintenance and crime control, some mores become codified and institutionalized even further as laws. Laws are norms that are considered to be so vital to the well-being of the group that their violation requires systematic and standard responses. Rather than relying on the idiosyncratic judgements of tribal elders to settle disputes, norms or prohibitions must now be committed to paper as legal documents (statutes) that explicitly state what the illegal act is and what sort of punishment will be meted out upon a finding of guilt.

Sumner argued forcefully that the folkways are the most important means by which the interests of the members of society are served. He suggested, further, that sociology ought to take the folkways as its core or primary object of study. He concluded that '[t]he life of society consists in making folkways and applying them. The science of society might be construed as the study of them'.

See also: Herbert Spencer.

See also in *Fifty Key Sociologists: The Contemporary Theorists*: Talcott Parsons.

Major works

What Social Classes Owe to Each Other. 1883. New York: Harper and Brothers.
Folkways: A Study of the Sociological Importance of Usages, Manners, Customs, Mores, and Morals. 1906. Boston, MA: Ginn and Co.
The Science of Society, 4 vols. 1927. With Albert Galloway Keller. New Haven, CT: Yale University Press.

Some extracts can be found in Robert C. Bannister, ed. 1992. *On Liberty, Society, and Politics: The Essential Essays of William Graham Sumner*. Indianapolis, IN: Liberty Fund.

JAMES J. CHRISS

GABRIEL TARDE

The great rival of **Durkheim** at the end of the nineteenth century, Gabriel Tarde's view of sociology lost out as the Durkheim school established its dominance over the development of French sociology. In recent years, Tarde's distinctive approach has been rediscovered and championed by some evolutionary psychologists, who hold that sociologistic explanations of human behaviour ignore the inherited instincts that drive human action and the propensity of individuals to imitate the behaviour of others. Tarde's ideas are more complex than his present-day advocates in evolutionary psychology suggest. Indeed, many of them have been central planks in the sociologistic approaches that he is sometimes held to have rejected.

Tarde was born in 1843 and trained as a lawyer. He became interested in the work of the Italian group of criminologists – Cesare Lombroso, Raffaele Garofalo and Enrico Ferri – who sought to explain criminal behaviour in terms of the racial and environmental factors that they believed to be associated with it. Impressed by their search for laws of social behaviour, Tarde nevertheless rejected their biological and environmental determinism and stressed, instead, the importance of socialized individual responses. Individuals learn through imitating those around them, he argued, and it is their socialized dispositions to act that explain the occurrence of high or low rates of criminality in particular populations and milieux. On the basis of his early work in comparative criminology and penal philosophy, Tarde was made director of criminal statistics in the Ministry of Justice, from which post he sought to popularize his ideas.

Tarde had already, however, begun to generalize his argument from the case of criminal behaviour to all forms of human behaviour. In 1890 he had published *The Laws of Imitation* and he used this model of human action and sociological explanation to construct general accounts of social institutions and social conflict in his subsequent books. The arguments of these were, in turn, summarized in *Social Laws*, of 1898. In these works – published at the same time as Durkheim was undertaking his analysis of suicide and the rules of the sociological method – Tarde constructed a form of methodological individualism in which variations in social phenomena were to be explained in terms of invariant, yet socially shaped, psychological dispositions.

Tarde's individualism was rooted in his belief in the existence of a natural tendency to imitate. It is through imitation that innovations are able to spread throughout a social group and across a society. In the absence of physical or social obstacles, innovations spread rapidly and uniformly. In real social situations, however, obstacles to the diffusion of innovations always exist and the rates and patterns of diffusion are constrained into specific channels and individuals may be unable to escape from particular circles of interaction and association. The social obstacles to diffusion that Tarde considered include such psychological barriers as the pride and prejudice of racial and class attitudes. People are less likely to copy those towards whom they are hostile or suspicious, but they are more likely to copy those whom they admire or with whom they identify.

These psychological barriers, Tarde held, correspond especially to social divisions and social inequalities of power and prestige. Influenced by the 'elite' theories emerging in the works of **Gumplowicz, Mosca** and **Pareto**, Tarde explored the unequal distribution of political power and the consequent social differentiation of a directive elite from the subordinate mass. Towards the end of the nineteenth century, he published a book, *La Transformation du pouvoir*, on the development of social power, highlighting this differentiation and postulating that imitation processes must be seen as shaped and constrained by power inequality. People tend to imitate the behaviour of those above them in the social structure, whom they treat as role models for emulation. The tendency of those in subordinate social positions to imitate those above them is greater than the tendency of those at the top to copy the behaviour of those below. Innovations, as examples of behaviour, spread from the elite to the mass in a trickle-down effect.

As a result of imitation, Tarde argued, innovations spread very rapidly: with each round of imitation the number of people who take up an innovation grows geometrically. Waves of 'imitative radiation' spread out at ever-increasing rates. Innovations occurring at a variety of locations radiate through interweaving and intersecting waves to form a complex network of imitative associations.

Early in the twentieth century Tarde left the Ministry of Justice and became a professor in the Collège de France, where he taught courses in the formation of public opinion and in the area of economic psychology. In his study of public opinion Tarde showed how the communication of ideas through the networks of diffusion that he had charted could lead to a social consensus within a group. Opinions formed within an elite spread exponentially through the whole society. Social consensus is limited by the existence of obstacles to communication that ensure the differentiation of attitudes and opinions around positions of power and privilege. Influenced by Gustav Le Bon, Tarde placed great emphasis on imitative influence in crowds. In the emotionally charged conditions of social effervescence that are generated in the anonymous mobs and crowds, whose collective actions are a major political factor, individuals are liberated from many normal constraints and are particularly prone to suggestibility and the influence of others. He had no opportunity to develop these ideas further, as he died in 1904.

The dominance of Durkheimian sociology in France prevented the successful diffusion of Tarde's ideas. Nevertheless, theorists in the United States and Britain did take up his emphasis on the propensity to imitate, and those interested in the diffusion of innovations and public opinion built on his structural arguments. Tarde has always, however, been a marginal figure within sociology. This reflects his reliance on the unexplained biological propensity to imitate as the basic variable in his social theory. While he had much to say about the consequences of imitation, he could not explain why innovations should occur, and nor could he explain why individuals imitate the particular ideas and practices that they do. Individuals encounter a vast array of behaviours in the others with whom they associate, and they must choose which – if any – of these they will imitate. Tarde had little to say about the factors leading people to choose one option rather than another.

The recent rediscovery of Tarde's laws of imitation by evolutionary psychologists takes no account of these problems. It is precisely Tarde's reliance on inherited dispositions that is his big attraction to them. Evolutionary psychologists posit that cultural evolution occurs through the spread of 'memes' – units of cultural reproduction – as individuals imitate each other's cultural responses. This welcome, if unintentional, recognition of the importance of social processes of communication and diffusion by evolutionary psychologists fails to consider the problems of Tarde's failure to provide us with an explanation for imitation. No inherited instinct, considered on its own, can explain the cultural choices that individuals must make.

See also: Ludwig Gumplowicz, Gaetano Mosca, Vilfredo Pareto.

Major works

*La Criminalité comparée.*1886. Paris: F. Alcan.
Penal Philosophy. 1890. New Brunswick, NJ: Transaction, 2001.
The Laws of Imitation. 1890. New York: H. Holt, 1903.
Monadologie et sociologie. 1893. Paris: Empêcheur de penser en rond, 1999.
La Logique sociale. 1895. Paris: F. Alcan.
L'Opposition universelle. 1897. Paris: F. Alcan.
Social Laws. 1898. New York: Macmillan, 1899.
La Transformation du pouvoir. 1899. Paris: Le Seuil, 2003.
L'Opinion et la foule. 1901. Paris: Presses Universitaires de France, 1989.
Psychologie économique, 2 vols. 1902. Paris: Félix Alcan.

Useful extracts from many of Tarde's works can be found in Terry N. Clark, ed. *Gabriel Tarde on Communication and Social Influence*. Chicago: ChicagoUniversity Press, 1969. Electronic versions of many of the full texts can be found at http://www.uqac.uquebec.ca/zone30/Classiques_des_sciences_sociales/classiques/tarde_gabriel/tarde_gabriel.html.

Further reading

Everett M. Rogers. 1962. *The Diffusion of Innovations*, 5th edn. New York: The Free Press, 2003.

JOHN SCOTT

ALEXIS DE TOCQUEVILLE

The reputation of Alexis de Tocqueville only seems to grow with time. A vast outpouring of new translations and editions of his works belies a rising enthusiasm for his vivid yet subtle writings. While

Tocqueville's contribution to sociological theory lies in his insights into the causes and outcomes of global democratization, he was never a deskbound theorist. Since he was a politician and traveller associating with a huge variety of people, Tocqueville's written work always reflected his life. Born into a Norman aristocratic family in 1805, Tocqueville was sensitized to the altered social and political realities after the French Revolution of 1789. Members of his family suffered imprisonment, execution, dispersal and loss of property during the Reign of Terror that followed the Revolution. The coming of democracy and the disempowerment of the aristocracy did not prevent him from training and working as a magistrate, being elected to the Chamber of Deputies and travelling widely in North America, Algeria and several European countries. He died in 1859.

Both politics and travel strongly influenced Tocqueville's writings, and his personal experiences of the spread of democracy are often woven into the texts. His period in office coincided with two journeys to Algeria, and some of the recently published papers based on these trips reveal him to be an advocate of French imperialism, even when it involved violence. In the reports on Algeria, Tocqueville attempted to reconcile the democratizing ideals of French occupation with the differing interests of the settler and indigenous populations. His more famous travels in North America in the company of Gustave Beaumont in 1831–2, ostensibly undertaken as research on US prisons, were the basis for a much wider investigation into the manners of the various peoples of North America. The encounters of travel imparted a personal and lyrical quality to his writing comparable with that of other nineteenth-century European visitors such as **Harriet Martineau** and Frances Trollope. Tocqueville recorded conversations with many different kinds of Americans, including slaves, farmers, prisoners and government officials. He even had an audience with President Andrew Jackson, whom he described as 'not a man of genius'. One major difference between his portraits of the US and Algeria was that, although he admired the Anglo-Saxon project of colonizing North America, he did not endorse it, as he did French imperialism in Algeria.

Taken in their totality, Tocqueville's works describe how the interplay of ideas and social institutions brought about social and political change in the United States, France and England. In doing this, he developed a comparative sociology by which differences and similarities between countries clarified past patterns and future directions in history. With the fall of the aristocracy and monarchy in France, democratic forms of governance, the power of merchant classes and less rigid patterns of social hierarchy became dominant. England was the exception, having moved to modernity without revolution by simply incorporating democratic institutions within an essentially feudal social structure. France, by contrast, violently decimated its feudal order and had installed democracy and egalitarianism through spreading a universalist doctrine of liberty. Differing from both European countries, the United States established a democratic social order without ever having to destroy feudalism, since it never existed in the American colonies. More broadly, European colonialism in Algeria and elsewhere made democracy a truly globalizing project.

Tocqueville's belief that the New World most starkly revealed a global future was solidified in his two volumes of *Democracy in America*, published in 1835 and 1840. Both volumes received numerous accolades, sold prolifically and contributed to Tocqueville's election to various prestigious academies. In this work, Tocqueville explained that the United States is unique among western nations because it is a pure form of democracy, untainted by feudalism. Without inherited social positions, each American was a citizen, equal under law to all others. Citizenship was enshrined in the Federal Constitution and backed up economically by the revision of the English legal system of primogeniture, which required the division of estates equally among all children. This diluted the power of inherited landed wealth and boosted the power of money, a more capricious basis for social distinctions. With universal male enfranchisement mandated from the earliest times of the Republic, Tocqueville argued that governance was the outcome of a participatory democracy. A 'bottom-up' political system emerged from local associations such as the New England township, and then counties, states and the Federal government evolved from this popular base. Each state administration had its own branches of government and constitution, as well as citizens' groups, all of which counterbalanced the power of Federal government. Additionally, certain 'inalienable rights' were granted citizens in the Federal Constitution. In sum, Tocqueville's America was a decentralized, rights-based state legitimated by the will of the populace.

This may sound like a ringing endorsement for democracy, but Tocqueville was always ambivalent towards it. He was singularly capable of sympathizing with features of old and new orders while also subjecting each to the most damning criticisms. This is evident in his understanding of the United States, but most poignant in his commentaries on France in *The Old Regime and the Revolution*, in which he pointed out that the quasi-religious doctrines of the

Revolution concealed the past and prevented people learning from history. For Tocqueville the past and present were inseparable, and the feudal history of France was indispensable in understanding many of the continuities of the Revolution. By adopting a more genealogical method, Tocqueville was able to argue that one form of absolutism was replaced with another, as inequality – under an often ineffective but sometimes innovative monarchy – was replaced by formal equality under the 'democratic despotism' of a rationalistic state regime. Paradoxically, the democratic Revolution enabled *and* destroyed freedom.

Tocqueville further speculated that democracy created peculiar cultural and psychological orientations. One of his most influential ideas in this respect was that individualism, although increasingly prevalent in France, was a character trait most sharply defined among Americans. Individualism was described as 'a mature and calm feeling which disposes each member of the community to sever himself from the mass of his fellows and to draw apart with his family and friends, so that after he has formed a little circle of his own, he willingly leaves society at large to itself'. This personality type signified a radical shift away from the more social and time-honoured webs of feudal relationships. The danger with individualism was that Americans would become so self-absorbed that future generations would be sacrificed to 'the satisfaction of immediate desires'. The continuing linkage between individualism and the destruction of social cohesiveness in the United States has been a theme pursued by contemporary American sociologists, including Robert Bellah, Robert Putnam and Amitai Etzioni, who have put forward proposals for a renewed communitarian ethos.

Democracy characterized the form of American society as a whole and was shaped by the unique historical and geographical circumstances that allowed both unbridled individualism and cultural invention. Most immediately, these qualities were nurtured by the vastness of the territory itself, something that had been impressed upon Tocqueville during his travels. The sheer space available to settlers imbued Americans with a sense of possibilities and fuelled personal ambition. The land represented the opportunity to better oneself. Once seized from the original Indian inhabitants, it could be claimed and owned. This meant that the American masses could attain social mobility through transforming what was to them a wilderness, under the woodsman's axe and the farmer's plough. These were possibilities denied most Europeans because deforestation and agricultural production for the manorial system had left no land to

claim. In turn, the wilderness created certain American cultural tendencies such as a veneration for nature (expressed later in landscape
painting, naturalism and transcendentalism), a certain 'restlessness of
heart,' insularity and practicality.

Clearly not an unleavened homage to the United States, *Democracy
in America* highlights many critical flaws of democracy. Of these, the
'tyranny of the majority' was perhaps one of the most pressing. In
several passages that anticipated Michel Foucault, Tocqueville argued
that social control in an absolute monarchy is achieved through harsh
punishment. In a democracy, on the other hand, the body is left
relatively free, but the soul is enslaved to the popular ethos of the
majority. Any social transgression is against society itself, since society
is predicated not upon the impositions of a monarch, but on the rule
of the majority. Therefore, strong pressures to internalize social control are created and expressed in affirmations of allegiance to collective symbols and 'the perpetual utterance of self applause'.
Individualism itself then actually becomes a form of conformity, and
the range of acceptable opinion constricts so much that, Tocqueville
declared, 'freedom of opinion does not exist in America'. This irony
stems from Tocqueville's view that loyalty to the will of the majority
dampened any desire to articulate criticisms of the social order itself.
Social conformism was also a tendency Tocqueville discerned in his
own country, noting in *The Old Regime* that the less regulated and
centralized feudal system allowed cultural variations, but the new
democratic society – being dominated by the strong state, bureau-
cracies, the city of Paris and the economic power of the bourgeoisie –
encouraged social homogenization and 'collective individualism'.
Similarly, the new forms of state authority were expressed, 'not
through destroying absolute power, but by converting it'.

When Tocqueville considered American ethnic relations, he
introduced yet another flaw of majority rule, invoking images of
shadow societies located parallel to American democracy. The black
population and American Indians were connected to democracy
without forming part of it. For Indians, this was partly a consequence
of continual territorial dispossession, which, although lamentable,
Tocqueville condoned under John Locke's premise that, as hunters
rather than agriculturists, 'Indians occupied without possessing' the
land. Such doctrines were inscribed into democratically established
law, the duplicity of which was not lost on the Indian orators Tocqueville came across. In an oft-cited phrase, Tocqueville remarked
that 'it is impossible to destroy men with more respect for the laws of
humanity'. With these laws backing them up, the westward march of

the settlers constantly disconnected Indians from their lands. The cruelty of this was reinforced when Tocqueville witnessed part of the 'Trail of Tears', in which the Choctaw Indians were forcibly expelled from their homelands to an area across the Mississippi.

The settlers had inherited the English model of colonial adminis-tration and maintained the 'rule of law' and the Puritan farmer's contempt towards Indians. Whites and blacks, by contrast, were irrevocably bound together. Slavery, 'the most formidable of all the ills that threaten the Union', had moulded the character of slaves and slaveholders alike, perverting and degrading both. Even the possibility of the abolition of slavery (still thirty years away at the time of Tocqueville's writing) offered only a false freedom. The ex-slaves had been so dehumanized that the scar of servility would always remain as a cause of resentment in their descendents. Maintaining that 'while the law may abolish slavery, God alone can obliterate the traces of its existence', Tocqueville anticipated the racial conflict that would erupt in the United States in the twentieth century. But despite his evident empathy with the slave and Indian populations, Tocqueville often fell back upon social evolutionism in depicting their demise as somehow inevitable.

The many paradoxes and subtleties in Tocqueville's writings have increasingly come to be important sources of sociological under-standing of the complex social processes through which societies move to and proceed with democracy. Tocqueville provided a nuanced account of both the gains and losses incurred by democracy, including when it is imposed by force, an issue that has startling contemporary relevance. His finer-grained studies of the United States and France proved to be incredibly prophetic. Tocqueville famously predicted the 1848 Socialist Revolution in France a few weeks before it happened, and his observations about the US have been cited repeatedly as encapsulating present-day American society.

See also: Harriet Martineau.

Major works

Democracy in America. 1835–40. Trans., ed. and with an intro. by Harvey C. Mansfield and Delba Winthrop. Chicago: University of Chicago Press, 2000.
The Old Regime and the Revolution. 1856. Ed. and with an intro. by François Furet and Françoise Mélonio, trans. by Alan S. Kahan. Chicago: Uni-versity of Chicago Press, 1998.
Writings on Empire and Slavery. Various dates. Ed. and trans. by Jennifer Pitts. Baltimore. MD: Johns Hopkins University Press, 2001.

Further reading

George Wilson Pierson. 1996. *Tocqueville in America*. Baltimore, MD: Johns Hopkins University Press.
Sheldon Wolin. 2001. *Tocqueville Between Two Worlds: The Making of a Political and Theoretical Life*. Princeton, NJ: Princeton University Press.

COLIN SAMSON

FERDINAND TÖNNIES

The leading figure in German sociology for a generation, Ferdinand Tönnies is today less well known than his contemporaries **Weber** and **Simmel**, neither of whom worked unambiguously in sociology. Tönnies was a founding figure in the formation of the German Sociological Society, held its presidency for many years and produced a pioneering text on general social theory. He is mainly remembered today, however, for contrasting 'community' with 'society' and, mistakenly, for holding to a romantic image of the communities of the past. Tönnies' view of 'society' was, in fact, strongly influenced by his socialist commitments and he was as critical of the past as he was of the present.

Tönnies was born in 1855 in Schleswig-Holstein, where his family came from a prosperous farming background. He studied at a number of universities, receiving his doctorate from the University of Tübingen. It was during his student career that Tönnies developed his commitment to socialist politics and it was because of his politics that he found himself denied an established chair until 1913, when he was appointed at the University of Kiel shortly before his official retirement from university teaching. In the early 1920s he returned to Kiel in an honorary position, remaining highly productive and influential within the discipline. The rise of the Nazi Party and the growth of opposition to any socialist or left-inclined politics put him under great pressure. He was persuaded by Hans Freyer, a Nazi supporter, to withdraw from the presidency of the Sociological Society in order to deflect any possible criticisms of the subject, and he was dismissed from his university post in 1933 – in the same year that many Jewish ands socialist sociologists were also losing their positions and being driven into exile. This wave of dismissals under the Nazi regime effectively marked the end of the formative period in German sociology, through most of which Tönnies had lived. He died three years later in 1936.

The book for which Tönnies is best known is variously translated as *Community and Society* and *Community and Association*, and was published a few years before **Durkheim** developed a related view of the relations between mechanical solidarity and organic solidarity. Tönnies followed this with studies of Hobbes and of **Marx**, a series of lengthy articles on such topics as custom and social stratification, and a book on the formation of public opinion. He was a great advocate of descriptive, empirical sociology, carrying out and sponsoring research on demography and criminology. His final work was a systematic introduction to social theory in which he drew out the underlying themes of his work and made a clear statement of the methodological and conceptual ideas shared widely among his sociological contemporaries.

Tönnies' most famous work contrasted two ideal types of social order. These were organized around, respectively, *gemeinschaftlich* relations of communal solidarity and the *gesellschaftlich* relations of calculative and contractual association. The former was approximated in many rural, agrarian localities in the past, where individuals occupied similar work roles and pursued similar ways of life to those of their neighbours. Homogeneity and similarity encouraged an emotional solidarity focused on shared values and concerns. Associative relations, on the other hand, are characteristic of the market and commercial relations of the towns and cities that had broken up traditional solidarities and established a complex division of labour in which individuals are linked purely through the cash nexus and by the rational calculation of their own profit and advantage.

The contrast was not unique to Tönnies. Similar ideas had figured in the evolutionary theories of Sir Henry Maine (who contrasted 'status' and 'contract' societies) and **Lewis Morgan** (who contrasted '*societas*' and '*civitas*'). Indeed, the rise of modern society had earlier been depicted in similar terms by such diverse writers as Hobbes and Hegel, and it was central to Marx's understanding of the specificity of capitalist society. In a simpler form it had become part of the taken-for-granted knowledge of contemporary sociologists in the form of the contrast between traditionalism and modernity. Tönnies' work was distinctive and important because of his rejection of evolutionism and his explicit presentation of the forms of social order as ideal or pure types. They nowhere exist in reality but describe tendencies within all societies and they can, therefore, be used as analytical tools in a vast range of sociological studies.

Tönnies saw each type of social order as rooted in distinctive orientations to social action. Action oriented towards the building and maintenance of communal relations is characterized by motives that Tönnies characterized as involving an 'essential' or 'natural' will: individual wills are driven by emotional commitments rooted deep in a person's character and temperament. Actions oriented towards associative encounters, on the other hand, involve an 'arbitrary' or 'rational' will – a will that reflects a willingness and ability to choose between alternatives on the basis of efficiency and advantage. This commitment comes close to that which Weber was to develop between traditional action and instrumentally rational action.

Much of Tönnies' later work sought to elaborate the various conceptual distinctions that were collapsed into the single contrast between community and association and to derive these concepts from his view of action and its orientation through will. His methodological individualism has much in common with that of Weber and was, indeed, something of a common assumption for many in his generation of social theorists. For all these writers, types of individual action were seen as the elements through which complex structures of social relations could be built. It was held that individuals in their actions build the social relations in terms of which they organize their lives, and sociologists must recognize this in their concepts. Social structures must not be reified, treated as things existing in their own right and independently of individual actions. All sociological concepts, therefore, must be understood as shifting complexes of action that may, under certain circumstances, come to be seen by actors as existing apart from them and, therefore, appear to exercise a causal influence on the individuals. In fact, it is only ever the internalized representations of the structures that can constrain individual actions; the structures themselves never exert any causal force.

Tönnies identified three distinct kinds of structural 'entities' produced through social action, each of which can take communal or associative forms. The simplest social entities are 'relations', among which Tönnies distinguishes the fraternal and familistic fellowship of communal relations from the contractual and exchange relations of association. Social relations can be compounded into 'collectivities' that appear to have a distinctive collective existence and of which individuals may feel themselves to be 'members'. The contrast drawn here by Tönnies is that between the communal forms of social estates and nations, on the one hand, and the associational forms of social classes and civil society, on the other. Finally, Tönnies identified 'corporations' or organizations that have a stronger collective reality and, by virtue of their constitutional rules and decision-making organs, have the appearance of acting. Communal organizations include guilds and churches, while associational organizatons include business enterprises, pressure groups and political parties.

See also: Emile Durkheim, Georg Simmel, Max Weber.

Major works

Community and Association. 1887. London: Routledge & Kegan Paul, 1955. New translation as *Community and Civil Society*. Cambridge: Cambridge University Press, 2001.
Thomas Hobbes: der Mann und der Denker. 1910. 2nd expanded edn. Stuttgart: F. Fromann. 1st edn published 1879–81.
Custom. 1909. New York: Free Press, 1961.
Karl Marx: His Life and Teachings. 1920. East Lansing, MI: Michigan State University, 1974.
A Theory of Public Opinion. 1922. Lanham, MD: Rowman and Littlefield, 2000.
'Estates and Classes'. 1931. In John Scott, ed. *Class*, vol. 1. London: Routledge, 1996.
Einführung in die Soziologie. 1931. Extracts in Werner J. Cahnman and Rudolphe Heberle, eds. *Ferdinand Toennies, on Sociology: Pure, Applied, and Empirical*. Chicago: University of Chicago Press, 1971.

Further reading

Werner J. Cahnman, ed. 1973. *Ferdinand Tönnies: A New Evaluation*. Leiden: E. J. Brill.

JOHN SCOTT

EDWARD TYLOR

Sir Edward Burnett Tylor was, after **Herbert Spencer**, the leading evolutionary theorist of the nineteenth century. He was a prodigious collector and collator of ethnographic data from across the world, and his writings presented the results of his reflections on these data as displays of evolutionary sequences of cultural traits and practices. The invention of systematic fieldwork anthropology seemed to make Tylor's method and approach irrelevant, and this was reinforced by the concurrent reaction against evolutionary theory.

Edward Burnett Tylor was born in London in 1832. Travelling in Mexico in his early twenties he encountered an amateur anthropologist who inspired in him the desire to pursue his own investigations into mythology, art and religion. He was soon to produce a book on Mexican culture and a compilation of studies on early civilization before producing, in 1871, his masterly *Primitive Culture*. He later produced a summary version of this as the first textbook in the subject: *Anthropology*. It was on the strength of these books that, despite having no degree, he became a lecturer and later professor of anthropology at Oxford. He retired in 1909 and died in 1917.

It was Tylor's definition of culture that became established as the defining disciplinary concept for anthropology and sociology. Culture, for Tylor, comprises the totality of knowledge, belief and emotional expression, together with legal and customary rules of behaviour and the various skills and habits acquired by individuals as members of a particular society. There is no differentiation to make between artistic culture and base expressions – all are equally cultivated through membership in a society. Each culture must be understood as a distinct and autonomous phenomenon, evolving according to its own integral principles. The diffusion of cultural traits is a reality, but a secondary one. Social evolution is a predominantly endogenous process. This evolution is, furthermore, directional. While cultural degeneration is possible, the long-term trend is in a progressive direction: a movement from lower to higher forms of cultural traits can be discerned.

Tylor rejected amateur fact-gathering in favour of the systematic analysis of co-variation using the comparative method. His method was to compare the cultural traits found in a range of societies in order to estimate what he called the 'adhesions' among them. By this he meant what later and more mathematically advanced writers would call *correlations*. Whenever cultural traits are associated together or are commonly associated with a particular way of life, Tylor argued, there is a uniformity of social conditions corresponding to the cultural patterns. In making this argument, Tylor made use of statistical measures of co-variation in social life. He examined the extent to which particular combinations of factors could be said to occur more often than would be expected on the assumption that they varied independently of each other. Where a combination occurs more frequently than expected, he argued, it is reasonable to assume that there is a causal connection between them. Most famously, Tylor used this method to demonstrate the causal relationship between the exogamous dual organization and classificatory systems of kinship terminology.

Tylor's evolutionism saw cultural items as subject to processes of natural selection that shaped the overall pattern of social development.

There are definite stages of social evolution that are invariant across human societies, and Tylor distinguished the 'savagery' of the Stone Age hunters and gatherers from the following stage of 'barbarism', where metal production became predominant, and the final stage of 'civilization'. He had little to say about variations across these stages or about any sequence of stages within the 'civilized' form of society.

See also: Leonard Hobhouse, Herbert Spencer.

Major works

Anahuac: Or Mexico and the Mexicans. 1861.
Researches into the Early History of Mankind and the Development of Civilization. 1865.
Primitive Culture. 1871. London: John Murray, 1920.
Anthropology. 1881. New York: David Appleton, 1897.

JOHN SCOTT

THORSTEIN VEBLEN

On 24 October 1929 the New York Stock Exchange crashed and the Great Depression began. Two months earlier, sociologist and economist Thorstein Bunde Veblen died. His books and papers had warned against exactly the kind of event that happened that October day and its consequences for 'the common man'.

Born in 1857 to immigrant farmers from Norway, he spent most of his childhood in Nerstrand, Minnesota. He attended Carlton College Academy, receiving his BA in 1880. In 1881 he started PhD studies in philosophy at Johns Hopkins, where he followed lectures by Charles S. Peirce, the founder of American pragmatism, who became a great inspiration for Veblen. Many of his works must be seen against the backcloth of pragmatist philosophy of science. He moved to Yale to complete his PhD in 1884. His dissertation on *The Ethical Grounds of a Doctrine of Retribution* is reported to have been lost. The next six years were spent at his parents' farm in Minnesota, though he seems not to have held down regular employment. In 1891–2 he went on to study political economy and American history at Cornell University, and when his department chair Laurence Laughlin was appointed head of the economics department at the newly founded University of Chicago in 1892, he brought Veblen with him. Veblen stayed at Chicago until 1906. He then taught economics at the University of Missouri (1911–18) and the New School for Social Research in New York (1918–26).

Veblen is often claimed as the founder of institutional economics, but he is also claimed as one of the great sociologists. He produced eleven books and many papers. His writings are often contradictory and cannot easily be placed in simple categories. In his time he was regarded as a politically radical thinker, drawing on diverse sources from different disciplines and from both Darwinian thought and Marxian theory, though he was often criticized for not referencing sources in his publications.

Veblen was writing at a time when America was shifting from an agrarian to an industrial society, and doing so more rapidly than elsewhere. By 1880, the non-agricultural labour force surpassed that of agriculture, and American society experienced rapid industrialization, urbanization and an influx of migrants from Europe. Finance capital gained ground over industrial capital, and the new society of mass production laid the grounds for a study of mass consumption.

The Theory of the Leisure Class, published in 1899, was Veblen's first book and was widely acclaimed as an original and groundbreaking work. The main theme of the study is a critique of the demonstration and display of social status. Chicago, where he lived while writing the book, was one of the fastest-growing urban communities in the United States during this period, and the difference between the wealthy and the poor was very evident indeed. He discussed the social stratification of contemporary America as resulting from an evolution from peaceful tribal societies to a higher form of barbarism where competition and combat underpin social life. The accumulation of wealth is the key marker of distinction – even more so if the wealth is gained passively through inheritance. Success is thought of in relative terms; it is dependent upon having *more* than others in the community to which one belongs. The 'leisure class' did not take part in productive work or the activities needed to uphold their everyday existence, but enjoyed high levels of wasteful consumption. Their 'conspicuous consumption' served no other purpose than to create social distinctions and uphold social hierarchies and a gendered division of labour. The originality of the study is undoubted. Veblen's style of writing borders on the ironic, and the book is said to have been thought of as entertaining among those he criticized. What raised eyebrows at the time was his concern with the plight of women in society, a topic that very few male social scientists had commented on.

Veblen's next book, *The Theory of the Business Enterprise*, looked at the formation of trusts in contemporary capitalism and at the increasing prominence of finance capital. His criticisms of market mechanisms for engendering waste and for exploiting labour continue and deepen the argument of *The Leisure Class*, but the conflict between 'men of waste' and 'men of work' is emphasized much more. The discussion of the conflict between production (industry) and profit (business) was also taken up in later works, where he concluded that industry would fare better if left to engineers than to financiers. *The Theory of the Business Enterprise* offered gloomy prospects for the future under capitalism. Veblen did not see the conflict between capital and labour as leading to a revolution, but to the submission of the working classes by their seduction into material improvement. He diagnosed the development of capitalism along a predatory and nationalistic trajectory, and saw this ending in some form of socialism or fascism that would lead to the downfall of capitalism itself. His scepticism about capitalism's ability to create stable and peaceful societies was again brought out in *An Inquiry into the Nature of Peace and the Terms of Its Perpetuation*, published during the First World War in 1917. The book was favourably received in radical circles, and it was hoped, in vain, that Veblen would play an important part in the peace settlements.

In *Absentee Ownership and Business Enterprise in Recent Times: The Case of America*, published in 1923, he concentrated on how ownership and control have increasingly been separated, creating a new form of alienation that is embedded in the system itself. This analysis thus deepens aspects of his discussions in *The Theory of the Business Enterprise* in important ways. The emerging large corporations were controlled and managed by a different class of people from those who owned them. They consequently presented themselves in ways that alienated and disempowered common people. This book in some ways echoes **Weber**'s nightmarish visions of bureaucracy but is more concentrated on aspects of economic exploitation. He also predicted that the instability of the contemporary economic system would lead to crises of the kind that happened on Wall Street shortly after his death.

Veblen's authorship covered a wide array of topics apart from those related to the dividing lines between 'pecuniary' and 'practical' men. In most of his books and papers, however, the discussion of any topic tended to gravitate towards this problem area. A case in point is *The Higher Learning in America*, which is a sweeping critique of how the universities are permeated by 'business culture's habituation of thought'. Pecuniary values underpin the management of universities and lie at the heart of the courses taught. This book was written years before it was published, while he was still an employee at the University of Missouri, and its first subtitle read *A Study in Total Depravity*. The management of the university advised against its publication.

In his will, Veblen expressed the wish that no biography of his life be written. By his contemporaries he was described as a person who was difficult to get to know. Nor did he seem to care much for the conventional, in thought, dress or behaviour. He never made a 'successful' academic career and his personality seemed to have held most people – friends and foes alike – at a distance. His first marriage was seemingly difficult and ended in divorce, and his second wife left him a widower in 1920. In 1926 he retired from the New School of Social Research and lived in California with his stepdaughter until his death only two months before the events on Wall Street turned all his bleakest forebodings into reality.

However strange the man, his writings speak of genius and have inspired other great thinkers of the twentieth century, most notably C. Wright Mills, John K. Galbraith and Pierre Bourdieu. In an age where Veblen's home country is the most powerful nation in the world, and where wars and global capitalism continue to affect people's everyday lives for better and for worse, Veblen's works, a century on, still offer fresh insight into important aspects of the development of contemporary society.

See also: Karl Marx.

See also in *Fifty Key Sociologists: The Contemporary Theorists*: C. Wright Mills.

Major works

The Theory of the Leisure Class. 1899. New York: Macmillan.
The Theory of the Business Enterprise. 1904. New York: Scribner.
The Vested Interests. 1911. London. George Allen and Unwin, 1924.
The Instinct of Workmanship and the State of the Industrial Arts. 1914.
Imperial Germany and the Industrial Revolution. 1915. London: Secker and Warburg, 1939.
An Inquiry into the Nature of Peace and the Terms of Its Perpetuation. 1917.
The Higher Learning in America. A Memorandum on the Conduct of the Universities by Businessmen. 1918. New York: Sagamore Press, 1965.
The Industrial System and the Captains of Industry. 1919. New York: Oriole Chapbooks.

The Engineers and the Price System. 1921. New York: Augustus M. Kelley, 1982.

Absentee Ownership and Business Enterprise in Recent Times: The Case of America. 1923. London: George Allen and Unwin, 1924.

Essays in Our Changing Order. Various dates. New York: Viking Press, 1934.

Further reading

John P. Diggins. 1978. *The Bard of Savagery. Thorstein Veblen and Modern Social Theory,* Hassocks, UK: Harvester Press.

Joseph Dorfman. 1934. *Thorstein Veblen and his America.* New York: Viking, 1966.

Irving Louis Horowitz, ed. 2002. *Veblen's Century. A Collective Portrait.* New Brunswick, NJ: Transaction Publishers.

David Riessman. 1953. *Thorstein Veblen.* New Brunswick, NJ: Transaction Publishers, 1995.

ANN NILSEN

LESTER WARD

Following hard on the heels of the Civil War and the Gilded Age, the Progressive Era was a period of American history in which Americans sought to deal with the negative effects of the rapid changes occurring all around them, especially in the areas of industrialization, urbanization and immigration. Progressive and municipal reformers in concert with groups and organizations representing such activities as philanthropy, charity, corrections, child welfare, social settlement and social work embarked upon the Progressive cause of social reconstruction. Sociology, at the time very much a fledgling, unproven discipline with only an amorphous sense of the topics and research agendas it could legitimately claim as its own, was well positioned then to take up the Progressive cause while adding to it a 'scientific' or 'systematic' legitimacy.

Lester Frank Ward, born in 1841 in the Illinois frontier, would by the time of the Progressive Era become the pre-eminent sociologist in America. Ward had cemented his position with the publication in 1883 of *Dynamic Sociology,* a large two-volume work that reflected his commitment to positivism and science. From the publication of *Dynamic Sociology* through all of his later works, including *Psychic Factors of Civilization, Outlines of Sociology, Pure Sociology, Applied Sociology* and his posthumously released six-volume *Glimpses of the Cosmos,* Ward argued that if sociology is to be of value in furthering the progressive agenda of societal reform and amelioration, it must separate itself from lay, popular and 'unscientific' claims about society and the suggestions for improvement associated with them. This can be accomplished only if sociologists are able to illustrate explicitly the scientific foundations upon which its knowledge rests. The social and psychological forces impelling human conduct and giving shape to human society must first be understood, then, before any programme of applied sociology can be implemented.

Ward's visions of science and society were forged by his impoverished childhood and the utilitarian belief in self and social betterment through hard work and effort. However, human beings cannot do this work as individuals alone because social systems are too vast and complex. A programme of universal or compulsory education would be absolutely crucial, then, as an element in the master trend of 'telesis', that is, in guiding planned change at the governmental and institutional levels to achieve the goals of societal betterment. (Indeed, Ward's call for universal education was pioneering, and informed John Dewey's position on the matter.)

Ward's belief in the importance of self-sacrifice for the public good appeared in concrete form as he served and was injured in the Civil War. Ward opposed slavery, eugenics and all forms of social arrangements that oppressed groups on the basis of sex, race, creed or social class. In many ways, Ward's thought laid the foundation for the emergence of the modern welfare state. After recuperating from his war-time injuries, Ward worked in government service in Washington, working as a botanist, geologist and palaeontologist. He received degrees in law and medicine, but practised neither. Ward was also fluent in a number of languages, and when he began keeping a personal diary in 1860 he wrote entries in French so as to learn better the nuances of the language.

Ward began writing *Dynamic Sociology* in 1869 while still engaged in his government work. It took him fourteen years to complete the work, which was published in two volumes covering some 1,400 pages. The work was a grand cosmology, as Ward linked together all that was known at the time from astronomy, geology, chemistry, palaeontology, biology, philosophy, ethnology and anthropology, psychology, economics and political science, and of course sociology. From sociology the two key figures with whom Ward dealt were **Auguste Comte** and **Herbert Spencer**. He took seriously Comte's theory of the hierarchy of the sciences, which holds that sociology is the 'queen' of the sciences to the extent that it is built upon and subsumes the basic principles of all the other sciences. As Ward explained,

Sociology is an advanced study, the last and latest in the entire curriculum. It should perhaps be mainly postgraduate. It involves high powers of generalization, and what is more, it absolutely requires a broad basis of induction. It is largely a philosophy, and in these days philosophy no longer rests on assumptions but on facts. To understand the laws of society the mind must be in possession of a large body of knowledge. This knowledge should not be picked up here and there at random, but should be instilled in a methodical way.

Ward did not take an academic position in sociology until the last few years of his life. In 1906 he was named chair of the newly formed sociology department at Brown University, where he remained until his death in 1913. Also in 1906, Ward was elected the first president of the American Sociological Society, and was re-elected for a second term in 1907. Again following Comte, Ward conceptualized sociology as the synthesis of all prior existing knowledge. This was reflected in a sociology course he taught at Brown University, which he titled 'A Survey of All Knowledge'.

Although he was influenced by Herbert Spencer as well as Comte, Ward repudiated the deterministic implications of evolutionary theory, and for this reason was critical of fellow American sociologist **William Sumner**'s support for *laissez-faire* government and economics. Although the 'survival of the fittest' may very well operate among sub-human species, Ward theorized that with the rise of the intellectual faculty and the emergence of government among humans, a better operating principle is the 'protection of the weakest'. Consistent with this, he believed that human beings were the master of nature, not its subject. Because of the psychic forces of mind and spirit, human beings alone can control and direct the iron laws of evolution that otherwise determine the fate of inorganic matter and the lower life forms. It is this mastery over nature that distinguishes human beings from all other creatures.

For Ward, nature is a domain of rigid laws, and although the human species is subject to these laws, since human beings (having reached the positive stage) can comprehend them, they can attempt to change them. Instead of a strict physical or organic evolution, Ward favoured a social evolution that implied an interventionist or 'producerist' government. Ward used the term 'meliorism' to refer to 'scientific utilitarianism inspired by faith in the law of causation and the efficacy of well-directed action'. In post-Civil War America, Ward felt, a new kind of government was needed, and this he termed the 'sociocracy'. This is a form of government that stands between individualist democracy (which tends to drift towards a *laissez-faire* doctrine, as seen especially during the Gilded Age) and socialism, which of course is a radically interventionist and collectivist government. The sociocracy would allow for rational planning of the economy without needlessly tying the hands of entrepreneurs and business. But rather than the individual making the rules, it would be the group (society) that takes charge of the production and distribution system.

Although many contemporaries of Ward, within both the natural and the social sciences, admired the depth and breadth of his scientific knowledge, they felt that his model of sociology would be difficult to implement because of the sheer vastness of the background knowledge required of students. Although **Albion Small** once remarked that Ward's *Dynamic Sociology* was the one book he wished he had written, he was also critical of Ward's cosmological vision in an era of increasing scientific specialization. For this reason, Ward was not long remembered by sociologists after his death in 1913. Yet today Ward's commitment to both science and humanitarianism appears to be an especially appropriate model for contemporary sociology, and his notion of sociocracy may be a viable alternative to both the egoistic individualism of capitalist democracy and the collectivist pathologies of socialism and communism.

See also: Auguste Comte, Albion Small, Herbert Spencer.

Major works

Dynamic Sociology, 2 vols. 1883. New York: Appleton.
Psychic Factors of Civilization. 1893. Boston, MA: Ginn and Co.
'The Place of Sociology among the Sciences'. 1895. *American Journal of Sociology* 1.
Outlines of Sociology. 1897. New York: Macmillan, 1913.
Pure Sociology. 1903. New York: Macmillan, 1914.
Applied Sociology. 1906. New York: Ginn and Co.

Further reading

Gale Largey. 2005. 'Lester Ward: A Life's Journey'. Film documentary, available at http://www.galelargey.com.
Edward C. Rafferty. 2003. *Apostle of Human Progress: Lester Frank Ward and American Political Thought, 1841–1913*. Lanham, MD: Rowman and Littlefield.

JAMES J. CHRISS

LLOYD WARNER

William Lloyd Warner was born in California in 1898 and studied anthropology at the University of California, Berkeley. His doctoral work took him to Australia, where he undertook fieldwork on the kinship organization of the Murngin tribes of Milingimbi in the eastern Arnhem Land district of the Northern Territories of Australia. His first academic appointment was at Harvard University, where he taught from 1925 until he moved to the University of Chicago in 1935. At Harvard he pioneered attempts to apply anthropological fieldwork methods to contemporary American society. He was closely associated with the experimental studies carried out by Elton Mayo into worker behaviour at the Hawthorne electrical works in Chicago, and he directed a major study of social stratification and community in the New England town of Newburyport (to which he gave the pseudonym 'Yankee City'). Following his move to Chicago, where he encountered the established tradition of urban sociology that had been built up in the Department of Sociology by Robert Park and his colleagues, he enlarged the comparative scope of his work. He directed a study of Morris in Illinois (known as 'Jonesville') and he was the inspiration behind Burleigh Gardner's study of Natchez ('Old City'), Mississippi (*Deep South*, 1941) and St Clair Drake's massive study of the black community in Chicago (*Black Metropolis*, 1945). At Chicago, Warner also set up the Social Research Institute, an organization that carried out consumer research and consulting work for private businesses. He died in 1959.

Warner's investigations into Australian kinship were firmly tied to the work of his later colleague **Alfred Radcliffe-Brown**, itself rooted in the tradition of **Durkheim** and his report on Aboriginal Australian patterns in *Elementary Forms of the Religious Life*. He documented variations in kinship terminology and the associated systems of cross-cousin marriage in terms of their contribution to specific patterns of social solidarity and religious life. Returning home, he sought to employ these same fieldwork methods to the small communities of the United States. Initially, his investigations were focused on the Hawthorne Studies for the Committee of Industrial Physiology, where Mayo's interviews had shown how important the family and community relations of workers are for their integration into their workplace. Warner was invited to participate in the research in order to apply his fieldwork experience in a study of family and community. Warner eventually concluded that the students and colleagues of Robert Park and Ernest Burgess, from the University of Chicago, were already undertaking comprehensive studies of the city and that, in any case, his particular fieldwork methods were better suited to smaller and less 'disorganized' areas.

He sought the same kind of small-scale, cohesive communities that he had studied in Australia, as laboratories for his methods, and he felt that the cities of New England – the heart of 'Yankee' America – would be ideally suited to his purposes. Investigating various localities, he settled on the small Massachusetts city of Newburyport and began his research in the late 1930s. His research drew on extensive and intensive interviews, a questionnaire survey, direct observations made by Warner and his team and documentary sources.

His basic assumption was that, while tribal societies were integrated through kinship, this role was played in more complex societies by systems of social stratification. Economic relations are fundamental to social structure and underpin people's value systems, and research must begin from an investigation of the patterns of solidarity that result from economic differences and inequalities. In any established city, he argued, a system of social classes would legitimate existing patterns of inequality and would be the basis from which people draw their identity and their sense of belonging to the community. Recognizing that the actual possession of economic resources was important, Warner nevertheless focused his own attention on the patterns of social solidarity associated with them. His concern was with matters of 'status' rather than economic class *per se*. Stratification, then, was seen as producing a hierarchy of social positions that are ranked as superior and inferior to each other and that are associated with distinctive rights and duties as well as patterns of living.

In Newburyport Warner identified a hierarchy of six social classes: the upper-upper, lower-upper, upper-middle, lower-middle, upper-lower and lower-lower classes. At the top was the patrician aristocracy of wealthy established families, closely integrated through kinship and social interaction and following distinctive rituals of interaction and social manners. They lived in the largest houses and in the most advantaged districts within the city. Below them were the 'new' rich of upwardly mobile families who had not yet secured acceptance at the very top of the hierarchy. They were often wealthier than the upper-upper class, but their money was looked down on as not being sufficiently 'old': they would secure acceptance, if at all, only after many generations living in the city. In a more modern city such as Morris, Warner noted, the division between old and new wealth was less socially significant and there was a single 'upper' class. The upper classes comprised the 'society' families.

The upper-middle class of small business families and professionals were the basis of local politics and civic participation in voluntary associations. They were distinct, however, from the lower-middle class of shopkeepers, clerks and skilled workers. The lower-middle class and the upper-lower class, however, together showed a degree of solidarity as the 'mass' of 'common men' who made up the majority of those living in the city. At the bottom of the hierarchy, and excluded from the mainstream, were those in the lower-lower class of unskilled workers, often living in poverty.

Newburyport was an ethnically homogenous society, in which ethnic migration of non-Yankees was relatively recent. There was, however, a distinct pattern of ethnic segregation across the city. It was in Natchez, however, that his co-workers found the pattern of stratification that Warner described as one of 'caste'. Natchez, in fact, consisted of two overlapping stratification systems: a white system and a black system, divided by a colour line that formed blacks and whites into distinct castes. Both black and white communities could be analysed in terms of their hierarchy of classes, but they remained distinctive. Upper-middle-class whites felt closer to lower-class whites than they did to upper-middle-class blacks. The caste line cut diagonally across the community, and Warner was concerned to investigate the conditions under which it might alter its angle and bring about greater ethnic equality. More complex patterns of caste and class division were found by his colleagues investigating Chicago.

Warner pioneered methods of social network analysis to investigate the cliques and friendship groups that he found within the various social classes, drawing once again on ideas that had, until then, been elaborated in anthropological studies of tribal societies. He showed that such ideas were relevant to more complex societies and opened the way for subsequent investigations into interpersonal social networks.

See also: Alfred Radcliffe-Brown, Oliver Cox, Emile Durkheim.

Major works

'American Caste and Class'. 1936. In John Scott, ed. *Class*. London: Routledge, 1996.
A Black Civilization. 1937. New York: Harper, 1958.

The Social Life of a Modern Community. 1941. With P. S. Lunt. New Haven,
CT: Yale University Press. Yankee City, vol. 1.
The Status System of a Modern Community. 1942. With P. S. Lunt. New
Haven, CT: Yale University Press. Yankee City, vol. 2.
The Social System of American Ethnic Groups. 1945. With Leo S. Srole. New
Haven, CT: Yale University Press. Yankee City, vol. 3.
The Social System of a Modern Factory. 1947. With J. O. Low. New Haven,
CT: Yale University Press. Yankee City, vol. 4.
The Living and the Dead. 1959. New Haven, CT: Yale University Press. Also
published as *The Family of God.* Yankee City, vol. 5.
Democracy in Jonesville. 1949. New York: Harper Brothers.
Social Class in America. 1949. New York: Harper and Row, 1960.
The Structure of American Life. 1952. Chicago: University of Chicago Press.
American Life: Dream and Reality. 1953. Chicago: University of Chicago
Press.
Yankee City. 1963. Abridged edn.

Further reading

Allison Davis, B. Gardner and M. Gardner. 1941. *Deep South.* Chicago:
University of Chicago Press.
St Clair Drake and Horace B. Cayton. 1945. *Black Metropolis.* New York:
Harcourt Brace.

JOHN SCOTT

BEATRICE WEBB

Beatrice Webb (née Potter) was born in 1858 into a large and affluent
family. Her parents were widely read and enjoyed intellectual and
political company. **Herbert Spencer** was a close family friend.
Despite her scepticism about Spencer's beliefs – expressed in her
autobiographical *My Apprenticeship* – Webb was influenced both by
Spencer's views on the role of women and his interest in classification.

Webb first ventured into the world of social problems and poverty
in 1883, when she undertook work for the Charity Organisation
Society (COS) as a rent collector. She found social work among the
poor uncongenial and she also rejected it as a means for solving the
problem of poverty, abandoning the work and the organization in
1885. She adhered to the COS's views on the perverse incentive
effects of handouts and of punitive attitudes to the 'idle unemployed',
but she felt that the individualized approach of the COS ignored the
central, structural causes of destitution. She accepted the standard

contemporary division between 'deserving' and 'undeserving' poor, but she felt it was the 'deserving' who were often beyond the power of COS workers to help. She was thereafter to seek the answers for social ills in administrative machinery rather than interpersonal solutions.

In the latter half of the 1880s she joined the band of investigators on **Charles Booth**'s massive survey into the *Life and Labour of the People in London*. Her remit was to research dock work and sweated labour. She had by this time fully determined that her existence would be that of a social investigator. The research work for Booth gave her the opportunity to extend and test skills of social investigation and analysis that she had begun to develop during her time with the COS. An article on dock labour was one of her earliest essays into publication. A further two articles covered tailoring sweatshops, where she had engaged in covert observation by working as a trouser hand. Here, she combined her observation with a structural analysis that, instead of putting the middlemen at the heart of the exploitative work, condemned the whole production process as an example of unregulated competition. In this she revealed her ability to link close observation to wider social structures, and her faith in the power and significance of regulatory structures.

This tailoring experience was not her first foray into working incognito to carry out research. In 1883 she visited the Lancashire town of Bacup as 'Miss Jones', a farmer's daughter from Wales. Here she became interested in the cooperative movement, and specifically the strength of consumer cooperation when contrasted with producer cooperation. She subsequently began work on a history of cooperation, which, in 1890, brought her into contact with the Fabian Society and the Fabian socialist Sidney Webb. They married in 1892, despite the fact that he was socially inferior to her and that his socialist politics and class dismayed her family. They agreed that marriage would not interfere with Beatrice's ambitions as a social investigator. Sidney emphasized the ways their work could be complementary, and she was to describe their marriage as *Our Partnership*.

Thereafter much of their work was undertaken jointly and published under both their names. But it depended less on the skills of observation and interviewing that Beatrice had developed and employed successfully, and more on the collection and collation of detailed documentary materials, predominantly on the history of institutions. For example, they jointly published a history of trade unionism and a voluminous history of local government. They were also both instrumental in establishing the London School of Economics, following a bequest to the Fabian Society in 1895.

Webb was concerned to develop principles of social method. She argued that any social researcher brings with them the baggage of their background and social and economic circumstances, but that by recognizing the bias this entailed it was possible to overcome it. Webb frequently described herself as an instrument of social investigation that she had developed and honed. As a result of such training she considered that it was possible to collect data from which principles and patterns would emerge. In practice, however, the general laws that she was looking for from her painstaking research often seemed to elude her. And it has been argued that she tended to neglect her real strengths in observation and for making imaginative leaps that might have led to a more focused analysis. Moreover, despite her criticism of Spencer for grasping illustrations for his ideas and then arguing from them as if from first principles, she was accused both by contemporaries and by subsequent analysts of using a similarly selective approach in her marshalling of 'the facts'.

In 1905, Webb was invited on to the Commission on the Poor Laws. Here she clashed with **Helen Bosanquet**, the stalwart of the COS and main author of the Commission's majority report. Webb wrote, again with Sidney, a minority report, which they publicized energetically. The proposal of the minority report was to 'break up' the poor laws, according separate provision to separate groups of the needy, such as the old, children and the disabled. It also proposed providing health care on a more general basis and not only for paupers. The justification for this was that disease could be constructed as a public nuisance and thus require state intervention for all the sick.

Support for state and administrative solutions to poverty did not, however, extend to the introduction of insurance benefits. With beliefs consonant with those of the COS, she remained convinced that any system which gave financial benefits to those not in work created incentives to 'malinger'. She therefore vehemently resisted the introduction of sickness insurance in 1911, while remaining a strong advocate of general health care provision on the basis of need.

During the First World War, Webb engaged extensively in committee work, as part of which she developed proposals for a minimum wage, something she had first argued for in relation to women's tailoring, following her investigations of the 1880s. Her proposal was not, however, taken up. Moreover, the war itself and the depression which it provoked in her undermined some of her faith both in the meaning of her work and in the rightness of her proffered solutions to social problems. Further challenge to the ability of her social prescriptions to match circumstances came with the rising unemployment of the 1920s and 1930s. The Webbs looked outside Britain for a society which could adequately reflect their faith in bureaucratic solutions, which had apparently solved the 'problem of poverty' and which did not display the collapse in morality they thought they were observing. For this they turned to the Soviet Union. Following a visit in the 1930s, when they were both in their seventies, they espoused the Soviet system as the most promising for society. They adhered to this view even after evidence of the brutality of its regime emerged. They saw in their picture of the Soviet Union a working example of what they had been promoting for decades past and thus, in a sense, a justification for their life's work. Beatrice Webb died in 1943.

See also: Charles Booth, Helen Bosanquet.

Major works

The Co-operative Movement in Great Britain (as Beatrice Potter). 1895. London: S. Sonnenschein.
Industrial Democracy. 1897. With Sidney Webb.
English Local Government, 11 vols. 1898–1929. With Sidney Webb. London: F. Cass, 1963.
A Constitution for the Socialist Commonwealth of Great Britain 1920. With Sidney Webb.
The Decay of Capitalist Civilization. 1923. With Sidney Webb. London: George Allen and Unwin.
My Apprenticeship. 1926. London: Longmans, Green & co.
Methods of Social Study. 1932. With Sidney Webb. London: Longmans, Green & co.
Soviet Communism. 1935. With Sidney Webb.
Our Partnership. 1948. Ed. B. Drake and M. Cole. London: Longmans, Green & co.
The Minority Report of the Poor Law Commission. 1909. With Sidney Webb. London: Stationery Office.

Further reading

J. Davis. 2004. 'Webb, (Martha) Beatrice (1858–1943) and Sidney James Webb (1859–1947)'. In H. C. G. Matthew and B. Harrison, eds. *Oxford Dictionary of National Biography*. Oxford: Oxford University Press.
Jane Lewis. 1991. 'Beatrice Webb, 1858–1943'. In *Women and Social Action in Victorian and Edwardian England*. Cheltenham: Edward Elgar.

LUCINDA PLATT

MAX WEBER

One of the greatest intellectuals of the twentieth century, with a truly virtuoso grasp of comparative historical, political, economic, social and cultural processes, Weber was one of the most influential sociologists that ever lived. It is only since the mid-1980s that a new understanding of Weber has emerged that works its way through the often obscuring veils spun by academic sociology to undertake the quest for the historical Weber and to reformulate a sociology that demonstrably bears a closer connection to Weber's actual work and ideas. Given the enormous range of Weber's output, however, even the best intended of interpreters, however, must narrow their focus at any one time. Overall, a consideration of Weber as a key sociologist cannot be separated from a consideration of how he has been received and utilized in a variety of ways within the discipline.

Max Weber was born in Erfurt, Germany, in 1864, the son of a politician and civil servant. He studied law at the University of Heidelberg and continued his studies in history while practising as a lawyer. He completed a doctorate in legal history in 1889 and became professor of economics at Freiburg in 1894, moving to the University of Heidelberg in 1897. Weber suffered a prolonged period of depressive illness and resigned from his chair in 1903. Release from his professorial duties allowed him to engage full time in research and he began to produce many of his most important studies. He also maintained a close interest in artistic and cultural movements, most notably the art of Max Klinger, the Stefan George Circle and the counter-cultural experiments in Ascona. Weber worked closely with other social scientists in professional bodies and became actively involved in the newly formed German Sociological Society in 1909. He was also politically active and was to become a member of the German negotiating team at the Treaty of Versailles after the First World War and a member of the commission drafting the Weimar Constitution. In 1918 he returned to university teaching, first at Vienna and then at Munich, where he headed the sociology department. He died in 1920.

The search for a thematic unit or set of organizing principles that hold across his work is difficult and may well be a chimera, but it is a central concern of contemporary Weber studies, which have involved very close work with the texts. What the thematic unity is taken to be and the texts in which it is supposed to be found determine which 'image' of Weber is promoted and what 'Weberian sociology' might then be constituted by it. It is no longer accepted that Weber's work can be mainly understood as 'a dialogue with the ghost of Marx': for one thing, such an emphasis ignores the importance of Nietzsche. For many years, his main work was considered to be *Economy and Society*, whereas Friedrich Tenbruch has more recently argued that 'The Economic Ethics of the World Religions' series – the investigations of the Protestant ethic and the religions of India and China and ancient Judaism – should be seen as more central to his articulation of the theme of the disenchantment of the world. Other scholars detect a life-long concern with the rise of western capitalism and prefer a very late work such as the *General Economic History*, underline a dominant interest in the rise of western rationalism or find the key in Weber's 'Author's Introduction' to his sociology of religion. Yet others have found the unity in Weber's own personality, expressed in his methodological views on cultural science and his essays on 'Science as a Vocation' and 'Politics as a Vocation'. More recently, Wilhelm Hennis has influentially argued that a central question for Weber was continually to consider the types of human beings that are moulded by various social groupings, organizations and systems and how this manifests itself in life-conduct.

The search for a thematic unity is a reaction to the sociological appropriation of Weber as the founder of a range of otherwise unconnected sub-disciplines. Weber's relation to various sub-disciplines in sociology perhaps finds its anchorage in the structure and content of *Economy and Society*. However, this has a complex textual history and Weber died before he could bring it to completion. The text can be divided into two parts: an earlier part written from 1910 to 1914 and largely unrevised; and a later part written from 1918 to 1920 that remained unfinished at Weber's death. There is therefore a degree of overlap between the two parts, and the discussion of the 'Basic Categories' of sociological analysis in the first chapter – where the famous definition of sociology as the study of social action is located – develops a conceptual vocabulary that is not reflected in Part Two. Weber's differential influence in various sub-disciplines in American and British sociology reflects its publishing history. Part One was translated in 1947 as *The Theory of Social and Economic Organisation*, while translations of sections on the city, bureaucracy, the sociology of law and the sociology of religion gave the impression of individual discrete Weber projects. A full translation appeared only in 1968, and it is only since then that Weber's contribution to the understanding of economic sociology and the sociologies of law, religion and the city has been re-assessed.

The case of bureaucracy is instructive. This had a major impact in industrial sociology, but it actually forms part of Weber's sociology of domination. The sociology of domination pays equal attention to traditional forms of domination based on custom, habit and the rule of the elders, to charismatic domination based on extraordinary abilities to challenge the everyday and to rational legal domination based on the acceptance of the rule of law. Examples of these forms of domination can be found in both historical and contemporary societies and are valuable tools for social analysis, but it is with bureaucracy that sociology has been mostly preoccupied given its concern to understand one of the dominant forms of organization and administration found in modernity. The ideal type of bureaucracy highlights the attributes of hierarchal organization, action guided by written documents, a strictly delimited area of specialization guarded by rules and full-time officers who require training and pursue a career and consider it their duty to fulfil administrative protocols.

There is much of interest to the sociology of politics in Weber's sociology of domination, in other parts of *Economy and Society* and many other texts. Weber's political writings, often engaging with the pressing issues of Wilhelmine Germany, are full of sociological insights. Examples include the typological contrast between a politician following an ethic of conviction and an ethic of responsibility found in *Politics as a Vocation*, lengthy articles on the Russian revolutions and on socialism, 'The President of the Reich' and 'Parliament and Government in Germany under a New Political Order'.

In recent times the whole range of Weber's work has become of interest. For example, Reinhard Bendix, a leading Weber scholar in the 1960s and 1970s, was well aware of Weber's entire output, and included commentary on such early works as 'On the History of Medieval Trading Companies', 'The Condition of Agricultural Workers in East Elbian Germany', 'The Stock Exchange', 'Social Causes for the Decay of Ancient Civilization' and the somewhat evolutionary and partisan 'The Nation State and Economic Policy'. Yet it is only lately that these works have been studied in depth and with an explicit aim to trace connections to the later works. Themes that link these include an interest in the social analysis of rural conditions, the use of social survey methods to investigate the social and psychological significance of work, the sociology of ancient societies and, of course, an interest in the workings of modern capitalism and its possible impacts on the way of life of social actors caught up in its cosmos. There is clearly much here that is more or less unknown in mainstream sociological appropriations of Weber.

Weber made crucial contributions to methodological discussions through his texts on '"Objectivity" in Social Science and Social Policy' and 'The Meaning of Ethical Neutrality in Sociology and Economics'. Weber's work is of considerable importance to the philosophy of the social sciences through his discussion of the processes of concept formation, the place of understanding and causal explanation in social science, and the roles of values. Not much of this discussion makes its way today into sociology methodology – now largely organized as a dispute between quantitative and qualitative approaches or as tolerant of relativistic stand-point epistemologies – but it is essential to appreciate the meaning of ideal types, typological analysis, value freedom, value relevance and understanding in Weber's work.

This can be illustrated through his ideas of the ideal type and *Verstehen* (understanding). Ideal types are purposive exaggerations of social phenomena, formulated into a mental construct and considered in relation to another similarly formulated type, in such a way as to bring out their significant differences and relations. The typological contrast between 'sect' and 'church', for example, is created to bring out the essential difference between them in relation to a particular set of questions that Weber is exploring in religious movements: in this instance, it is the principle of membership (voluntary or compulsory) and its consequences. Weber's commitment to the understanding of social action (presented in his idea of *Verstehen*) can be clearly seen in the worldviews and motives of social actors that he discusses in *Protestant Ethic*. Weber's argument that the early Calvinists were faced with a psychological anxiety that sought release in certain types of ethical conduct and ways of working illustrates his empathy with a human subject together with an imaginative reconstruction of the available solutions derived from the theological and ethical ideas found in the cultural context. Moreover, the essential difference between the 'carriers of the ethic' – the ascetic Protestants, persons of Benjamin Franklin's Enlightenment rationality and entrapped modern individuals – is precisely a difference in their motivations to devote themselves to a vocation.

Whilst the *Protestant Ethic* essays began life as a separate and discrete study, they eventually came to form a part of the 'Economic Ethics of World Religions' series and were paraphrased and retold in his other works. The essays comprise a truly labyrinthine text whose full meaning cannot be achieved until after many re-readings. Essentially, Weber shows an affinity between the way of life that is demanded in modern capitalist culture and the way of life pursued on religious grounds by ascetic Protestants in the past. Whilst *Protestant Ethic* focuses on individual psychological motivations and devotion to a vocation, an essay on 'The Protestant Sects and the Spirit of Capitalism' illustrates how ascetic Protestants proved themselves to their peers, through joining a sect in which the values of a vocation determined who was gifted to be a member and, moreover, disciplined members, through monitoring and the threat of expulsion, to maintain and demonstrate those values.

After completing *Protestant Ethic*, Weber turned his attention to the analysis of economic ethics in the world religions of China and India and a study of ancient Judaism. These studies have been seen as counter-cases of the postulated relation between religious ethics and the development of a capitalistic way of life that work to support Weber's original thesis. Understood correctly, this is not far off the mark. However, it must not be thought that this is all one can find of sociological significance in the essays, and it should not lead to the conclusion that Weber was somehow operationalizing his thesis to test it against a universal data set. Rather, the sociological importance of the series can be best gathered from the essays that introduce the series known as 'Social Psychology of the World Religions' and the essay published 'in between' the China and India essays as 'The Religious Rejections of the World and Their Directions' (also known as 'The Intermediate Reflections').

The reception in sociology of Weber's analysis of class and of bureaucracy as the most significant elements of his legacy shows a bias of interest in the modern and processes of modernization. This is understandable as an interest of contemporary persons, but it forgets that Weber was concerned with social forms and ways of life in both modern and pre-modern times. He was an historical sociologist. His interest in pre-modern times was to better illustrate and understand the uniqueness of the modern, but it is important to remember that Weber does not periodize history or posit unilinear developments. The modern human being, for Weber, is faced with a conflict between values rather than the support of an overarching and consensual moral framework. Rationalization and bureaucratization have created a cosmos that cannot be escaped through wishful thinking or mystical utopias, and in which individuals make choices with consistency in line with their deeply held, if irrational, personal beliefs.

Weber's sociology also appears to be a sociology of culture, since he is concerned with worldviews and values and gives ideal interests a considerable role in explanation. However, Weber at no time defended a one-sided approach to social explanation: material interests and conditions had an equal role to play. A better appreciation of Weber's relation to a sociology of culture will be gathered through a detailed analysis of Weber's use of the term 'culture' in his entire work. At the same time, of course, Weber was interested in the arts and in the cultural institutions of societies. There are many references and allusions that relate to culture, texts and images that require a good deal of scholarly spade work before we can assess their full significance to Weber's sociology of culture or before we can complete our cultural interpretation of Weber.

See also: Karl Mannheim, Georg Simmel, Ferdinand Tönnies.

See also in *Fifty Key Sociologists: The Contemporary Theorists*: Alvin W. Gouldner, Talcott Parsons.

Major works

The History of Commercial Partnerships in the Middle Ages. 1889. Lanham, MD: Rowman and Littlefield, 2003.
'Developmental Tendencies in the Situation of East Elbian Rural Labourers'. 1894. In Keith Tribe, ed. *Reading Weber*. London: Routledge, 1989.
'Stock and Commodity Exchanges'. 1894. *Theory and Society* 29, 2000.
'The National State and Economic Policy (The Freiburg Address)'. 1895. *Economy and Society* 9, 1980.
'Commerce on the Stock and Commodity Exchanges'. 1896. *Theory and Society* 29, 2000.
'The Social Causes of the Decline of Ancient Civilizations'. 1896. In Max Weber. *The Agrarian Sociology of Ancient Civilizations*. London: New Left Books, 1976.
'"Objectivity" in Social Science and Social Policy'. 1904. In Max Weber. *The Methodology of the Social Sciences*. New York: Free Press, 1949.
'The Protestant Ethic and the Spirit of Capitalism'. 1904–5. In Peter Baehr and Gordon C. Wells, eds. *Max Weber: The Protestant Ethic and the 'Spirit' of Capitalism, and Other Writings*. Harmondsworth: Penguin, 2002.
'Replies to Critics (1907–10)'. In David J. Chalcraft and Austin Harrington, eds. *The Protestant Ethic Debate. Max Weber's Replies to his First Critics, 1907–10*. Liverpool: Liverpool University Press, 2001.
'Agrarian Relations in Antiquity'. 1909. In Max Weber. *The Agrarian Sociology of Ancient Civilizations* (as chs 1 and 2). London: New Left Books, 1976.
The Rational and Social Foundations of Music. 1911. Carbondale, IL: Southern Illinois University Press, 1958.
'The Social Psychology of the World Religions' (the so-called *Einleitung*. 1915. Revised 1920). In Hans Gerth and C. Wright Mills, eds. *From Max Weber*. London: Routledge, 1948.

'Religious Rejections of the World and Their Directions' (the so-called 'Intermediate Reflections'. 1915. Revised 1920). In Hans Gerth, and C. Wright Mills, eds. *From Max Weber*. London: Routledge, 1948.

The Religion of China. 1915. New York: Macmillan, 1951.

The Religion of India. 1916. New York: Macmillan, 1958.

Ancient Judaism. 1917. New York: Macmillan, 1952.

The Russian Revolutions. (Essays of 1905–8 and 1917.) Ed. Gordon C. Wells and Peter Baehr. Cambridge: Polity Press, 1995.

'Science as a Vocation'. 1919. In Peter Lassman and Irving Velody. *Max Weber's 'Science as a Vocation'*. London: Unwin Hyman, 1989.

Political Writings. (Essays of 1895–1919.) Ed. by Peter Lassman and Ronald Speirs. Cambridge: Cambridge University Press, 1994. Includes the essay on 'Politics as a Vocation'.

General Economic History. 1919–20. New York: Greenberg, 1927.

Economy and Society. 1910–14 and 1918–20. Ed. by Guenther Roth and Claus Wittich. Berkeley, CA: University of California Press, 1968.

'The Protestant Ethic and the Spirit of Capitalism'. Revised version 1920. In Stephen Kalberg, ed. *Max Weber: The Protestant Ethic and the Spirit of Capitalism*. Oxford: Blackwell, 2002.

'The Protestant Sects and the Spirit of Capitalism'. Revised version 1920. In Hans Gerth and C. Wright Mills, eds. *From Max Weber*. London: Routledge, 1948.

For definitive German texts the reader is referred to the ongoing Collected Works project, the Max Weber *Gesamtausgabe* (www.mohr.de/mw/mwg.htm).

Further reading

Dirk Kaesler. 1988. *Max Weber: An Introduction to His Life and Work*. Cambridge: Polity Press.

Richard Swedberg, ed. 2005. *The Max Weber Dictionary: Key Words and Central Concepts*. Stanford, CA: Stanford University Press

Alan Sica. 2004. *Max Weber: A Comprehensive Bibliography*. New Brunswick, NJ: Transaction.

DAVID CHALCRAFT

FLORIAN ZNANIECKI

Znaniecki has the double honour of being both an intellectual founder member of the Chicago school of sociology and the founder of academic sociology in Poland. In America and Western Europe his name has most often been associated with that of William I. Thomas, with whom he collaborated on the methodologically groundbreaking project *The Polish Peasant in Europe and America*. His own sociological contributions to what has come to be termed 'humanistic' sociology, an approach that puts the experiences of the acting individual at the centre, continued, however, throughout his life both in the US and in Poland.

Florian Witold Znaniecki's cultural approach to sociology grew out of a scholarly rich upbringing. He was born in Poland in 1882. He learned several European languages before becoming a published poet and a student at the University of Warsaw. His anti-Russian political activities led to his expulsion from the university and to a period of travel and study visits to several universities across Europe, including a period as a student of **Simmel**. After receiving a doctorate in philosophy from Cracow University, his continuing political activities prevented him from gaining an academic post and he became director of the Polish Emigrants' Protective Association. In this capacity he met in 1913 the American sociologist William I. Thomas, one of the original members of the Chicago school. Thomas' interest in Chicago immigrant communities led to several trips to Europe in search of their social and cultural origins and the impact of these on often painful processes of integration and Americanization. On Thomas' suggestion, Znaniecki travelled to Chicago and one of the most significant research collaborations in sociological history was set in train.

The early work of the Chicago school developed as a pragmatic and progressive response against the theoretical abstractness of earlier sociological thinkers in Europe and America. The work of Robert Park and William I. Thomas reflected the search for more accurate reporting of the major social and economic upheavals that characterized rapid industrialization and urbanization, much of it fuelled by a culturally mixed immigrant labour force. It was also influenced by social reformers and philanthropists, many of them women, such as **Jane Addams**, and their demands for a more practical and empirical approach to welfare without moralistic and religious overtones. It also, with **George Herbert Mead**, saw the concept of the 'self' as an important cornerstone in the understanding of how conflicting social values could be brought together better to accommodate rapid social change and culturally sensitive integration. Znaniecki fitted well into this melting pot of peoples and ideas.

The paradox at the centre of attention in *The Polish Peasant* was the problem of the dependency of the individual upon social organization and culture and the dependence of social organization and culture on the individual, outlined in its 'Methodological Notes'. Whereas **Durkheim**'s aim had been that of explaining the predictable universality of human behaviour irrespective of individual human motivations, the explanatory challenge tackled by Znaniecki and Thomas was that of its inherent unpredictability and malleability in the face of change. This required a different kind of empirical research methodology than that of searching for statistical commonalities. The attempt to understand individual meanings led to a search for culturally shared values and practices 'outside' the mind of any particular individual – shared 'definitions of the situation' framed by religious ideas and cultural heritages of nationhood – as well as for evidence of their individual interpretations in particular contexts. The vast amount of material presented in the book (15,000 documents examined, comprising 60 percent of the work as a whole) derived from a series of different sources: letters from immigrants, letters to emigrants' associations in Poland, newspaper articles, life histories and information from Polish immigrant institutions in the US. The evidence presented continues, almost a century later, to provide meaningful and moving evidence of individual tenacity and collective capacity for organizational transformation in the face of social conflict and hardship.

Znaniecki did not himself find life as an immigrant sociologist easy, and in 1920 he returned to Poland, where he became professor of sociology at the University of Poznan and founder of the Polish Sociological Institute. The concept of the 'definition of the situation', as outlined in *The Polish Peasant*, and the Polish material assembled by Znaniecki were taken further in subsequent work by Chicago sociologists, and added to them was similar material from other immigrant groups, such as Italians, Jews and Scandinavians. The concept has also become enshrined in what has, in view of Znaniecki's contribution, somewhat misleadingly come to be referred to as 'the Thomas dictum', that if people define situations as real, then they are real in their consequences: a theoretical cornerstone of symbolic interactionism.

During the next decades, Znaniecki wrote several books (published both in Polish and in English). These were on the sociology of education, on social psychology and on *The Method of Sociology*. In the latter work he elucidated his concept of 'the humanistic coefficient', the notion that cultural data are always 'somebody's', and as such 'belong to somebody else's active experience and are such as this active experience makes them'. His largest theoretical work, *Social Actions*, was an important, yet often sidelined, groundbreaker for developments in American sociological theory: for example that of Talcott Parsons on the distinct components of the social actions of 'culture-bearing' human beings. Znaniecki's work was also an acknowledged source of influence on the work of, for example, Howard S. Becker. In 1938 the methodological challenges raised by the use of selectively assembled documents became the subject of a major conference, the proceedings of which were published in a volume edited and introduced by Herbert Blumer, ensuring continuing debate over the validity and reliability of such methods.

At the time of the German invasion of Poland in 1939, Znaniecki's position as a Polish patriot and academic again brought dangers and he was forced to return to the United States. He spent the last part of his life as professor of sociology at the University of Illinois, by now a well-known 'man of knowledge', on whose varied social roles he wrote a classical text. In 1952 he published his last major works, *Modern Nationalities* and *Cultural Sciences*. He never returned to Poland and he died in 1958. It was not until the end of Communist rule in 1999 that his contribution to a more humanistic sociology than that fostered under the Soviet hegemony could yet again be celebrated in his country of birth.

The legacy of Znaniecki goes well beyond the discipline of sociology itself. Contemporary public opinion and market research, including more recent methodological tools such as focus groups, rely heavily on the concept of the definition of the situation as a tool for ascertaining group responses, as does much contemporary work in qualitative sociology. Much of the credit for what today is taken for granted in sociology belongs to Znaniecki and his insistence that the reflections of individual human beings need to be heard and understood, theoretically and empirically, if we are fully to appreciate their responses to social change.

See also: George Herbert Mead, Georg Simmel.

See also in *Fifty Key Sociologists: The Contemporary Theorists*: Howard S. Becker.

Major works

The Polish Peasant in Europe and America. 1918–20. With W. I. Thomas. Vols I and II, Chicago: University of Chicago Press, 1918; vols III–V, Boston, MA: Badger, 1919–20. A 2nd edn in two abridged vols was published by Alfred A. Knopf, New York, 1927.
Cultural Reality. 1919. Chicago: University of Chicago Press.
The Laws of Sociology. 1925. Chicago: University of Chicago Press.
The Method of Sociology. 1934. New York: Octagon Books, 1968.
Social Actions. 1936. New York: Farrar and Reinhart (with the Polish Sociological Institute, University of Poznan).

The Social Role of the Man of Knowledge. 1940. New York: Columbia University Press.

Cultural Sciences, Their Origin and Development. 1952. Urbana, IL: University of Illinois Press.

Modern Nationalities: A Sociological Study. 1952. Urbana, IL: University of Illinois Press.

Extracts from his work can be found in *On Humanistic Sociology: Selected Papers.* Ed. and with a biographical intro. by Robert Bierstedt. Chicago: University of Chicago Press, 1969.

Further reading

Herbert Blumer, ed. 1939. *Critiques of Research in the Social Sciences 1: An Appraisal of Thomas and Znaniecki's The Polish Peasant in Europe and America.* New Brunswick, NJ: Transaction, 1979.

E. STINA LYON

INDEX

Entries in **bold** refer to principal entries in the book.

SOCIOLOGY: THE BASICS

Martin Albrow

This is a book for anyone who wants to know what sociology is and what sociologists do. In a subject that has changed dramatically over the last twenty years, *Sociology: The Basics* offers the most up to date guide to the major topics and areas of debate. It covers among other things:

- Sociology and society
- Laws, morality and science
- Social relations
- Power and communication
- Society in the future
- Becoming a socialist

Clearly written, concise and comprehensive, *Sociology: The Basics* will be an essential text for anyone thinking of studying the subject.

0-415-17264-0
978-0-415-17264-6

Available at all good bookshops
For ordering and further information please visit
www.routledge.com

SOCIOLOGY: THE KEY CONCEPTS

John Scott

Sociology: The Key Concepts brings together a strong group of well-known experts to review ideas from all areas of this diverse and pluralistic discipline. Exploring the key debates and founding ideas of this exciting field of study, the book is fully cross-referenced and covers such topics as:

- Community
- Childhood
- Emotion
- Discourse
- Race and racialisation
- Modernity
- McDonaldisation
- Gender
- Consumption
- Social capital
- Identity

0-415-34406-9
978-0-415-34406-7

Available at all good bookshops
For ordering and further information please visit
www.routledge.com

Lightning Source UK Ltd.
Milton Keynes UK
UKOW04f2320180614

233684UK00004B/136/P